D1076168

Locomotive Compendium

SOUTHERN

Colin Boocock

Handsome 'Lord Nelson' 4-6-0 No 30863 Lord Rodney *stands outside the shed at Eastleigh on 24 April 1959. This was one of just two examples that did not receive Bulleid's new cylinders and extended smokebox.*
Author

Ian Allan
PUBLISHING

On the frosty morning of Sunday 4 January 1959 Bulleid 'Merchant Navy' Pacific No 35006 Peninsular & Oriental S. N. Co. *restarts the 11am Waterloo–Exeter from Andover Junction.* Author

First published 2010

ISBN 978 0 7110 3423 5

Published by Ian Allan Publishing

an imprint of Ian Allan Publishing Ltd, Hersham, Surrey KT12 4RG. Printed in England by Ian Allan Printing Ltd, Hersham, Surrey KT12 4RG.

Code: 1004/B2

Visit the Ian Allan Publishing website at www.ianallanpublishing.com

Distributed in the United States of America and Canada by BookMasters Distribution Services.

Mixed Sources
Product group from well-managed forests and other controlled sources
www.fsc.org Cert no. SGS-COC-005526
© 1996 Forest Stewardship Council

CONTENTS

INTRODUCTION

This book, the second in the 'Locomotive Compendium' series, illustrates and describes all classes of locomotive that British Railways inherited in 1948 from the Southern Railway, and also those SR types that were introduced, built or rebuilt in the early years of BR.

The Southern Railway was formed in 1923 by the amalgamation of three large railway companies plus several small ones. These were the:

South Eastern & Chatham Railway (SECR)
London & South Western Railway (LSWR)
London, Brighton & South Coast Railway (LBSCR)
Plymouth, Devonport & South Western Junction Railway (PDSWJR)
Isle of Wight Railway (IWR)
Isle of Wight Central Railway (IWCR)
Freshwater, Yarmouth & Newport Railway (FYNR)
Lynton & Barnstaple Railway (L&BR — narrow-gauge)
Halwill & Torrington Railway

The Southern Railway jointly owned (with the London, Midland & Scottish Railway) the Somerset & Dorset Joint Railway, which linked Bournemouth and Bath over the Mendip hills. After 1930 the SR managed the S&DJR infrastructure and provided carriages for many of the local trains; the LMS provided all the locomotives and some carriages for locals at the northern end of the line. In BR days SR-type locomotives also ventured on the S&D main line. When BR was formed in 1948 the Southern Railway was joined by the Kent & East Sussex Railway and the East Kent Railway to form BR's Southern Region.

The SR was primarily a passenger railway, including the London suburban area south of the Thames, an area penetrated by few London Underground routes. The conductor-rail electrification of most of the suburban area within SR boundaries was a logical business move. However, the cost of electrifying suburban and main lines had a knock-on effect on the capital available for renewal of its diverse fleet of locomotives. By World War 2 the SR still operated some very old steam locomotives, most of which were needed during the war to support the very heavy traffic demands which the SR had to meet. Thus a large number of ancient if interesting locomotives was brought into British Railways' stock at nationalisation on 1 January 1948, at which time the nascent Southern Region found that it owned a total of 1,810 locomotives of 87 different classes. It is these locomotives, plus subsequent further builds and rebuilds of the SR-based classes, that

are the subject of this Compendium. Even experimental locomotives that were actually built by or delivered to the Southern Region of BR are included in this book, notably the 'Leader' class and the early Southern diesels.

The three main pre-Grouping railways' locomotives when absorbed by the Southern kept their original class designations, with some odd results. For example there were two 'B4' classes, the 4-4-0s from the Brighton line and the ex-LSWR 0-4-0 dock tanks. More confusing were the two 'R1' classes, both of which came via the SECR — the Class R1 0-4-4T and Class R1 0-6-0T locomotives.

This book attempts to place all these diverse classes in a sequence that relates to their railways of origin, and also to the engineer mostly responsible for their design or acquisition.

After BR was formed early building of locomotives for the Southern Region concentrated on Bulleid Pacifics and on 2-6-4Ts of LMS and, later, BR design, built at Brighton, and Ivatt 2-6-2Ts built at Crewe. Under BR's Modernisation Plan the Hastings line was 'dieselised' with multiple-units in 1957, electrification of the Kent main lines was opened in two phases in 1958 and 1962, and diesel and electric locomotives were supplied to handle freight. Displacement of more modern steam locomotives westwards to the Western Section (the former LSWR lines) saw the end of most of the pre-Grouping stock, supported by 'dieselisation' of branch and secondary lines in Hampshire, Berkshire and the few remaining non-electrified lines in Sussex and Kent. BR Southern Region planned to electrify to Bournemouth and to Exeter, hoping to reach the latter by about 1970, but the BR Board did not wish steam to last that long in just one area of the country. By transferring all ex-SR routes west of Salisbury to the Western Region in 1963, the BRB enabled the WR, which was rationalising its own routes, to roster surplus diesel-hydraulic locomotives on Waterloo–Exeter trains. This, and the inauguration of electrification to Bournemouth, enabled SR steam to finish in July 1967. The Southern Region's last steam-hauled passenger train ran from Weymouth to Waterloo behind rebuilt 'Merchant Navy' 4-6-2 No 35030 *Elder-Dempster Lines* on 9 July 1967.

All tractive-effort figures for steam locomotives are conventionally calculated at 85% boiler pressure, and all dimensions are given in imperial measurements. Weights quoted are for locomotives in working order.

Left: *The Southern Region inherited a plethora of ancient and wondrous locomotives from the pre-Grouping era. This entire scene at Allhallows-on-Sea (across the Thames Estuary from Southend) on 2 June 1952 is reminiscent of the Victorian age! Former London, Chatham & Dover Railway Class R1 0-4-4T No 31697 heads old non-corridor carriages forming a train for Gravesend.* Neil Sprinks

Above: *The three cylinders of Maunsell 'U1' 2-6-0 No 31903 are put to good use as the locomotive heads away from Bournemouth Central with the daily through train to Brighton on 12 March 1955.* Author

Numbering

After the Grouping in 1923 locomotives at first retained their previous numbers. As many of these duplicated or triplicated others, the SR added letter prefixes denoting their Works allegiance, *i.e.* 'A' for Ashford (ex-SECR locomotives), 'B' for Brighton (LBSCR) and 'E' for Eastleigh (LSWR). From 1931 the prefixes were removed and the locomotives (but not ex-LSWR or SR designs) were renumbered by the addition of 1,000 to SECR numbers and 2,000 to LBSCR numbers. In the tables that accompany the text in this book the 1931 scheme numbers are shown after the original numbers where appropriate, separated by an oblique stroke.

Acknowledgements

The author would like to thank all those who have helped him obtain information and photographs to complete this record of all Southern Railway-inspired locomotives that ran on the Southern Region of British Railways. Particular thanks are due to Hugh Ballantyne, John Harvey, Brian Morrison, Neil Sprinks, Alan Thorpe, Martyn Thresh, Don Townsley, Charles Woodland and Eric Youldon. The book could not have been completed without the wonderful collections in the Ian Allan Library and at Colour-Rail.

LONDON & SOUTH WESTERN RAILWAY

The London & South Western Railway was the largest component of the Southern Railway at the 1923 Grouping. With territory stretching from Waterloo to the north coast of Devon and Cornwall and taking in all the South Coast of England from Portsmouth to beyond Plymouth, it was indeed a major railway. It had had the foresight, through its CME, Dugald Drummond, to relocate its locomotive- and carriage-building and overhaul workshops from London Nine Elms and to set them up in new, modern (for the day) factories at Eastleigh, plumb in the middle of its network.

The LSWR had several famous names among its locomotive engineers, including the Beattie brothers (Joseph and William), William Adams, Dugald Drummond and Robert Urie, of whom all but the earliest produced locomotives that would survive to become parts of the British Railways fleet in 1948. William Beattie begat his fine express 2-4-0 tender engines that unusually had floating leading axleboxes suspended from the outside slide bars; these were additional to the inside axleboxes within the main frames and were added to control any tendency to roll. This design had derived from similar locomotives in the form of 2-4-0 well tanks that for many years worked suburban trains out of Waterloo. Amazingly, three of these reached the BR period, their story being related on page 7. William Adams designed some most graceful express 4-4-0s, one of which is in the National Railway Museum, as well as some very useful mixed-traffic 0-4-2s, nicknamed 'Jubilees'. Many of his freight 0-6-0s and most of his passenger 0-4-4Ts served BR before their eventual withdrawal.

Dugald Drummond's locomotives included many successes as well as a few somewhat dubious performers. Particularly good were his inside-cylinder 4-4-0s, culminating in the 'T9' and 'D15' designs, both of which were outstanding for their day, while the 0-6-0s of the '700'

class, although somewhat mundane, performed well on their freight duties. It was when he tried to extrapolate his ideas into bigger locomotives that Drummond met with difficulties. His first classes of big 4-6-0 were not successful, seemingly unable to use well such steam as was produced by their large boilers, and his best were the fine-looking 'T14s', which were improved in later years by Urie and Maunsell. Urie's 4-6-0s, on the other hand, became better and better with each new design and with each new modification and rebuild — a process that continued into the Maunsell era on the Southern Railway. Nor was Urie entirely tied to convention when it came to producing powerful tank engines for hump shunting and for cross-London freights; his 'G16' and 'H16' respectively were masters of their task, if perhaps a little cumbersome.

The LSWR's system of locomotive classification was based on the number of the order placed with the works for the first batch of each class. Order numbers were needed for everything produced by the works, and locomotives were only a small part of the list. The system should have started at A1, working its way through the alphabet to Z1 and then resuming with A2 to Z2 and so on; how one of the first orders was numbered A12 is something of a mystery! Locomotives ordered from outside contractors took their classification from the running number of one of the locomotives (*e.g.* '700').

Below: *LSWR trains retained their character even after nationalisation. Here, on 9 May 1955, the 5.16pm stopping service from Fawley to Romsey approaches Eastleigh behind Drummond Class M7 0-4-4T No 30032. Apart from numbering and liveries very little has changed since the pre-Grouping era.* Author

Among the longest-living steam locomotives in the UK, the three Beattie 2-4-0 well tanks that became part of BR's locomotive stock in 1948 had actually been saved by fate some 49 years earlier. W. Beattie had designed these locomotives for working suburban trains out of London's Waterloo station. Eighty-five such locomotives were built, based on an earlier design of passenger 2-4-0 tender engine but improved. Introduced in 1863, the class was still being expanded more than 10 years later. However, the Class 415 'radial' 4-4-2Ts, introduced in 1883 by William Adams, displaced many of the Beattie tanks from their suburban duties, and 31 of the class were converted to run with tenders. However, withdrawal of the 2-4-0Ts had already started, and all but three had gone by the end of 1899.

The quirk of fate that led to the prolonged lives of Nos 298, 314 and 329, which had been built in 1874 and 1875, was the difficulty in finding any alternative motive power for the Bodmin–Wenford Bridge branch line in Cornwall. This lightly laid line had sharp curves and needed locomotives with relatively short or flexible wheelbases and light axle loads. The Beattie well tanks were ideal but old. When their Beattie high-topped fireboxes wore out they were replaced with new Adams-style boilers. These in turn were replaced by Drummond boilers with the safety valves on the domes, the boiler type that they carried into the BR years. The locomotives also gained enclosed cabs at some stage. Of the three, No 329, built in 1875, had rectangular splashers over the coupled wheels, the other two having conventional curved splashers.

Having been placed on the duplicate number list (with the '0' prefix added to their running numbers) in 1899 and 1901, the trio were renumbered by BR as 30585-7. It was only in 1962 that the Southern Region, having put Class 04 diesel shunting locomotives to work on Weymouth Quay, was able to send three ex-GWR '1366' 0-6-0 pannier tanks to Wadebridge depot to work the Bodmin–Wenford Bridge line, allowing the Beattie tanks finally to be withdrawn. No 30586 was scrapped, but the two with curved splashers were preserved. No 30587 forms part of the National Collection and is based at Bodmin, while No 30585 is at Quainton Road. Both have been restored to working order, and at a special event in 2008 the pair were active together on the preserved railway at Bodmin.

Class	0298 2-4-0WT
Engineer	W. Beattie
Designed for	LSWR
Built by	Beyer Peacock
Number in class	3*
Introduced	1874**
BR power rating	0P
Cylinders (2 outside)	16½in x 20in
Coupled wheels	5ft 7in
Boiler pressure	160lb/sq in
Grate area	14sq ft
Tractive effort	11,050lb
Weight	37 tons 16cwt
SR numbers	E0298, E0314, E0329 / 3298, 3314, 3329
BR numbers	30585-30587

* Originally 85 locomotives, of which 82 had been withdrawn by the end of 1899
** Date relates to oldest survivor in 1948; class introduced 1863

Above right: *On 23 July 1960, not long after its last general overhaul at Eastleigh Works, Class 0298 2-4-0WT No 30587 stands outside the depot at Wadebridge. Note the additional axlebox suspension supported by the lower slide bar.* Author

Right: *Pictured at Eastleigh depot on 2 March 1960, newly overhauled No 30586, with rectangular splashers, waits to be returned to its home depot at Wadebridge. This locomotive would not be preserved.* Author

Other classes of LSWR locomotive did military service in the 1914-18 war, but the 0-6-0s of the '395' class exceeded them all. During that conflict no fewer than 50 of the 70 locomotives went overseas with the War Department's Railway Operating Division, mostly to Palestine and Mesopotamia (later Iraq), although a few went to Serbia. Regrettably, four '395s' that were on their way to Palestine were in the *SS Arabic* when it was torpedoed and sunk in the Mediterranean Sea, where they rest to this day. No locomotives of this class that went overseas appear to have been repatriated to the UK, probably because by the end of the war they were more than 30 years old.

The '395' was Adams's first main-line goods design, and all 70 were built by Neilson & Co. That the '395s' were chosen for war service indicates how the authorities considered them to be useful and reliable, perhaps justifying their nickname 'Jumbos'. Even though the 50 war veterans were not required again, others of the class survived, 18 reaching BR stock.

There were originally two variants. Those built from 1885, known initially as the '496' class, had a longer front overhang and thus were heavier by over a ton. Some received Drummond boilers with safety valves on the domes, and in SR days some gained second-hand boilers from withdrawn ex-LCDR Class M3 4-4-0s. When built the design had a sloping front to the smokebox; during later overhauls some locomotives received more orthodox vertical fronts. In the early years of the 20th century the locomotives were placed on the duplicate list, with an '0' prefix added to their running numbers. In later years the surviving 18 '0395s' were used for local goods workings and for shunting in depots such as Nine Elms, as well as serving as works shunters at Eastleigh. All varieties survived until the last six were withdrawn by BR in 1958/9. Up until then the Eastleigh Works shunters were usually Nos 30566 and 30568; these were surprisingly displaced on that duty by the transfer of the two ex-Plymouth, Devonport & South Western Junction Railway 0-6-2Ts.

Class	0395 0-6-0
Engineer	W. Adams
Designed for	LSWR
Built by	Neilson & Co
Number in class	18*
Introduced	1881
BR power rating	2F
Cylinders (2 inside)	17½in x 26in
Coupled wheels	5ft 1in
Boiler pressure	140lb/sq in**
Grate area	18sq ft
Tractive effort	15,535lb**
Weight	37 tons 12cwt / 38 tons 14cwt***
SR numbers	E029, E083, E0101, E0154, E0155, E0163, E0167, E0397, E0400, E0433, E0436, E0439-E0442, E0496, E0506, E0509 / 3029, 3083, 3101, 3154, 3155, 3163, 3167, 3397, 3400, 3433, 3436, 3439-3442, 3496, 3506, 3509
BR number series	30564-30581

*   Survivors of a class of 70
**   Those that received LCDR boilers pressed at 150lb/sq in had tractive effort raised to 16,645lb
***   Locomotives with long front overhang

Left: Class 0395 No 30566 rattles towards Eastleigh after a stint of shunting at Fawley on 6 July 1955. This locomotive had a long frame overhang forward of the wheels, and a sloping smokebox front. Author

Left: Pictured at Eastleigh on 8 October 1959, '0395' No 30567 illustrates the short-frame variety. It has a vertical smokebox front and an ex-LCDR boiler. Author

Built from 1882 to 1885, the 71 4-4-2Ts of the LSWR's '415' class were graceful locomotives intended for suburban passenger traffic. The rear axle was of the radial type, which incorporated curved horn guides within which the axleboxes and wheelset could take up angular positions in line with track curvature. The side water tanks were small, but there was also a well tank situated between the frames underneath the long coal bunker. The total water capacity was 1,200 gallons, which, with three tons of coal being carried, was sufficient for most out-and-back duties. With the arrival of the 'T1' 0-4-4Ts (and later the bigger 'M7s') the '415s' were displaced from the heaviest duties, though they still served many years in the London area.

Two of the class were moved in 1913 to take over the branch line between Axminster and Lyme Regis. This line had sharp curves and steep gradients, and more rigid locomotives — even the little Class A1X 'Terriers' — caused track damage. During the period 1904-24 most of the class were renumbered into the duplicate series, becoming the '0415' class. Aside from two locomotives sold into Government service during World War 1, withdrawals did not begin in earnest until 1922. By 1928 all had gone except locomotives sold for further service elsewhere and the two locomotives then working the Lyme Regis branch — Nos E0125 and E0520. These were kept for that duty and duly overhauled, though they did have some difficulty in covering all services on occasions when both suffered from mechanical defects, working as they did so far from their home depot at Exmouth Junction. To alleviate this situation the two survivors were joined in 1946 by the former No 0488. This locomotive had been in Government service from 1917 to 1919, when it was sold on to the East Kent Railway, becoming EKR No 5. In 1946 the SR bought it back and numbered it in the duplicate list as 3488, whereupon it joined the other two at Lyme Regis. This is the locomotive that is now preserved on the Bluebell Railway. The '0415' class soldiered on into the early BR years, and the locomotives were finally withdrawn from service in 1961, displaced by diesel railcars.

Class	0415 4-4-2T
Engineer	W. Adams
Designed for	LSWR
Built by	LSWR Nine Elms
Number in class	3*
Introduced	1885**
BR power rating	1P
Cylinders (2 outside)	17½in x 24in
Coupled wheels	5ft 7in
Boiler pressure	160lb/sq in
Grate area	18sq ft
Tractive effort	14,920lb
Weight	55 tons 2cwt
SR numbers***	E045, E050, E054, E055, E058, E059, E0106, E0125, E0126, E0129, E0169, E0416, E0422, E0426, E0428, E0429, E0431, E0480, E0481, E0483, E0485, E0486, E0487, E0490, E0517, E0519, E0520, E0521, E0522, E0524 / 3125, 3488, 3520
BR number series	30582-30584

* Survivors of a class of 71, of which 41 withdrawn before 1923
** Date relates to oldest survivor in 1948; class introduced 1882
*** All bar Nos E0125 and E0520 withdrawn by the end of 1928, No 3488 being acquired from the East Kent Railway in 1946

Right: On 14 April 1960, after its last general overhaul at Eastleigh Works, Class 0415 4-4-2 radial tank No 30582 awaits transfer back to Exmouth Junction for its last years on the Lyme Regis branch. This locomotive started life in 1885 as LSWR No 125, became 0125 in 1911, was renumbered 3125 after 1931 and in 1948 became BR No 30582 — its first transfer off the duplicate list in 37 years! Author

Above: *Class A12 0-4-2 No E603 was built at Nine Elms in 1894 as one of the then 'O4' class. This picture illustrates the locomotive in early SR condition. The boiler has the hallmarks of Adams, with safety valves over the firebox and a tall dome.* Ian Allan Library

It was an unusual wheel arrangement for the LSWR. The LBSCR had its 'Gladstone' 0-4-2 express locomotives, but nothing quite like it had been seen on the South Western. William Adams resumed construction of locomotives at Nine Elms Works with the first of this class, 30 locomotives being built to order No A12. They proved to be very successful and were used for main-line stopping services and also for heavy excursion and troop trains. They also became common on the lines in north Devon and Cornwall. Their 'Jubilee' nickname arose from the fact that the first year of their build was the 50th of Queen Victoria's reign.

The 'A12s' had two inside cylinders, the slide valves positioned below the cylinders. Most of the tenders of the first batch were second-hand, being taken from Beyer Peacock goods locomotives. In due course another 60 locomotives were ordered, known officially as Class O4. Detail differences from the original 'A12s' included the slide valves' being between the cylinders, offering more direct steam passages. New tenders were provided, of 3,300gal water capacity. The first 40 of the second batch were built by Neilson & Co of Glasgow, the remainder at Nine Elms.

These were generally long-lived locomotives, the first withdrawals taking place in 1928, the last in 1948. Four entered British Railways service, but as they were withdrawn in 1948 they did not receive their allotted five-figure running numbers. No 612 had passed into

Class	A12 0-4-2
Engineer	W. Adams
Designed for	LSWR
Built by	LSWR Nine Elms (527-556, 637-656*) / Neilson & Co (597-636*)
Number in class	90
Introduced	1887
BR power class	unclassified
Cylinders (2 inside)	18in x 26in
Coupled wheels	6ft 0in
Boiler pressure	160lb/sq in
Grate area	17sq ft
Tractive effort	15,900lb
Weight	43 tons 8cwt
SR number series	E527-E556, E597-E656 / 527-556, 597-656**
BR numbers	30618***, 30627***, 30629***, 30636***, DS3191

*   Known originally as Class O4
**   No 612 renumbered 3191S in 1946
*** Never carried

departmental stock in 1946 as a stationary boiler at Eastleigh Locomotive Works and lasted thus until, nominally DS3191, it was scrapped in 1951. Regrettably, no 'A12' is preserved.

William Adams's ordering of locomotives to replace the ageing Beattie well tanks included the build of 60 Class O2 0-4-4Ts, smaller locomotives than the Class T1 described on page 13. The 'O2s' were neat locomotives that had a good turn of speed despite their relatively small coupled wheels of 4ft 10in diameter. They were deployed across the LSWR system. In BR days the 47 survivors included among their duties working the steeply graded railway from Weymouth to Easton on Portland Bill, several branch lines around Plymouth and south Devon, and virtually all passenger services on the Isle of Wight.

To work on the Isle of Wight the locomotives needed Westinghouse brake air pumps, because all the carriages on the island had air brakes. They also received enlarged coal bunkers. Their performance was excellent on the Ryde–Ventnor line on which six-coach trains were the norm in summer, their only significant problem being the need for smokeboxes to be cleared of ash after arrival at Ventnor!

Justifiably, all Isle of Wight locomotives received names of locations on the island. After 1938 the SR painted them in malachite green livery, this being replaced from 1949 onwards by BR lined black. In 1949 two additional 'O2s' were converted to work on the island, equipped for push-pull working to displace the two 'A1X' 0-6-0Ts remaining there. Nos W35 and W36 had second Westinghouse pumps fitted to the right-hand side of the smokebox to provide air for the push-pull system. They worked the Bembridge and Ventnor West branches until closure in the early 1950s, following which the push-pull apparatus was removed. The 'O2s' were withdrawn when the Isle of Wight network was cut back and electrified in 1966. No W24 *Calbourne* is preserved on the Isle of Wight Steam Railway.

Class	O2 0-4-4T
Engineer	W. Adams
Designed for	LSWR
Built by	LSWR Nine Elms
Number in class	60
Introduced	1889
BR power rating	0P
Cylinders (2 inside)	17½in x 24in
Coupled wheels	4ft 10in
Boiler pressure	160lb/sq in
Grate area	17sq ft
Tractive effort	17,235lb
Weight	46 tons 18cwt / 48 tons 8cwt*
SR number series	E177-E236 / 177-236 W14-W34*
BR numbers	30177, 30179, 30181** (W35*), 30182, 30183, 30192, 30193, 30197, 30198** (W36*), 30200, 30203, 30204, 30207, 30212, 30213, 30216, 30221, 30223-30225, 30229-30233, 30236, W14-W34*, plus (from 1949) W35* and W36*

* Modified to work on Isle of Wight; the 'W' prefix was not applied after the SR's 1931 renumbering, nor by BR, except on the bunker numberplates
** Never carried this number

Above: *The neat outline of an Adams 'O2' is exemplified by No 30225, standing at Eastleigh shed on 28 April 1959 after a general overhaul at the nearby locomotive works.* Author

Below: *Fitted with a Drummond boiler with safety valves on the dome, 'O2' No 30223 is pictured at Bournemouth Central on 11 April 1955.* Author

Right: *Class O2 0-4-4T No W30* Shorwell *stabled at Ryde St John's depot, on the Isle of Wight, on 1 July 1961. Note the extended coal bunker; also the air-brake pump on the far side of the smokebox.* Author

CLASS B4

Among the LSWR's many quaint and delightful locomotive types, the Adams 'B4' 0-4-0Ts must rank highly. They were low-slung, yet relatively long for their short wheelbase, and the use of outside cylinders gave them a waddling gait when heading along the main-line railway. Intended for working over the sharp curves of industrial sites such as docks, they spent a large portion of their working lives at Southampton.

For working at Southampton Docks, which had restricted clearances in some locations, the normal, enclosed cabs were changed to a rather attractive canopy design. The Docks Superintendent also arranged for the locomotives to carry painted names on their tank sides, names that covered many of the Continental ports, provinces and islands that were accessible from Southampton. The names were carried throughout their lives until British Railways painted them out when applying all-over black — its standard livery for goods locomotives. Prior to nationalisation the wide spaces in the canopy cabs had been plated over.

Drummond made small modifications to the design before ordering the last five locomotives. Initially classified as 'K14' (though eventually absorbed under the generic 'B4' designation), these locomotives had slightly smaller boilers and longer frames. All the locomotives eventually received Drummond flared chimneys, replacing the Adams stovepipes on the earlier locomotives. Oddly, the 'B4s' lacked power-operated brakes and thus had to rely on handbrakes; most if not all were eventually fitted with vacuum ejectors for handling passenger stock and fitted freight wagons.

Aside from their duties at Southampton Docks, from which they were ousted by the 'USA' 0-6-0Ts (page 112), these useful locomotives also worked at harbours at Dover, Poole and Hamworthy, were the preferred shed shunters at Bournemouth depot and shunted the small yards at Winchester. Nos 30092 and 30096 — and possibly others — were sold into industrial service. No 30102 was for several years mounted on a plinth at a holiday camp near Ayr before moving to Bressingham, its present home. At the time of writing No 30096, restored as No 96 *Normandy*, is preserved on the Bluebell Railway after its period of industrial service at Northam.

Class	B4 0-4-0T
Engineer	W. Adams
Designed for	LSWR
Built by	LSWR Nine Elms
Number in class	25
Introduced	1891
BR power rating	1F
Cylinders (2 outside)	16in x 22in
Coupled wheels	3ft 9¾in
Boiler pressure	140lb/sq in
Grate area	10.8sq ft
Tractive effort	14,650lb
Weight	33 tons 9cwt / 32 tons 18cwt*
SR numbers	E81, E82-E84*, E85-E100, E101*, E102, E103, E147*, E176 / 81-103, 147, 176
BR numbers**	30081-30103, 30147, 30176

* Originally Class K14
** Not all locomotives had these applied

Right: *Drummond 'K14' No 30084 still carried its Drummond boiler, with safety valves atop the dome, when photographed at Dover shed on 26 July 1959.* Author

Above: *Adams Class B4 0-4-0T No 30089 at Eastleigh on 2 December 1958, showing the basic, original design hardly changed apart from the Drummond chimney.* Author

Below: *Formerly Southampton Docks shunter* Normandy, *'B4' No 30096 is seen at Eastleigh depot on 21 July 1959 after a general overhaul in the nearby works. Note the simple plating of the cab front and back that covered the original canopy spaces.* Author

Above: *Formerly* Granville, *No 30102 retained its Adams dished plate smokebox door. Seen at Eastleigh depot in 1958, it displays different spectacle openings in the cab front, compared with No 30096 above. The mesh in the spark-arrestor over the chimney top would appear to let most small sparks through!* Author

An odd feature of the locomotive fleets of the 'Big Four' railways was that each had a No 1 and on three of them the locomotive carrying that number was a humble tank engine. As already intimated, the SR had three locomotives carrying the No 1. That in the main fleet list was an Adams Class T1 0-4-4T, but the number was also carried by a diesel shunter (page 102) and an 'E1' (officially No W1 — see page 57) on the Isle of Wight.

Adams introduced his Class T1 as a tank version of the 'A12' 0-4-2, with the same cylinders and boiler but with smaller coupled wheels. Thus it was suitable for suburban and empty-stock working and for mixed traffic on branch lines. The first order for 20 locomotives was executed at Nine Elms Works in 1888, a further 30 being delivered from 1894 and a final 10 in 1896. They were not built in numerical order, No 1 being the first of the second batch.

The first 20 locomotives used the same cylinders as the first 'A12s', with the slide valves underneath; the later locomotives, originally designated 'F6', had the later 'A12' (strictly 'O4') arrangement, with the slide valves between the cylinders. The 'F6s' had a slightly greater firebox heating surface, an increased grate area and more weight, distributed differently — the increase in weight was all on the bogie, and the coupled wheels actually had 11cwt less adhesion weight. In later years all 50 locomotives were designated 'T1'.

The 'T1s' worked suburban trains out of Waterloo as well as being the main power for a time on South Devon branch lines, and in SR days they were scattered throughout the Western Section. Thirteen survived to become part of the BR fleet in 1948 but were destined for early withdrawal in the great cull of the late 1940s and early '50s, none escaping the cutter's torch.

Class	T1 0-4-4T
Engineer	W. Adams
Designed for	LSWR
Built by	LSWR Nine Elms
Number in class	13 (plus 37 withdrawn before 1948)
Introduced	1894*
BR power rating	1P
Cylinders (2 inside)	18in x 26in
Coupled wheels	5ft 7in
Boiler pressure	160lb/sq in
Grate area	17sq ft / 17.85sq ft**
Tractive effort	17,100lb
Weight	53 tons 0cwt; 55 tons 2cwt**
SR number series	E1-E20**, E61-E80, E358-E367** / 1-20**, 61-80, 358-367**
BR numbers***	30001-30005, 30007-30010, 30013, 30020, 30361, 30367

*   Date relates to oldest survivor in 1948; class introduced 1888
** Originally Class F6
*** Never carried

Below: *In full SR Maunsell green livery, Adams Class T1 0-4-4T No 1 is seen shunting at Eastleigh before World War 2. During and after the war it was in plain black with 'sunshine' lettering and numbers shaded in green. The last locomotives of the class were early withdrawals, and few if any received their BR numbers. D. Sutton collection / Ian Allan Library*

CLASS G6

To provide a useful shunting locomotive Adams used as much of the 'O2' design as possible in producing the Class G6 0-6-0T. Boiler, cylinders and coupled wheels were the same, as were the cab and side tanks. Indeed, the only visible differences were the six coupled wheels and the absence of a bogie. The class had some variations. Two were fitted with Drummond boilers, which were moved among other locomotives in the class as works overhauls progressed. The last 10 had boilers with bigger fireboxes and correspondingly shorter barrels, giving a slight weight reduction. These were initially classified 'M9' but in time were absorbed into the 'G6' class.

The 'G6s' were used in yards all over the system. One tough duty for the Exmouth Junction allocation was banking heavy trains between Exeter St Davids and Exeter Central stations, though they were displaced on this by the advent of the Class E1/R 0-6-2Ts (page 85).

All the class entered BR service, but the advent of diesel shunting locomotives, together with a spate of yard closures, rendered them redundant. Two passed into departmental stock at Meldon Quarry; No 30272 (DS3152) went there in 1949 and was replaced in 1960 by No 30238 (DS682). The latter was withdrawn in 1962, the last survivor. None was preserved.

Class	G6 0-6-0T
Engineer	W. Adams
Designed for	LSWR
Built by	LSWR Nine Elms
Number in class	34
Introduced	1894
BR power rating	2F
Cylinders (2 inside)	17½in x 24in
Coupled wheels	4ft 10in
Boiler pressure	160lb/sq in
Grate area	17sq ft
Tractive effort	17,235lb
Weight	47 tons 1cwt; 46 tons 15cwt*
SR numbers	E160, E162, E237-E240, E257-E275, E276-E279*, E348-E354* / 160, 162, 237-240, 257-275, 276-279*, 348-354*
BR numbers**	30160, 30162, 30237-30240, 30257-30275, 30276-30279*, 30348-30354*; DS3152 (30272), replaced by DS682 (30238)

* Formerly Class M9, with boiler differences
** Most never applied

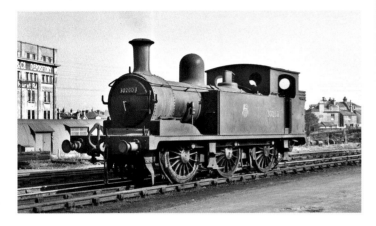

Left: *The Adams Class G6 0-6-0T design was essentially an 'O2' with six coupled wheels and no bogie. No 30260, with an Adams boiler with safety valves on the firebox top, shunts the east yard at Bournemouth on 22 September 1956.* Author

Below: *Adams Class G6 0-6-0T No 30274, with a Drummond boiler (safety valves on the dome), stands at Eastleigh depot on 2 April 1959 after an intermediate overhaul.* Author

Dugald Drummond will always be remembered for his Class T9 4-4-0s, partly because they were excellent and good-looking locomotives but also because they were the last Drummond 4-4-0s to survive on BR. Introduced in 1899, the 'T9s' were intended to be the LSWR's front-line express passenger locomotives. While Adams had wavered between giving his express designs 7ft 1in or 6ft 7in coupled wheels, Drummond standardised on 6ft 7in — a size that was subsequently adopted by Urie and, in SR days, Maunsell. The 'T9s' had slide valves for the two inside cylinders. The first 50 locomotives had narrow cabs and splashers, necessitating small additional splashers to accommodate the throw of the coupling rods; all these locomotives were built with conventional six-wheeled tenders. The next 15 were built with wider cabs and did not need the coupling rod splashers, and these later locomotives were coupled to 4,000gal tenders with eight wheels having inside frames, giving them an exposed look that earned the nickname 'watercarts'. The 66th locomotive of the class was built by Dübs as its main exhibit in the 1901 Glasgow Exhibition; subsequently acquired by the LSWR, it was originally numbered 773 but was renumbered 733 by the SR in 1924. This locomotive had a narrow cab and splashers and a six-wheeled tender. Tenders were later mixed up so that both narrow and wide-cab locomotives could be seen with either type of tender.

The 'T9s', with good-steaming boilers, excelled in performance from the first and were soon nicknamed 'Greyhounds' on account of their fast running. Urie's addition of superheating served to raise their performance from good to excellent. Upon rebuilding the smokebox was extended to accommodate the superheater. Urie also fitted his cast stovepipe chimney, with short capuchon, in place of Drummond's more elegant flared design, although the capuchon was eventually removed from all but one locomotive (No 119) in order to meet the SR's composite loading-gauge.

Demoted to secondary passenger duties, all 66 'T9s' lasted into the BR era. The last was withdrawn in 1963 and is preserved as SR No 120.

Above: *Drummond 'T9' No 30117 poses at Fratton shed on 22 April 1961. One of the last survivors, it has a narrow cab and splashers necessitating separate small splashers to clear the coupling rods, while the chimney shows the remnant of a capuchon that has been incompletely removed by grinding. The locomotive is coupled to an eight-wheeled 'watercart' tender.* Author

Below: *No 30300 had a wide cab and splashers. When photographed at Eastleigh depot on 4 April 1960 it was paired with a six-wheeled tender.* Author

Class	T9 4-4-0
Engineer	D. Drummond
Designed for	LSWR
Built by	LSWR Nine Elms, Dübs (702-733)
Number in class	66
Introduced	1899
BR power rating	3P
Cylinders (2 inside)	19in x 26in
Coupled wheels	6ft 7in
Boiler pressure	175lb/sq in
Grate area	24sq ft
Tractive effort	17,670lb
Weight	46 tons 4cwt, 48 tons 17cwt*
SR number series	E113-E122, E280-E289, E300-E305*, E307*, E310-E314*, E336-E338*, E702-E733 / 113-122, 280-289, 300-305*, 307*, 310-314*, 336-338*, 702-733
BR number series**	30113-30122, 30280-30289, 30300-30305, 30307, 30310-30314, 30336-30338, 30702-30733

*   Locomotives with wider cabs
**   Not all locomotives received their allocated BR numbers

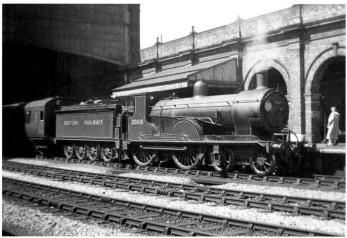

Above: *Specially painted and cleaned for working VIP trains to and from Royal Ascot, No 30119 stands at Bournemouth Central on 29 June 1952, having arrived from Brockenhurst with a stopping train via Ringwood and Wimborne. Formerly No 119, this locomotive had been repainted in or after 1938 from its Maunsell dark green into malachite green, a colour which BR retained at its final repaint.* Author

CLASS M7

The first truly Drummond design to emerge from Nine Elms Works after his arrival on the LSWR was his Class M7 0-4-4T, intended for use on suburban and main-line stopping passenger trains. This used the same boiler as would later be fitted to his '700' class (page 18) and was in effect an enlargement of Adams's Class T1 (page 13). Drummond features included the positioning of the two safety valves on top of the dome, redesigned cab side openings and the flared cast-iron chimney that was to replace the Adams stovepipe on all classes that survived into the Drummond era.

The class, which at its peak totalled 105 locomotives, was constructed over a period of 15 years, and during this time there were several changes in design. The first 45 locomotives, built from 1897 to 1899, had short front frames, and the sandboxes were combined with the front wheel splashers. The 10 built in 1900 had the leading sandboxes inside the smokebox, although these would later be re-sited in a forward position beneath the side running plates. Ten further, similar locomotives were built in 1903, but these had longer front frames. From 1904 the front sandboxes were once again combined with the leading splashers; these and subsequent locomotives received balanced crank axles. Locomotives built from 1903, all with long frames, were initially classified 'X14', though all later reverted to the all-embracing 'M7' designation.

Early use of 'M7s' on express trains between Plymouth and Exeter via Okehampton was curtailed as a result of derailments, caused allegedly by the lack of a leading pony truck or bogie wheels. When the 'M7s' were displaced from suburban working by electrification they were sent to work branch-line services all around the LSWR system and, indeed, later ventured eastwards into Central and Eastern Section areas. The LSWR fitted some with a cable-operated push-pull system, but the SR replaced this with the LBSCR type of air-operated system, and 36 'M7s' were so fitted in the 1930s; these latter were all

long-underframe locomotives, the front overhang allowing space for a large air reservoir fixed behind the buffer-beam, and could be distinguished easily by the Westinghouse air pump on the fireman's side of the smokebox.

In 1921 No 126 was rebuilt by Urie with features similar to those incorporated in his rebuilding of the '700' class. However, in this form it proved too heavy for many 'M7' passenger duties and was withdrawn in 1937. Its frames were subsequently used for No 254, and the practice of swapping good frames for bad resumed during at least two overhauls at Eastleigh in the late 1950s.

In the late 1940s a few 'M7s' that were used for bringing empty stock for prestige trains into Waterloo station were painted in SR malachite green, and at least two received their BR numbers when carrying this smart livery.

The second 'M7' withdrawal was of No 30672, which had fallen down the Waterloo & City line rolling-stock lift shaft at Waterloo station and was cut up on site in May 1948. The rest of the class survived to be withdrawn by BR in the years 1957-64. Nos 30053 and 30245 are preserved, the latter a static exhibit at the National Railway Museum, York, in near-original condition as LSWR No 245. Initially sold into preservation in the USA, No 30053 was later repatriated to the UK and has for some years been based on the Swanage Railway in Dorset, on which line a number of 'M7s' worked for many decades.

Below: *The early style of 'M7' 0-4-4T with splasher sandboxes and short front-frame overhang is illustrated by No 30033 at Eastleigh station on 17 July 1956. Typical Drummond features are the cab shape, the safety valves on top of the dome and the flared cast-iron chimney.* Author

Right: *The next variation in the 'M7' design came with the group that had the leading sandboxes placed initially in the smokebox. Later these would be moved to beneath the front frame, as on No 30112, station pilot at Bournemouth Central in August 1954.* Author

Below: *Later 'M7s' had longer front frames, and No 30030's home depot took advantage of this by fitting a small snowplough. The locomotive is seen at Eastleigh station on 4 July 1955.* Author

Above: *Thirty-six Class M7 0-4-4Ts were fitted for push-pull operation using the LBSCR air-operated system. No 30481, photographed at Eastleigh depot on 14 December 1957, shows the Westinghouse compressed-air pump on the smokebox side and the regulator-operating cylinder on the tank front. The air reservoir for the system fits neatly behind the buffer-beam under the longer frame.* Author

Class	M7 0-4-4T
Engineer	D. Drummond
Designed for	LSWR
Built by	LSWR Nine Elms (95) / LSWR Eastleigh (10)
Number in class	104 (plus 1 withdrawn before 1948)
Introduced	1897
BR power rating	2P
Cylinders (2 inside)	18½in x 26in
Coupled wheels	5ft 7in
Boiler pressure	175lb/sq in
Grate area	20sq ft
Tractive effort	19,755lbf
Weight	60 tons 4cwt, 62 tons 0cwt*
SR numbers	E21-E60**, E104-E112**, E123-E133**, E241-E256, E318-E324, E328**, E356, E357, E374-E379**, E479-E481**, E667-E676 / 21-60, 104-112, 123-133***, 241-256, 318-324, 328, 356, 357, 374-379, 479-481, 667-676
BR numbers****	30021-30060, 30104-30112, 30123-30125, 30127-30133, 30241-30256, 30318-30324, 30328, 30356, 30357, 30374-30379, 30479-30481, 30667-30676

* Applies to locomotives with push-pull apparatus (Nos 30021, 30027-30029, 30045-30060, 30104-30111, 30125, 30128, 30129, 30131, 30328, 30379, 30480, 30481)
** Nos E21, E27-E30, E45-E60, E104-E111, E123-E133, E328, E374-E379, E479-E481 originally Class X14
*** No 126 withdrawn in 1937
**** No 30672 never carried this number

CLASS 700

The LSWR had a collection of ancient 0-6-0s for its goods services, plus the competent mixed-traffic 'Jubilee' 0-4-2s (page 10), but when Drummond came on the scene he met a need for replacements for some of the older locomotives. His design of 0-6-0 bore similarities to locomotives he had produced in Scotland. It had two inside cylinders, with slide valves, and used the same saturated boiler that was being built for the new Class M7 0-4-4Ts (pages 16 and 17) and which also appeared on locomotives of Classes C8 and K10 (page 19). Cylinders and motion were also standard LSWR items.

In the last years of the booming 1890s there was no surplus locomotive-building capacity at Nine Elms, so the railway placed its order for 30 0-6-0s with Dübs & Co of Glasgow, which delivered the entire class in 1897. The locomotives were originally numbered from 687 to 716, so it seems odd that the class designation should have been '700' rather than '687', after the first locomotive, in line with normal practice for contractor-built locomotives. Nos 702-716 were later renumbered in a scattered range of numbers to make way for new 'T9' 4-4-0s.

R. W. Urie took on the superheating of the '700' class, incorporating this in quite a significant rebuild. The boiler was enlarged and pitched 9in higher, the frames extended forwards by 1ft 6in to clear the extended smokebox, larger-diameter cylinders were fitted, and the locomotives received stovepipe chimneys, originally with capuchons (subsequently cut off). Later, all locomotives received Maunsell superheaters.

As vacuum-fitted locomotives the '700s' could be used on passenger trains, but they were normally confined to goods work. As time went on they were relegated from main-line operation to secondary routes and branch lines, but all 30 were still active when BR was formed in 1948. Indeed, so useful were they that only two had succumbed by 1960. Mass withdrawals followed in 1961 and 1962 following the cascading of larger locomotives such as Woolwich Moguls, themselves displaced by modernisation of the Kent lines. Few older goods tender engines survived into preservation, and regrettably the '700s', despite their 65-plus years of service, proved no exception.

Class	700 0-6-0
Engineer	D. Drummond
Designed for	LSWR
Built by	Dübs
Number in class	30
Introduced	1897
BR power rating	3F
Cylinders (2 inside)	19in x 26in
Coupled wheels	5ft 1in
Boiler pressure	180lb/sq in
Grate area	20sq ft
Tractive effort	23,540lb
Weight	46 tons 14cwt
SR numbers	E306, E308, E309, E315-E317, E325-E327, E339, E346, E350, E352, E355, E368, E687-E701 / 306, 308, 309, 315-317, 325-327, 339, 346, 350, 352, 355, 368, 687-701
BR numbers	30306, 30308, 30309, 30315-30317, 30325-30327, 30339, 30346, 30350, 30352, 30355, 30368, 30687-30701

Below: *The Class 700 0-6-0s were rebuilt by Urie with superheaters and extended smokeboxes and thereafter always looked heavy at the front end. No 30699 had just been outshopped from overhaul when photographed at Eastleigh shed on 9 December 1958. Author*

Before producing the 'T9s' (page 15) Drummond had delivered his Class C8 4-4-0 express locomotives. These were saturated-steam 4-4-0s, with the same boiler design as the 'M7' 0-4-4T (pages 16 and 17). Good-looking locomotives, the 'C8s' ran for 35 or more years but were never modernised in the way that the 'T9s' were, and none survived into the 1940s. However, longer-lived was the 'K10' variant, introduced by Drummond in 1901, with smaller (5ft 7in) coupled wheels for mixed-traffic use and with boiler heating surface increased by 100sq ft. Like the 'T9s' and other Drummond designs of the period these locomotives had his patented firebox water tubes that crossed the firebox space in an attempt to increase heating surface. These proved a liability in terms of maintenance, and when Urie took over as CME in 1912 he set about removing this feature from all locomotives that had it. However, neither he nor Maunsell endowed the 'K10s' with superheaters. In consequence the locomotives spent most of their lives on secondary duties; the author recalls them working stopping trains on the relatively rural line between Salisbury, West Moors and Bournemouth. However, during World War 2 several 'K10s' were transferred temporarily to work in places outside the SR such as Gloucester, Bristol and Nottingham.

The 'K10s' all started life with six-wheeled tenders, but as the years went by several received eight-wheeled 'watercarts' as tenders were switched at works overhauls.

Being suited to their more menial tasks, the 'K10s' comfortably outlasted the 'C8s', and withdrawals did not begin until early 1947. The remainder were withdrawn by BR in the late 1940s and early '50s, and none survived to be preserved.

Class	K10 4-4-0
Engineer	D. Drummond
Designed for	LSWR
Built by	LSWR Nine Elms
Number in class	31 (plus 9 withdrawn before 1948)
Introduced	1901
BR power rating	1MT
Cylinders (2 inside)	18½in x 26in
Coupled wheels	5ft 7in
Boiler pressure	175lb/sq in
Grate area	20sq ft
Tractive effort	19,760lb
Weight	46 tons 14cwt
SR numbers	E135-E146, E149-E153, E329, E340-E345, E347, E380-E394/ 135-146*, 149-153*, 329, 340-345*, 347*, 380-394*
BR numbers**	30135, 30137, 30139-30146, 30150-30153, 30329, 30340, 30341, 30343, 30345, 30380, 30382-30386, 30389-30394

*   Nos 136, 138, 149, 342, 344, 347, 381, 387, 388 withdrawn 1947
** Only No 30382 received its BR number

Below: Class K10 4-4-0 No E344 photographed between the wars in SR Maunsell lined green livery and with six-wheeled tender. W. J. Reynolds

CLASS L11

By 1903 Drummond must have realised the limitations of the 'M7' boiler for main-line work when compared with the more productive 'T9' type. He decided that the next batch of mixed-traffic 4-4-0s should develop the 'K10' design by incorporating the 'T9' boiler. Accordingly, because the firebox was longer and deeper, the Class L11 4-4-0s had a coupled wheelbase 1ft longer at 10ft, and the boiler was pitched 3in higher. As with the 'K10s', a total of 40 'L11s' was built. They were in effect 'T9s' with smaller coupled wheels, which could equally be expressed as 'K10s' with 'T9' boilers, so closely related were these designs.

Like the 'T9s', the 'L11s' lived with a mixture of six-wheeled and eight-wheeled tenders. Eleven were built with inside-framed eight-wheeled tenders, but the rest standardised for a time on the six-wheeled outside-frame type. Tenders were exchanged between locomotives and the other similar classes as developments continued. For example, when a few 'T9s' were temporarily converted to oil burning these received 'watercart' tenders in exchange for six-wheelers, which were adequate for the secondary duties of the 'L11s'.

It had been customary for Drummond tenders to have feed-water-heating tubes in the tender-tank well, adding 382sq ft to the overall heating surface. The 'L11s' also had these, but in later years they were removed as a means of reducing maintenance costs. Like the 'K10s', the 'L11s' did not receive superheaters.

The 'L11s' worked successfully over all the Southern Railway's Western Section and also gravitated further east on occasions. All the class survived to be taken into BR stock, and many received their allocated five-figure BR numbers. Withdrawal began in the late 1940s and was completed in the early '50s — not an era that was conducive to locomotive preservation — and in consequence none of the class survives today.

Class	L11 4-4-0
Engineer	D. Drummond
Designed for	LSWR
Built by	LSWR Nine Elms
Number in class	40
Introduced	1903
BR power rating	1MT
Cylinders (2 inside)	18½in x 26in
Coupled wheels	5ft 7in
Boiler pressure	175lb/sq in
Grate area	24sq ft
Tractive effort	19,760lb
Weight	50 tons 11cwt
SR numbers	E134, E148, E154-E159, E161, E163-E175, E405-414, E435-E442 / 134, 148, 154-159, 161, 163-175, 405-414, 435-442
BR numbers*	30134, 30148, 30154-30159, 30161, 30163-30175, 30405-30414, 30435-30442

* Most never applied

Below: *Class L11 4-4-0 No 148, paired with a Drummond 4,000gal 'watercart' tender. The 'T9s' aside, all Drummond 4-4-0s that survived into the BR era had wide cabs and splashers.* Ian Allan Library

The step-by-step development of Drummond's 4-4-0 designs continued with the Class 'S11', a mixed-traffic type based on the 'L11' but with a bigger boiler, higher pitched, and a small increase in cylinder diameter. However, the boiler pressure and grate area remained unchanged from the 'T9', possibly limiting the locomotives' potential effectively to feed the bigger cylinders when working hard on gradients such as the 1 in 75 of Honiton Bank.

The 10 'S11s', though outwardly mixed-traffic locomotives, were intended to work express trains over the difficult, hilly main line west of Salisbury. They were originally coupled to 'watercart' tenders but in the 1940s gave these up to several of the 'T9' class. Drummond fitted these 10 locomotives with his patented design of balanced crank axle; this employed extensions to the inside crank webs on the driving axle that in theory balanced the reciprocating parts and would eliminate the need for balance weights on the wheels themselves and thus reduce the repetitive vertical forces on the track, known as hammer-blow.

Urie rebuilt the 'S11s' with superheaters which required extended smokeboxes — an improvement in their appearance, in the author's view. Maunsell later fitted his more effective superheater. Most locomotives lost their handsome Drummond chimneys in favour of short, stubby Urie-type stovepipes, a work not completed even in the 1950s.

During World War 2 the 10 locomotives were loaned to the LMS (being classified by that railway as '2P'), and worked mainly out of Bath Green Park on the Somerset & Dorset line, although some ventured further afield, working from Saltley, Burton-upon-Trent and Peterborough. All were returned to the SR in 1945.

BR withdrew the 'S11s' in the early 1950s and scrapped the entire class.

Class	S11 4-4-0
Engineer	D. Drummond
Designed for	LSWR
Built by	LSWR Nine Elms
Number in class	10
Introduced	1903
BR power rating	3P
Cylinders (2 inside)	19in x 26in
Coupled wheels	6ft 1in
Boiler pressure	175lb/sq in
Grate area	24sq ft
Tractive effort	19,400lb
Weight	53 tons 15cwt
SR number series	E395-E404 / 395-404
BR number series*	30395-30404

* Nos 30395 and 30401 never carried these numbers

Right: *Class S11 4-4-0 No 30404 stands at Salisbury with a Bournemouth train. This locomotive was one of the last to retain its Drummond-type chimney.* Author

Left: *Most of the 'S11s' later gained Urie stovepipe chimneys, as seen on No 30400, standing by the coaling plant at Guildford depot on 1 September 1951 — three years before it was finally condemned.* Brian Morrison

CLASS L12

For an express-passenger version of his Class S11 4-4-0 Drummond ordered 20 similar locomotives but with 6ft 7in coupled wheels for use on the flatter main lines out of Waterloo. The resulting 'L12' had a boiler pitched slightly higher than the 'S11', on account of the larger coupled wheels. Under R. W. Urie the locomotives were superheated and given extended smokeboxes and short stovepipe chimneys. In common with the 'T9' and 'S11' classes the 'L12s' continued the practice of combining superheating with slide valves, which worked well in all three types. Maunsell later fitted them all with his own design of superheater. For many years half the 'L12s' had 'watercart' tenders and half had the six-wheeled type, though most ended up with the latter.

The 'L12s' worked far and wide over the main lines of the Western Section of the SR. On 1 July 1906 No 421 was allowed to pass through Salisbury station at too high a speed with the overnight Plymouth–Waterloo boat train and rolled over at the sharp exit curve. The accident resulted in much loss of life, but the locomotive was repaired and returned to service.

Having been displaced from main-line expresses by newer locomotives such as the 'King Arthurs', the 'L12s' were used on secondary lines and main-line stopping services. Their end came quickly in the early 1950s, by which time BR Standard locomotives were being delivered to the Southern Region's South Western Division, and all had been scrapped by the end of 1955.

Above: *Following rebuilding by Urie 'L12' 4-4-0 No E424 carried his design of stovepipe chimney with capuchon; however, this was outside the SR composite loading-gauge, and on most locomotives such adornments were later removed. Visible high on the side of the smokebox is one of the snifting valves, which Bulleid would have removed from all SR locomotives in the 1940s.* Ian Allan Library

Class	L12 4-4-0
Engineer	D. Drummond
Designed for	LSWR
Built by	LSWR Nine Elms
Number in class	20
Introduced	1904
BR power rating	3P
Cylinders (2 inside)	19in x 26in
Coupled wheels	6ft 7in
Boiler pressure	175lb/sq in
Grate area	24sq ft
Tractive effort	16,755lb
Weight	55 tons 5cwt
SR number series	E415-E434 / 415-434
BR number series*	30415-30434

* No 30430 never carried this number

Like the 'T9' (but unlike most Drummond 4-6-0s that came between) the Class D15 4-4-0 proved to be an excellent design and, indeed, has been described as his masterpiece. The 'D15' was, in fact, Drummond's last express-locomotive design and was effectively an enlargement of his 'L12' 4-4-0. The boiler was larger, and the firebox had a usefully increased grate area, achieved by lengthening the firebox and sloping the grate so that the back was high enough to clear the rear coupled axle. The cylinders in their original form were ½inch larger in diameter than those of the 'L12', and the boiler pressure was an exciting (for the period) 200lb/sq in. Like the 'L12' and 'S11' classes the 'D15s' had wide cabs without coupling-rod splashers. They were coupled initially to eight-wheeled 'watercart' tenders but later received six-wheeled tenders, with which they ended their lives.

Urie rebuilt the 'D15s' by adding superheaters, enlarging the cylinders (by ½in in diameter) and reducing the boiler pressure (to 180lb/sq in). The superheater header was accommodated in an extended smokebox. In the mid-1920s Maunsell fitted his own superheaters, and the locomotives received somewhat stubby stovepipe chimneys which did not improve their appearance. Nevertheless, the 'D15s' performed superbly and economically, initially on the Bournemouth expresses and then later on the Portsmouth Direct line, being employed there until the advent of electrification. Later they worked secondary, cross-country and stopping passenger services, but, being heavier than the 'T9s', they had a more limited route availability and were withdrawn in the 1950s. The last was condemned in 1956, and none was preserved.

Class	D15 4-4-0
Engineer	D. Drummond
Designed for	LSWR
Built by	LSWR Eastleigh
Number in class	10
Introduced	1912
BR power rating	3P
Cylinders (2 inside)	20in x 26in*
Coupled wheels	6ft 7in
Boiler pressure	180lb/sq in*
Grate area	27sq ft
Tractive effort	20,140lb
Weight	61 tons 11cwt
SR number series	E463-E472 / 463-472
BR number series	30463-30472

* Before superheating, boiler pressure was 200lb/sq in, cylinder diameter 19½in, and tractive effort 21,270lb

Below: *The Class D15 4-4-0s were handsome and effective machines and, like all Drummond's larger 4-4-0s, ended up with six-wheeled tenders. No 30464 is seen being prepared for service at Nine Elms depot in July 1954.* Brian Morrison

CLASS T14

Probably the best of Drummond's many attempts at producing a big, powerful 4-6-0 was the 'T14'. This was a four-cylinder simple, with four sets of Walschaerts valve gear. The 10 locomotives were built with large, straight splashers covering the six coupled wheels down to the level of the straight valances; the deep splashers had a circular inspection window that earned them the nickname 'paddleboxes'.

Within five years of their construction Urie had started rebuilding the 'T14s' with extended smokeboxes and superheaters. Like the 'D15s', the 'T14s' had their boiler pressure reduced, this time from 200lb/sq in to 175lb/sq in, although the cylinder dimensions remained unchanged. In the early 1930s Maunsell opened up the area behind the outside cylinders by raising the running plate and providing separate wheel splashers, giving the locomotives an altogether more modern appearance; at the same time Maunsell superheaters were fitted.

Some commentators have noted that the exhaust passages on the 'T14s' were very clear and direct, giving the potential for free exhaust emissions. That the locomotives were a bit sluggish may therefore have come more from inadequacies in the design of live steam passages or in the ability of the boiler to feed the four quite large cylinders. Mechanical problems beset the axleboxes, which were a weak point in the design, running hot with unwarranted frequency, so Maunsell fitted them with mechanical lubricators, which brought a sufficient improvement.

As express passenger locomotives the 'T14s' did not excel, performing no better than the 'D15' 4-4-0s, but they were nonetheless adequate for secondary passenger duties. They were undoubtedly Drummond's best 4-6-0s, lasting far longer than any of his other LSWR designs of this wheel arrangement, and their performance is said to have improved a little when, late in SR days, they were fitted with short Urie-style stovepipe chimneys. Having been eased off the top duties early on by the Urie 4-6-0s, the 'T14s' spent the rest of their lives on secondary workings such as Waterloo–Basingstoke semi-fast workings and stopping trains to Salisbury and Bournemouth, the last example being withdrawn in 1951.

Class	T14 4-6-0
Engineer	D. Drummond
Designed for	LSWR
Built by	LSWR Eastleigh
Number in class	9 (plus 1 withdrawn before 1948)
Introduced	1911
BR power rating	4P
Cylinders (4)	15in x 26in
Coupled wheels	6ft 7in
Boiler pressure	175lb/sq in*
Grate area	32sq ft
Tractive effort	20,140lb
Weight	76 tons 10cwt
SR number series	E443-E447, E458-E462 / 443-447, 458-462**
BR number series***	30443-30447, 30459-30462

*   Before superheating, boiler pressure was 200lb/sq in, and tractive effort 23,017lb
**   No 458 was withdrawn in 1940 after being hit by a German bomb at Nine Elms
*** Only Nos 30446, 30447 and 30461 received their allocated BR numbers

Below: *Even after two heavy rebuilds Drummond's four-cylinder Class T14 4-6-0s remained handsome locomotives. Complete with 'watercart' tender, No 460 is pictured in wartime Southern livery.* Ian Allan Library

Three Class C14 0-4-0Ts entered BR service after long lives that started in 1906. The trio had originally formed part of a class of 10 2-2-0T locomotives fitted for push-pull operation, in an attempt to replace unsuccessful steam railmotors with something more substantial. That this was not the end result is evident from the fact that, at the start of World War 1, all 10 had ventured onto other work, seven having passed variously to the War Department, the Admiralty (two) or to the Ministry of Munitions (four, one of these being on loan). The three that remained with the LSWR were converted as 0-4-0Ts, enabling them to perform useful shunting work and ultimately prolonging their lives well beyond those of the unrebuilt examples. The conversion was achieved by moving the cylinders from their original position between the leading and driving wheels, so that they were more conventionally in front of the four wheels.

The 'C14' design had a short wheelbase, a single-plate rolled boiler barrel, driving wheels of just 3ft diameter and cylinders of 10x14in stroke. Cylinder diameters were progressively enlarged to the final 14in, giving the locomotives an unusual square cylinder section in side elevation. They were side-tank engines with standard Drummond style cabs, flared chimneys and very small rear coal bunkers. As ever, the safety valves were atop the dome. In the 1910s all three locomotives were transferred to the duplicate list, to make way for Urie 'N15' 4-6-0s in the LSWR's numbering system.

The very short length of the 'C14s' gave them a truncated appearance, but the short wheelbase served the three 0-4-0T conversions well in that they were considered suitable for working in Southampton Docks. In 1927 one locomotive, No E0745, was transferred to service stock as No 77S and became the regular shunting locomotive at Redbridge track-engineering depot. The other two found their final employment shunting on the tightly curved Southampton Town Quay lines. Interestingly, following the withdrawal of Nos 30588 and 30589 in 1957, the departmental locomotive became the last steam locomotive regularly to work the Town Quay, and did so without ever being re-absorbed into capital stock. No 77S was withdrawn in 1959 without being renumbered. All three were scrapped.

Class	C14 0-4-0T
Engineer	D. Drummond
Designed for	LSWR
Built by	LSWR Nine Elms
Number in class	3*
Introduced	1913
BR power rating	0P (0F until 1952)
Cylinders (2 outside)	14in x 14in
Coupled wheels	3ft 0in
Boiler pressure	150lb/sq in
Grate area	10sq ft
Tractive effort	9,720lb
Weight	25 tons 15cwt
SR numbers	E0741, E0744, E0745** / 3741, 3744, 77S
BR numbers	30588, 30589, DS77

*   Survivors of a class 10 locomotives built in 1906/7 as 2-2-0Ts; rebuilt as 0-4-0Ts in the years 1913-23
** Renumbered 77S in 1927

Above right: *The diminutive yet full-height Class C14 0-4-0Ts were unusual for small LSWR tank engines in having outside Walschaerts valve gear. Converted in 1922 from a 2-2-0T railmotor locomotive (in which form it had been numbered 0741), No 30588 was later employed on shunting duties at Southampton Town Quay. It was photographed at Eastleigh depot on 14 May 1955.* Author

Right: *Towards the end of steam operation at Southampton Town Quay, where this photograph was taken on 20 September 1958, the regular locomotive was 'C14' No 77S, which by now had been relieved of its duties at Redbridge civil-engineering depot.* Author

With experience in Scotland behind him it was not surprising that Robert Wallace Urie eschewed the rather unorthodox 4-6-0s that Drummond had provided for the LSWR, instead drawing on what he had seen in Scotland in the form of simple, rugged 4-6-0s for mixed-traffic working. In 1914 Eastleigh Works outshopped the first of his 'H15' class. This created quite a sensation, being much more impressive in appearance than anything previously seen south of the River Thames. Its large-diameter boiler was matched by enormous cylinders, of 21in diameter, with a stroke of 28in — long by all but GWR standards. Urie, however, was not of the Churchward school of locomotive design and had not fully applied the benefits of large-diameter and long-travel piston valves, wide steam passages and free exhausts. Thus, although the big boiler of a Urie 'H15' could produce quite a lot of steam, the locomotive was not able to use it effectively, apart from at relatively slow speeds such as when pulling long, heavy freight trains. Use of 'H15s' on main-line expresses showed that the Drummond 'D15' 4-4-0s were altogether more fleet-of-foot and economical machines, a fact Urie was man enough to acknowledge.

The 'H15' was a mixed-traffic locomotive with 6ft 0in coupled wheels and took its place in the middle of the three classes of standard 4-6-0s that the SR later inherited from the LSWR, most of which would be developed further by Maunsell in the 1920s. Indeed, the Southern Railway-built examples were of broadly similar external appearance except for the differences in their driving-wheel sizes and in the various tenders to which the locomotives were coupled.

Below: *Urie's beefy Class H15 4-6-0s, with their high-pitched, large-diameter parallel boilers, created a sensation when they first appeared from Eastleigh Works. Attached to a high-capacity (5,200gal) bogie tender, No 30487 waits outside Bournemouth Central with stock for an up working on 24 March 1956.* Author

On eight of his 10 'H15' locomotives Urie experimented with Schmidt and Robinson superheaters, and two locomotives had saturated boilers; he then settled on his own design, which became known as the 'Eastleigh' superheater. In Maunsell's time locomotive No 491 received a Class N15 tapered boiler with a Maunsell-designed superheater, a type that was fitted in due course to all other 'H15s', though the original parallel boilers were retained on these.

Urie had recognised the need to develop and improve the 'H15' 4-6-0 design before ordering 10 more new locomotives. Completed in 1924, these locomotives have always been credited to Maunsell because they emerged from Eastleigh Works in Southern Railway days when he was CME. In fact they had been ordered before the Grouping of 1923, the order being ratified by Maunsell before construction began, and were essentially to Urie's improved design.

In the 1920s all the 'H15s' received standard smoke-deflectors; those on the parallel-boilered locomotives were aligned slightly outwards at the top, whereas those on the taper-boilered examples sloped inwards and were attached to the handrails at the top.

In service the 'Maunsell' locomotives were employed variously on stopping passenger trains, parcels trains and freights. When called upon they could deputise satisfactorily for their faster 'N15' siblings on express trains (which the original examples could not), albeit with the penalty of a limited top speed. Indeed, on summer Saturdays it was not unusual to see a Maunsell 'H15' heading a 10-coach train of holidaymakers down the main line to Bournemouth (having taken over from a 'foreign' locomotive at Oxford) or on a relief train from Waterloo. However, the heaviest work for the class involved sharing Southampton Docks–Feltham/Nine Elms freight workings with the 'S15' 4-6-0s. Being well suited to heavy slogging, the 'H15s' were in their element on such work.

The introduction of BR Standard Class 4 and Class 5 4-6-0s resulted in the withdrawal of all the 'H15s' in the late 1950s and early '60s, none being preserved.

Class	H15 4-6-0
Engineer	R. W. Urie
Designed for	LSWR
Built by	LSWR and SR Eastleigh
BR power rating	4P5FA
Number in class	20
Introduced	1914
Cylinders (2 outside)	21in x 28in
Coupled wheels	6ft 0in
Boiler pressure	180lb/sq in
Grate area	30sq ft
Tractive effort	26,240lb
Weight	81 tons 15cwt* / 79 tons 19cwt**
SR number series	E482-E491, E473-E478, E521-E524 / 482-491, 473-478, 521-524
BR number series	30482-30491, 30473-30478, 30521-30524

* Urie 'H15s' Nos 30482-30490 with parallel boilers
** Maunsell 'H15s' Nos 30473-30478, 30521-30524 plus Urie 'H15' No 30491, all with taper boilers

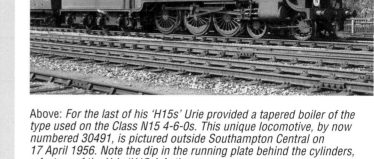

Above: *For the last of his 'H15s' Urie provided a tapered boiler of the type used on the Class N15 4-6-0s. This unique locomotive, by now numbered 30491, is pictured outside Southampton Central on 17 April 1956. Note the dip in the running plate behind the cylinders, a feature of the Urie 'H15s'.* Author

Below: *Shortly after the formation of the SR Maunsell ordered some modified 'H15s', with better cylinders and draughting. They were visually distinguishable by their straight running plates and valances, as seen on No 30474 at Eastleigh on 9 December 1958.* Author

CLASS H15

Being reasonably satisfied that his 'H15' locomotives were significantly better than the preceding Drummond 4-6-0s, Urie in 1915 rebuilt the 1907-built Class E14 4-6-0 No 335 to become an 'H15' look-alike. The rebuild utilised the existing boiler, now superheated, and the frames, tender and wheels appear to have been reused as well. Two new outside cylinders replaced the original four cylinders fed by piston valves actuated by outside Walschaerts valve gear. The locomotive's tender was a large Drummond 'watercart' of 4,500gal water capacity.

Later, in 1924 and 1925, Maunsell rebuilt the five Drummond Class F13 4-6-0s in similar fashion. Doubts remain as to how much of the Drummond locomotives remained, though it is safe to assume that the boilers and tenders were original. In appearance these five locomotives looked similar to No E335 but had straight, high running plates, No E335 displaying the characteristic Urie lower section behind the cylinders. These locomotives also retained their Drummond 'watercart' tenders to the end. Like their Urie brethren, all these locomotives received standard SR smoke-deflectors.

All six 'rebuilt' locomotives officially formed part of Class H15. Being no more improved than Urie's original 'H15s', they were mainly used on freight workings. They were the first 'H15s' to be withdrawn, being displaced by new BR Standard 4-6-0s; the first was condemned in 1957, the rest following in 1958/9 with the exception of No 30331, which survived 1961. None was preserved.

Class	H15 4-6-0
Engineer	R. W. Urie* / R. E. L. Maunsell**
Designed for	LSWR and SR
Rebuilt by	LSWR and SR Eastleigh
BR power rating	4P5FA
Number in class	6
Introduced	1914*, 1924**
Cylinders (2 outside)	21in x 28in
Coupled wheels	6ft 0in
Boiler pressure	175lb/sq in
Grate area	31.5sq ft
Tractive effort	25,510lb
Weight	82 tons 1cwt* / 80 tons 11cwt**
SR number series	E330-E335 / 330-335
BR number series	30330-30335

*   No 335, rebuilt from Drummond Class E14 4-6-0 built 1907
** Nos E330-4, rebuilt from Drummond Class F13 4-6-0s built 1905

Left: *Urie rebuilt Drummond's unique Class E14 four-cylinder 4-6-0 as a two-cylinder simple, in which guise formed part of the 'H15' class. No 30335, seen at Eastleigh depot in 1957, had a dipped running plate and was visually very similar to the standard Urie 'H15s' except for its large-capacity Drummond inside-framed tender.* Author

Below: *When Maunsell similarly rebuilt the five Drummond Class F13s the result was almost identical in appearance apart from the straight running plates. No 30332 was photographed running through Eastleigh station towards the depot on 5 May 1955.* Author

Each stage of locomotive development by Urie brought an improvement in performance, which must have endeared him to the LSWR directors, used to the frequent disappointments of the Drummond era. Needing 20 express passenger locomotives to take on the principal workings westwards out of Waterloo, he adapted and improved the 'H15' design. The first 'N15s' had the standard 6ft 7in coupled wheels for express locomotives, but innovations included a boiler in which the front barrel ring was tapered, an Eastleigh superheater from new and 11in-diameter piston valves. From the start the boiler proved to be free-steaming, and the locomotives were noticeably better than the parallel-boiler 'H15s', doing what they were built to do and becoming popular locomotives with crews.

Maunsell later modified the Urie 'N15s' by increasing the valve travel and adding his own superheater, at the same time lining the enormous 22in-diameter cylinders (as big as the loading-gauge could accommodate!) to reduce them to 21 inches (except on No E755). Freer running resulted, encouraging Maunsell to develop the design further in the next batches of 'N15s' built by or delivered to the SR (see pages 76-78). In the early 1930s Maunsell modified six locomotives — Nos 740, 743, 745, 746, 748 and 752 — with double-exhaust-ported valves to improve exhaust release.

The Urie 'N15s' were included in the SR's programme of naming express passenger locomotives and received robust names from Arthurian legend. All the 'N15s' were given smoke-deflectors that sloped slightly inwards towards the top.

When Bulleid joined the SR he modified cylinders and valves on four locomotives that Maunsell had not improved, these being Nos 738, 750, 751 and 755. He also began to fit some locomotives with Lemaître five-jet blastpipes and wide chimneys to reduce their exhaust back pressure, Nos 736, 737, 741, 752 and 755 being so equipped; on Nos 736, 752 and 755 the smoke-deflectors were modified to lean slightly outwards towards the top, the other two remaining unaltered. Five locomotives that in 1947 ran for a short time as oil-burners were fitted with electric lighting (which they retained), current being supplied from a steam turbo-generator; these were Nos 740, 745, 748, 749 and 752.

Displaced by BR Class 5 4-6-0s, the Urie 'N15s' were the first 'King Arthurs' to be withdrawn, all going for scrap in the period 1953-8.

Above: *No 30746* Pendragon *was one of the 20 Urie 'N15s' that were later brought into the generic 'King Arthur' class by the SR. With a tapered boiler and sloping smoke-deflectors, the locomotive was photographed at Bournemouth Central on 2 October 1954.* Author

Below: *Also pictured at Bournemouth Central, this time on 26 June 1953, is No 30737* King Uther, *with wide chimney and Lemaître exhaust as provided by Bulleid in an attempt to improve performance.* Author

Class	N15 4-6-0
Engineer	R. W. Urie
Designed for	LSWR
Built by	LSWR and SR Eastleigh
BR power rating	5P
Number in class	20
Introduced	1918
Cylinders (2 outside)	21in x 28in*
Coupled wheels	6ft 7in
Boiler pressure	180lb/sq in
Grate area	30q ft
Tractive effort	23,915lb*
Weight	80 tons 7cwt
SR number series	E736-E755 / 736-755
BR number series	30736-30755

*	No 30755 retained 22in-diameter cylinders, producing a tractive effort of 26,250lb

Right: *Three of the Urie 'N15' 4-6-0s with Lemaître exhausts and wide chimneys had their smoke-deflectors set wider at the top. One such locomotive was No 30736* Excalibur, *seen on the Battledown flyover on 4 August 1951.* E. D. Bruton

CLASS S15

For heavy, fast goods traffic and occasional use on heavy passenger trains Urie produced a small-wheeled version of his 'N15' 4-6-0. The 'S15' thus had 5ft 7in coupled wheels, while the boiler was pitched 4½in lower than on either the 'N15' or the 'H15'. In common with the latter, the side running plates and valances were two-level over and behind the cylinders, and the cabs retained Drummond's style of arched roof, with side gutters inboard of the cab sides. The boiler was the standard tapered design used on the early 'N15s' and later 'H15s' and was pressed at 180lb/sq in.

Following the Grouping Maunsell had the Eastleigh superheaters replaced with his own type and (in the early 1930s) added smoke-deflectors, while the Urie stovepipe chimneys with which these locomotives were originally fitted were replaced by a more elegant Maunsell design, with all-round lip and capuchon. Maunsell also developed the 'S15' design for further construction, from 1927, and these locomotives are described on page 83. Bulleid made no changes other than his usual modification of removing the snifting valves on the smokebox sides.

As freight locomotives the 'S15s' were regarded highly. Their most successful workings were the heavy 60-wagon loads that they hauled out from Southampton Docks to take to Feltham Yard in West London, or on occasions to Nine Elms Yard. The locomotives had a capacity for long, heavy slogging at moderate speeds, which suited their characteristics well. They were, however, sufficiently fleet of foot to manage summer weekend passenger specials on the Bournemouth line and were often used for stopping services on the West of England main line, on which their hill-climbing ability proved particularly advantageous. Indeed, so useful were these locomotives that withdrawal did not begin until late 1962, although all the Urie examples had gone by early 1964. Two — Nos 30499 and 30506 — survive in preservation on the Mid-Hants Railway.

Class	S15 4-6-0
Engineer	R. W. Urie
Designed for	LSWR
Built by	LSWR Eastleigh
BR power rating	6F
Number in class	20
Introduced	1920
Cylinders (2 outside)	21in x 28in
Coupled wheels	5ft 7in
Boiler pressure	180lb/sq in
Grate area	30sq ft
Tractive effort	28,200lb
Weight	79 tons 16cwt
SR number series	E496-E515 / 496-515
BR number series	30496-30515

Left: *The Class S15 4-6-0s were handsome locomotives, with tapered boilers and the typical Urie drop in the height of the running plate behind the cylinders. When photographed at Eastleigh depot on 16 April 1960 No 30506 was coupled to a Drummond 'watercart' tender.* Walter Gilbert

Left: *By the late 1950s most 'S15s' had standard Urie double-bogie tenders. No 30510 is seen ex works at Eastleigh depot on 30 April 1959.* Author

The LSWR, being a forward-looking railway, opened its new marshalling yard at Feltham soon after World War 1. The yard had a hump over which trains were to be propelled slowly, groups of wagons or individual wagons being uncoupled so that they could run down from the hump to the specific sidings to which the yard controller directed them.

Trains arriving from the South West behind big 4-6-0s were heavy and needed a strong locomotive to propel them over the hump, and to meet this requirement Urie designed a massive 4-8-0T. Introduced in 1921, the 'G16' used the standard 5ft 1in wheel size of earlier Drummond goods locomotives and was driven by 22in x 28in cylinders, the biggest that could fit into the loading-gauge. Indeed, the four locomotives of this class, together with the 'T14' and 'H16' types, were the widest steam locomotives in Britain, having a maximum width of 9ft 2in. The boiler, slightly smaller than that of Urie's 4-6-0 designs, had a parallel barrel and Eastleigh superheater (later updated by Maunsell). The superheat was intended to facilitate the use of these locomotives on trip workings in the London area, but in reality they tended to stay at Feltham and were used largely as intended as hump shunters — a duty thought by many to be better handled with saturated steam. The upper surface of the side tanks was angled to afford the driver a clear view of ground staff and of the locomotive's front end when buffering up. The Urie stovepipe chimney was never replaced by a Maunsell design, though the capuchon was at some time removed.

The advent of the competent and reliable English Electric 350bhp diesel shunters heralded the end for these unusual locomotives, though the last two were not withdrawn until 1962.

Class	G16 4-8-0T
Engineer	R. W. Urie
Designed for	LSWR
Built by	LSWR Eastleigh
BR power rating	8F
Number in class	4
Introduced	1921
Cylinders (2 outside)	22in x 28in
Coupled wheels	5ft 1in
Boiler pressure	180lb/sq in
Grate area	27sq ft
Tractive effort	33,990lb
Weight	95 tons 2cwt
SR number series	E492-E495 / 492-495
BR number series	30492-30495

Below: *The SR's largest eight-coupled tank engines were Urie's four Class G16 4-8-0Ts, built for shunting heavy freight over the sorting hump at Feltham marshalling yard in West London. Pictured ex works at Eastleigh on 9 April 1958, No 30495 shows the short, high side tanks with sloping top affording the locomotive crew a clear view of ground staff.* Author

CLASS H16

Shunting requirements aside, the LSWR also had need of a large tank engine to work cross-London freight trains, on which distances were relatively short but loads and gradients could be difficult. The solution came in the form of the Class H16 4-6-2T, five of which were built in 1921/2.

In some respects the 'H16' might be regarded as a tank version of the Urie 'S15', being similar in certain dimensions, but there were in fact several differences; equally it had features in common with the 'G16' class but also various differences, reflecting its intended work. The cylinders and wheels were common to the Urie 'S15' 4-6-0s, while the boiler was that designed for the 'G16s', although the cab and bunker were narrower, and the tanks both longer (there being no need of the angled top of the 'G16' tanks) and lower, aiding stability at speed — not that high speeds featured in these locomotives' regular duties. The boiler, smaller than that of an 'S15', was deemed sufficient for the shorter routes that these locomotives were expected to traverse. Even so, at 96 tons 8cwt the 'H16' design was the heaviest locomotive (minus tender) on the LSWR.

Although only five were built, the 'H16s' could be found far and wide around the London area, on occasion appearing as far west as Reading. They also helped out on empty-stock workings between Waterloo and Clapham Junction. In the late 1950s the introduction of Bo-Bo diesels on cross-London transfer freights allowed them to broaden their horizons still further, and from 1960 they spent a couple of years working oil trains between Fawley and Southampton. However, the entire class was summarily withdrawn in November 1962, none being retained for posterity.

Class	H16 4-6-2T
Engineer	R. W. Urie
Designed for	LSWR
Built by	LSWR Eastleigh
BR power rating	6F
Number in class	5
Introduced	1921
Cylinders (2 outside)	21in x 28in
Coupled wheels	5ft 1in
Boiler pressure	180lb/sq in
Grate area	27sq ft
Tractive effort	28,200lb
Weight	96 tons 8cwt
SR number series	E516-E520 / 516-520
BR number series	30516-30520

Below: *For cross-London freights Urie built five Class H16 4-6-2Ts. These were even heavier than the 'G16s', and the side tanks were lower and straight-topped. Fresh from overhaul, No 30520 stands in Eastleigh Works yard on 14 May 1955.* Author

SOUTH EASTERN & CHATHAM RAILWAY

The early locomotive history of the two railways that combined under a management committee in 1899 to form the South Eastern & Chatham Railway includes some famous names, most particularly those of James Stirling and William Kirtley. Because of the financial situation of these railways and of the Southern Railway during the Great Depression and in wartime, many very old locomotives survived to the middle of the 20th century. Their longevity was in part explained by the fact that many had earlier been rebuilt by Harry Wainwright, the SER's Locomotive, Carriage & Wagon Superintendent from 1899 to 1913. Hence a few Stirling and Kirtley locomotives were absorbed into British Railways stock in 1948 along with a large number attributed to Wainwright himself. The Wainwright locomotives were notable for their designer's combination of solid (if not advanced) engineering and an eye for superb styling, and the surviving Class D 4-4-0 is one of the most beautiful locomotives in the National Railway Museum.

Both constituent railways were troublesome to operate because of the gradients necessary to enable their main lines to cross the North and South Downs. The LCDR main line from Ramsgate along the North Kent coast had the 1 in 100 of Sole Street Bank, which heavily loaded morning trains to London had to overcome, while SER trains heading south out of Tonbridge for Hastings or northwards for Sevenoaks were also faced with long climbs. The SER route from Charing Cross to Dover carried heavy boat-train traffic for the Channel ports of Folkestone, Dover and Deal, yet the SECR was basically a 'small locomotive' railway.

When Wainwright retired he was succeeded by Richard Maunsell, who had previously served on the Great Southern & Western Railway in Ireland. Maunsell had a gift of recruiting talented engineers to his team of designers. This team, based at the Ashford drawing office, set about rebuilding the important passenger locomotives of Classes D and E. Though not all were so treated, the result was some of the most effective express locomotives of their size in the country.

For goods traffic the SECR had 109 Class C 0-6-0s, most of which lasted into the British Railways era. These were well-designed locomotives that were left more or less in their original form throughout their lives. The same could be said for the Wainwright Class H 0-4-4Ts. The author rode one of these to show a customer who wanted one for preservation, and all involved were impressed with the lively performance of this '1P' machine; indeed, in the author's view the Class H tanks were well capable of out-performing the bigger 'M7' 0-4-4Ts of the LSWR, which BR classed as '2P'.

The SECR's finest legacy to the Southern Railway was undoubtedly Maunsell's Class N 2-6-0 design and all the classes that flowed from that engineering masterpiece. Despite the unfortunate riding characteristics of the 2-6-4T versions, which led to several derailments, the basic design was very sound, and the fleet of 172 Maunsell 2-6-0s and 2-6-4Ts inherited by BR needed no substantial rebuilding, although there was some technical tweaking of cylinders and exhaust layouts in the late 1950s when replacement parts were needed.

SER locomotives were classified by the simple expedient of using the next available letter in the alphabet, Stirling having started with the 'A' class. The SECR — and, indeed, the Southern Railway under Maunsell — continued the practice until the SR's 'V', 'W' and 'Z' classes appeared. Significant modifications were expressed by means of a numeric suffix, the rebuilt 'R' class becoming Class R1, for example.

Below: *Typical of the ancient locomotives and rolling stock bequeathed to British Railways by the Southern is this train approaching Reading South station in August 1948. It is headed by Class B1 4-4-0 No 31446, built as a Stirling Class B in 1898 and rebuilt by Wainwright as a 'B1' in 1915. It was withdrawn in September 1949. The leading three vehicles form a 'birdcage' set, so called because of the raised guard's observation windows at each end.* H. C. Casserley

Not to be confused with the SER Class R 0-6-0Ts, the 18 LCDR 0-4-4Ts of W. Kirtley's Class R were brought into SECR stock when the railways merged in 1899. The SECR made no attempt to reclassify its locomotives, and the parallel class designations have confused some lay people even to this day! An order for 15 Class R1 0-4-4Ts was placed for delivery in 1900, these locomotives having larger-diameter cylinders, larger coal bunkers and bigger bogie wheels. Later all the 'Rs' were rebuilt with the larger cylinders, and Wainwright subsequently fitted both classes with boilers designed for his Class H locomotives (page 43), so there was then little to choose between them. (To add to the confusion, the SECR then rebuilt some of the SER Class R 0-6-0Ts, which also became Class R1!)

The 'R' and 'R1' 0-4-4Ts were intended for suburban passenger work, a rôle they fulfilled until ousted to more rural parts by electrification. All but four of the 'Rs' and seven of the 'R1s' were later fitted with push-pull apparatus and worked branch-line services. Two 'R' and two 'R1' 0-4-4Ts were scrapped in 1940 and 1929 respectively, all the others entering BR stock in 1948. Withdrawals began in earnest in 1949, most locomotives having gone by the end of 1953, although the final example, No 31704, lasted until 1956. None is preserved.

Class	R / R1 0-4-4T
Engineer	W. Kirtley
Designed for	LCDR
Built by	LCDR Longhedge, Sharp Stewart*
Number in class	18, 15*
Introduced	1891, 1900*
BR power rating	1P
Cylinders (2 inside)	17½in x 24in
Coupled wheels	5ft 6in
Boiler pressure	160lb/sq in
Tractive effort	15,150lb
Weight	42 tons 10cwt, 51 tons 9cwt*
SR number series	A658-A675, A696-A710* / 1658-1675, 1696-1710*
BR number series**	31658-31675, 31696-31710*

*   Details refer to Class R1
** Nos 31672, 31673, 31699 and 31707-31709 never carried these numbers

Left: In early BR lined black livery, ex-LCDR Class R 0-4-4T No 31662 stands at Ashford on 3 October 1953. The lack of a BR emblem and power rating suggests the locomotive had been repainted in 1949 before supplies of crests became available and that it had been well cleaned thereafter. A. R. Carpenter

Below: Ex-LCDR 'R1' 0-4-4T No 31704 coaled up and ready to go at Tonbridge shed on 26 March 1953. Comparison with the previous view reveals that there was little difference visually between the 'R' and 'R1' types, but the bogie wheels on this locomotive were 6in larger in diameter than those on the 'R' class. Brian Morrison

At the formation of British Railways in 1948 there were three remaining Class T 0-6-0Ts of LCDR origin. The class of 10 locomotives had been introduced by LCDR Locomotive Superintendent William Kirtley, whose drawing office at Longhedge produced some competent locomotive designs, many of which formed the basis of the steam-locomotive developments under H. S. Wainwright after 1899. Two of the class were built in 1879, the rest in the years 1890-3.

The 'T' class had the same size-cylinders as the Class R 0-4-4Ts and the same boiler pressure but had smaller coupled wheels, at 4ft 6in diameter. Thus they were relatively sturdy machines, well able to shift heavy loads in marshalling yards. A characteristic feature of the design was the curved tops to the side tanks. The class was numbered from 141 to 150 in the LCDR fleet. Upon its formation in 1899 the SECR added 459 to all LCDR locomotive numbers, the Class Ts becoming Nos 600-9.

The 'T' 0-6-0Ts were basic shunting locomotives that worked in sidings, principally at Victoria and Herne Hill, and in some of the SECR's numerous small goods yards. During World War 1 two of them worked for a time at Boulogne. As the railways south-east of London concentrated more and more on their passenger services, goods traffic became a lower priority, and the class dwindled. Most were withdrawn in the 1930s, but No 1607 was transferred to service stock and went to work at Meldon Quarry as No 500S. The three that survived into BR ownership were soon withdrawn, and only one (No 31604) received its BR number. The last to be condemned was No 1602 (still carrying its SR number) in 1951. No LCDR locomotive survives in preservation.

Class	T 0-6-0T
Engineer	W. Kirtley
Designed for	LCDR
Built by	LCDR Longhedge
Number in class	3 (plus 8 withdrawn before 1948)
Introduced	1879
BR power rating	2F
Cylinders (2 inside)	17½in x 24in
Coupled wheels	4ft 6in
Boiler pressure	160lb/sq in
Tractive effort	18,510lb
Weight	40 tons 13cwt
SR number series	A600-A609 / 1600-1609*
BR numbers**	31602, 31604, DS500

*   No 1607 was transferred to service stock in 1938 as No 500S
** Only No 31604 received its BR number

Below: *Class T 0-6-0T No 1602 at Reading shed on 31 May 1937. This locomotive had been built at the LCDR's Longhedge Works in 1893 as No 143. When the LCDR locomotives became part of the joint SECR fleet their numbers were increased by 459, this example becoming No 602. After the 1923 Grouping it was given an 'A' prefix by the SR, and in the 1931 renumbering it became 1602, finally being withdrawn by BR in 1951 as No 31602. Ian Allan Library*

Two 0-4-0 crane tank engines built by Neilson & Co were delivered to the SER in 1881 and 1896. Inside-cylinder machines, they were almost identical except that the second, No 409, had a longer crane jib than the original, No 302. The consequence of the longer crane jib was that No 409's lifting capacity was 2 tons, against the 2½ tons of No 302. Each crane had its own two-cylinder steam engine to work the hoist chain. Both locomotives weighed a little less than 18 tons, were low-set, with a long rear overhang to balance the weight of the crane, and originally had open cabs, each with a light steel canopy above, and raised wooden buffer blocks on which were bolted conventional spring buffers.

Following the Grouping No 409 was taken into service stock and renumbered A235S, then 235S, finally being withdrawn in 1935. No 302 on the other hand had a much longer career. Having from 1881 to 1905 worked at Folkestone Harbour, where its crane proved useful in the goods sidings, it was used from 1905 to 1914 at Ashford Works; thereafter it aided the war effort at Dover and at Richborough before returning to Ashford, where it stayed from the end of the war until 1927, by which time the Southern Railway had numbered it A234S in service stock. The period 1929-38 saw No A234S (or 234S, as it soon became), now fitted with the Westinghouse brake, working at Lancing Carriage Works. In 1938 it went for overhaul, receiving a covered cab, and, having been reinstated to capital stock as No 1302, was sent to Stewarts Lane to work at a milk depot. It duly passed to British Railways in 1948 but was set aside at Stewarts Lane depot and never received its allocated BR number (31302), being withdrawn and scrapped in 1949 after a life of 68 years.

Class	1302 0-4-0T
Engineer	J. Stirling
Designed for	SECR
Built by	Neilson & Co
Number in class	1 (plus 1 withdrawn before 1948)
Introduced	1881
BR power rating	- (not classified)
Cylinders (2 inside)	11in x 20in
Coupled wheels	3ft 3in
Boiler pressure	120lb/sq in
Tractive effort	6,330lb
Weight	17 tons 17cwt
SR numbers	A234S, A235S / 234S, 235S* / 1302
BR number**	31302

* Withdrawn 1935
** Never applied

Below: *In British Railways days former SER crane tank engine No 1302 was set aside at Stewarts Lane depot. Note the simple construction, the flat plate smokebox door, the high wooden blocks to which the buffers are bolted and the cab that was fitted in 1938, by which time the locomotive was already 57 years old! This photograph was taken on 19 April 1949, five months before the locomotive's withdrawal. A. F. Cook*

Given the hilly nature of the Southern Eastern Railway's main line between Charing Cross and Dover, it is surprising that James Stirling designed for it two classes of express 4-4-0s with 7ft 0in coupled wheels! Both his 'F' and 'B' classes were high-stepping locomotives, built between 1883 and 1898 ('F') and between 1898 and 1899 ('B'). From 1903 and 1910 respectively these near-identical classes were rebuilt by Wainwright; all but two of the 29-strong 'B' class were rebuilt as Class B1, while of an original total of 88 'Fs', 76 became 'F1s'. Wainwright replaced the domeless 160lb/sq in Stirling boilers with domed boilers pressed at 170lb/sq in, these being pitched higher above rail level, and the 'F1s' were fitted with new cabs, giving better protection to the crews. Externally, the two classes appeared practically identical. Their tenders were different, however, those coupled to 'F1s' having outside frames with the leaf springs outside the tender tanks and above the valances; the 'B1' tenders were more conventional, with inside frames and the springs below the valances. Maunsell superheated them and fitted extended smokeboxes; he also reduced the cylinder diameter by 1in.

Despite their large coupled wheels the 'F' and 'B' classes performed well, although they were later outclassed by more modern locomotives, particularly when Maunsell rebuilt the Wainwright 'D' and 'E' classes. Their duties still included main-line work, but increasingly on secondary routes around Kent and across to Guildford and Reading, and their last duties were on such lines as Tonbridge–Reading. The last of these handsome 4-4-0s was withdrawn in 1951. None is preserved.

Classes	F1 and B1 4-4-0
Engineer	H. S. Wainwright*
Designed for	SECR*
Rebuilt by	SECR Ashford*
Number in class	'F1': 9 (plus 67 withdrawn before 1948)
	'B1': 16 (plus 11 withdrawn before 1948)
Introduced	1903 (F1)*, 1910 (B1)*
BR power rating	1P
Cylinders (2 inside)	18in x 26in
Coupled wheels	7ft 0in
Boiler pressure	170lb/sq in
Tractive effort	14,490lb
Weight	45 tons 2cwt
SR numbers	'F1': A2, A9, A11, A24, A25, A28-A32, A35, A42, A43, A53, A56, A60, A62, A74, A78, A79, A84, A87-A89, A94, A97, A103, A105, A110, A114, A116-A118, A130, A133, A137, A140, A143, A148, A149, A151, A156, A183, A185, A187, A188, A190, A192, A195-A157, A159, A201-A206, A208, A209, A212-A216, A226, A228, A230-A233, A236, A240, A249, A250 / 1002, 1009, 1011, 1024, 1025, 1028, 1030-1032, 1035, 1042, 1043, 1053, 1056, 1060, 1062, 1074, 1078, 1079, 1084, 1087-1089, 1094, 1103, 1105, 1110, 1114, 1117, 1118, 1130, 1133, 1137, 1140, 1143, 1148, 1149, 1151, 1156, 1183, 1185, 1187, 1188, 1190, 1192, 1195-1157, 1159, 1201-1206, 1208, 1212, 1214, 1215, 1216, 1228, 1230-1233, 1236, 1240, 1249, 1250
	'B1': A13, A17, A21, A101, A132, A186, A189, A217, A440-A457, A459 / 1013, 1017, 1021, 1101, 1132, 1186, 1189, 1217, 1440-1457, 1459
BR numbers**	'F1': 31002, 31028, 31031, 31042, 31078, 31105, 31151, 31215, 31231
	'B1': 31013, 31217, 31440, 31443, 31445, 31446, 31448-31455, 31457, 31459

*   Rebuilt from J. Stirling SER Classes F (introduced 1883) and B (introduced 1898), built by Neilson Reid (SER Nos 440-459) or at Ashford Works (remainder)
**   Only Nos 31078, 31105, 31151, 31231 and 31446 received their allocated BR numbers

Right: *Few good photographs exist of Class F1 4-4-0s. This one predates the period covered by this book but shows No 1249 in the form (though not the livery) in which nine others of this class entered BR service. Note the outside-framed tender, Maunsell's extended smokebox and the enlarged cab, which replaced a much less commodious one when the locomotive was rebuilt by Wainwright in 1906. No 1249 would be withdrawn in 1944.*
O. J. Morris

CLASS C

It is said that success breeds success, and the development of the 'O'-series 0-6-0s that became the SECR's new Class C was no exception. The detailed design work is reported to have been carried out by draughtsmen previously employed by the London, Chatham & Dover Railway at Longhedge, though the work was clearly done under the guidance of H. S. Wainwright. The result was a sturdy, reliable and competent goods locomotive that had a good turn of speed and good riding characteristics to go with it. Indeed, the design remained unchanged in any significant respect over the 60-plus years that most of the class were in service — itself an unusual feature in British locomotive design. One locomotive, SECR No 685, was rebuilt in 1917 as an 0-6-0ST for general shunting and became Class S (page 51), but no further similar rebuilds were authorised.

In traffic the 'C'-class 0-6-0s were employed chiefly on main- and secondary-line goods, including cross-London workings to other railways' yards. In summer they were often called upon to handle extra passenger workings, such as hop-pickers' specials and holiday trains, which they were able to haul at useful speeds. They thus gained themselves a reputation of being most useful locomotives, and it is little wonder that a large number (109) was constructed, or that the majority enjoyed a 60-year service life.

Over time the Class C 0-6-0s found themselves allocated to all depots on the Southern Railway's Eastern Section. After the Kent Coast electrification some were to be found further west on the Southern Region, notably at Nine Elms, though they did little work there before being withdrawn.

The entire class survived to enter BR stock in 1948, thereafter suffering only piecemeal withdrawals until the late 1950s and early '60s, when the majority were withdrawn. The last was taken out of revenue-earning service in 1963, but two locomotives survived to enter the Southern Region's departmental stock. No 31272 was renumbered DS240 and served for a few years as a stationary boiler at Ashford. No 31592 became DS239, its duties including snowplough working, and survived until 1967; it then passed into preservation as SECR No 592 and, restored in the ornate SECR goods livery of fully lined dark green, can nowadays be found on the Bluebell Railway.

Right: *Virtually original in all details except livery, Wainwright Class C 0-6-0 No 31112 stands at Nine Elms depot on 16 August 1959.* Author

Below right: *Class C 0-6-0 No 31592 was loaned to departmental stock to be fitted with a 3S-type snowplough, as seen at Ashford Works on 15 March 1963. The loan was consummated in 1966 and the locomotive renumbered DS239, only to be withdrawn in 1967. It is now preserved on the Bluebell Railway as SECR No 592.* Author

Class	C 0-6-0
Engineer	H. S. Wainwright
Designed for	SECR
Built by	SECR Ashford (71) / SECR Longhedge (8) / Neilson Reid (15) / Sharp Stewart (15)
Number in class	108*
Introduced	1900
BR power rating	2FA
Cylinders (2 inside)	18½in x 26in
Coupled wheels	5ft 2in
Boiler pressure	160lb/sq in
Tractive effort	19,520lb
Weight	43 tons 16cwt
SR numbers	A4, A18, A33, A37, A38, A54, A59, A61, A63, A68, A71, A86, A90, A102, A112, A113, A150, A191, A218, A219, A221, A223, A225, A227, A229, A234, A242-A245, A252, A253, A255-A257, A260, A262, A267, A268, A270-A272, A277, A280, A287, A291, A293, A294, A297, A298, A317, A460, A461, A480, A481, A486, A495, A498, A499, A508, A510, A513, A572, A573, A575, A576, A578-A585, A588-A590, A592, A593, A681-A684, A686-A695, A711-A725 / 1004, 1018, 1033, 1037, 1038, 1054, 1059, 1061, 1063, 1068, 1071, 1086, 1090, 1102, 1112, 1113, 1150, 1191, 1218, 1219, 1221, 1223, 1225, 1227, 1229, 1234, 1242-1245, 1252, 1253, 1255-1257, 1260, 1262, 1267, 1268, 1270-1272, 1277, 1280, 1287, 1291, 1293, 1294, 1297, 1298, 1317, 1460, 1461, 1480, 1481, 1486, 1495, 1498, 1499, 1508, 1510, 1513, 1572, 1573, 1575, 1576, 1578-1585, 1588-1590, 1592, 1593, 1681-1684, 1686-1695, 1711-1725
BR numbers**	31004, 31018, 31033, 31037, 31038, 31054, 31059, 31061, 31063, 31068, 31071, 31086, 31090, 31102, 31112, 31113, 31150, 31191, 31218, 31219, 31221, 31223, 31225, 31227, 31229, 31234, 31242-31245, 31252, 31253, 31255-31257, 31260, 31262, 31267, 31268, 31270, 31271, 31272***, 31277, 31280, 31287, 31291, 31293, 31294, 31297, 31298, 31317, 31460, 31461, 31480, 31481, 31486, 31495, 31498, 31499, 31508, 31510, 31513, 31572, 31573, 31575, 31576, 31578-31585, 31588-31590, 31592***, 31593, 31681-31684, 31686-31695, 31711-31725

*   Excludes SECR No 685, rebuilt 1917 as a Class S 0-6-0ST
**   Nos 31257 and 31460 never carried these numbers
*** 31272 was renumbered DS240 in 1965, and No 31592 became DS239 in 1966

CLASS D

The quest for more powerful express locomotives prompted Harry Wainwright to lead the design of a new class of 4-4-0 for the Dover, Ramsgate and Hastings lines. These were considerably more powerful than the 'B1' class, with more modestly sized coupled wheels of 6ft 8in and larger cylinders. The 51 Class D 4-4-0s were graceful locomotives, with short smokeboxes, round-topped fireboxes and flowing curves over the driving-wheel splashers leading past the cabsides. They initially wore a most spectacular livery of green with multi-coloured lining but later received the plain-grey livery that was suitable for wartime service and which was retained by the SECR until the Grouping. Following the SR takeover in 1923 they were painted in Maunsell dark green with cream lining but donned unlined black for

World War 2. BR applied its standard mixed-traffic livery of black with red, cream and grey lining to those that survived long enough to be overhauled at Ashford Works.

In terms of performance the 'Ds' were regarded as sure-footed machines capable of hard work — a necessary attribute when confronted with the gradients on the SECR main lines across the North and South Downs. From 1913, 21 locomotives were rebuilt by Maunsell as Class D1 (page 53); of the remaining 30, 28 were absorbed into British Railways stock in 1948. By then they were very much relegated to secondary work, appearing mainly on the Tonbridge–Reading line. The last example in service was No 31075, which was withdrawn from Guildford shed in 1956.

Class	D 4-4-0
Engineer	H. S. Wainwright
Designed for	SECR
Built by	SECR Ashford (21 locomotives) / Sharp Stewart (10) / Dübs (10) / Robert Stephenson (5) / Vulcan Foundry (5)
Number in class	28 (plus 2 withdrawn before 1948 and 21 rebuilt from 1921 as 'D1')
Introduced	1901
BR power rating	2P
Cylinders (2 inside)	19in x 26in
Coupled wheels	6ft 8in
Boiler pressure	175lb/sq in
Tractive effort	17,455lb
Weight	50 tons 0cwt
SR numbers	A57, A75, A92, A477, A488, A490, A493, A496, A501, A549, A574, A577, A586, A591, A726, A728-A734, A737, A738, A740, A742, A744, A746, A748, A750 / 1057, 1075, 1092, 1477, 1488, 1490, 1493, 1496, 1501, 1549, 1574, 1577, 1586, 1591, 1726*, 1728-1734, 1737, 1738, 1740, 1742*, 1744, 1746, 1748, 1750
BR numbers**	31057, 31075, 31092, 31477, 31488, 31490, 31493, 31496, 31501, 31549, 31574, 31577, 31586, 31591, 31728-31734, 31737, 31738, 31740, 31744, 31746, 31748, 31750

*   Withdrawn 1944 (1742) and 1947 (1726)
**   Not all locomotives received their allocated BR numbers

Right: *The last Class D 4-4-0, No 31075, at Ashford Works on 7 July 1956.* Author

Following the success of his 'D' class Harry Wainwright's design team developed a more powerful 4-4-0 known as Class E, introduced from 1905. The 'E' class had the same size cylinders, a higher boiler pressure, coupled wheels 2in smaller than the 'D' class and a 6in-longer wheelbase. The boiler had a Belpaire firebox, and from 1908 the locomotives received extended smokeboxes, ensuring they were always visually distinct from the 'D' class.

Twenty-six Class E 4-4-0s were built, at Ashford Locomotive Works, 11 later being rebuilt to Maunsell's specification as Class E1 (page 52). Two locomotives were experimentally superheated in 1912, No 36 having a Robinson-type superheater, and No 275 a Schmidt type. Both had their boiler pressures reduced to 160lb/sq in and cylinder diameter increased to 20½in. Later the class was fitted with Maunsell superheaters.

Like the 'D' class, the 'E' class worked main-line expresses on the SECR system, being relegated to secondary passenger duties when ousted by later, larger or more effective locomotives. All became part of British Railways' stock and were withdrawn between 1950 and 1955; none was retained for preservation.

Class	E 4-4-0
Engineer	H. S. Wainwright
Designed for	SECR
Built by	SECR Ashford
Number in class	15 (plus 11 rebuilt from 1919 as Class E1)
Introduced	1905
BR power rating	2P
Cylinders (2 inside)	19in x 26in*
Coupled wheels	6ft 6in
Boiler pressure	180lb/sq in*
Tractive effort	18,410lb*
Weight	52 tons 5cwt
SR numbers	A36, A157, A159, A166, A175, A176, A273, A275, A315, A491, A514-A516, A547, A587 / 1036, 1157, 1159, 1166, 1175, 1176, 1273, 1275, 1315, 1491, 1514-1516, 1547, 1587
BR numbers**	31036, 31157, 31159, 31166, 31175, 31176, 31273, 31275, 31315, 31491, 31514-31516, 31547, 31587

* SECR Nos 36 and 275, superheated in 1912, had boiler pressure reduced to 160lb/sq in and cylinder diameter increased to 20½in; tractive effort was then 19,050lb

** Not all received their allocated BR numbers

Below: *The graceful form of Wainwright's Class E 4-4-0 is displayed well in this view of No 31273 at Ashford on 8 October 1949 after repainting in early BR lined black livery but without the BR emblem on the tender.* W. Beckerlegge

CLASS O1

The 'O1' design was a rebuild of James Stirling's Class O 0-6-0, of which 122 were built from 1878 to 1899. The 'O' was a successful main-line goods locomotive, 55 examples being built by Sharp Stewart, the remaining 67 at Ashford Locomotive Works. When H. S. Wainwright assumed the locomotive-engineering chair at Ashford he initiated the rebuilding of 59 examples as Class O1, with domed boilers and bigger cabs; some also received tenders from London, Chatham & Dover Railway locomotives. The non-rebuilt Class O 0-6-0s were withdrawn during the SECR and SR years.

In appearance the 'O1s' were neat, compact locomotives, but their tenders, which had outside frames and springs alongside the narrow tender tanks, gave a hint as to their age. It would be unusual were such a large class of locomotives not to have detail differences.

This was true particularly with regard to the sandboxes, which on some locomotives were combined with the leading splashers while on others were mounted below the running plate behind the buffer-beam.

Fifty-five 'O1s' entered BR stock on 1 January 1948. By this time they had been relegated to menial goods and shunting duties around the Eastern Section, having been superseded on main-line freights by the 'C' class (pages 46 and 47) and later by Maunsell 2-6-0s. Among their last duties was yard shunting at Ashford and Dover. Under BR their withdrawal continued, though not precipitously, the last one surviving in service until June 1961. This was No 31065, which is now preserved and is sometimes operational on the Bluebell Railway in Sussex.

Above: *Class O1 0-6-0 No 31048 shunts at Ashford on 7 July 1956. This locomotive had its leading sandboxes below the running plate and behind the buffer-beam.* Author

Below: *Within a month of withdrawal, 'O1' 0-6-0 No 31434 is serviced at Dover Marine depot on 26 July 1959. This locomotive had its leading sandboxes combined with the leading-wheel splashers, the curved smokebox wing plates adding to its style.* Author

Class	O1 0-6-0
Engineer	H. S. Wainwright*
Designed for	SECR*
Rebuilt by	SECR Ashford*
Number in class	55 (plus 4 withdrawn before 1948**)
Introduced	1903*
BR power rating	2F
Cylinders (2 inside)	18in x 26in
Coupled wheels	5ft 2in
Boiler pressure	150lb/sq in
Tractive effort	17,300lb
Weight	41 tons 1cwt
SR numbers***	A3, A7, A14, A39, A41, A44, A46, A48, A51, A64-A66, A80, A93, A106, A108, A109, A119, A123, A238, A248, A251, A258, A316, A369-A374, A377-A381, A383-A386, A388-A391, A393, A395-A398, A425, A426, A428-A430, A432, A434, A437-A439 / 1003, 1007, 1014, 1039, 1041, 1044, 1046, 1048, 1051, 1064-1066, 1080, 1093, 1106, 1108, 1109, 1123, 1238, 1248, 1251, 1258, 1316, 1369-1374, 1377-1381, 1383-1386, 1388-1391, 1395-1398, 1425, 1426, 1428-1430, 1432, 1434, 1437-1439
BR numbers****	31003, 31007, 31014, 31039, 31041, 31044, 31046, 31048, 31051, 31064-31066, 31080, 31093, 31106, 31108, 31109, 31123, 31238, 31248, 31258, 31316, 31369-31374, 31377-31381, 31383-31386, 31388-31391, 31395-31398, 31425, 31426, 31428-31430, 31432, 31434, 31437-31439

*   Rebuilt from Stirling Class O 0-6-0s built 1891-9 by SER Ashford or Sharp Stewart

**   Includes SER No 282, withdrawn 1912

***   Nos A119, A393 and 1251 withdrawn 1925, 1926 and 1946 respectively

**** Most locomotives never received their allocated BR numbers

Forming a significant component of London's suburban rail network, connecting the capital with a heavily populated area of north Kent, the SECR soon after its formation needed some more powerful suburban tank engines that would also be suitable for secondary-line passenger trains away from London. The Class H 0-4-4T design used the same boiler as the Class C 0-6-0, its cylinders were just ½in smaller in diameter (being the same as those on the 'O1s'), and the coupled wheels were of 5ft 6in diameter, giving the class a useful turn of speed and reasonable haulage capacity. The cab roof had a pronounced side overhang, giving it a 'pagoda' appearance, similar to that on the Class R1 0-6-0T (page 45). All locomotives were fitted with vacuum brakes as standard, but 16 also had Westinghouse air brakes. Sandboxes were located under the running plates.

The 'H' 0-4-4Ts were sprightly runners with a good turn of speed and were free-steaming locomotives, being popular with their crews. In later years, as they were displaced from heavy suburban trains by electrification, they ended up on branch and secondary lines. Two were withdrawn in the 1940s, but the rest, 64 in total, entered BR stock in 1948, and from 1949 no fewer than 46 were fitted for push-pull operation. Their later duties included the Westerham branch and local services between Three Bridges and East Grinstead. BR began to withdraw the type in earnest in 1959, and the last ran until 1964. No 31263 was held at Ashford for preservation and is now at the Bluebell Railway in full SECR passenger livery as No 263.

Class	H 0-4-4T
Engineer	H. S. Wainwright
Designed for	SECR
Built by	SECR Ashford
Number in class	64 (plus 2 withdrawn before 1948)
Introduced	1904
BR power rating	1P
Cylinders (2 inside)	18in x 26in
Coupled wheels	5ft 6in
Boiler pressure	160lb/sq in
Tractive effort	17,360lb
Weight	54 tons 8cwt
SR numbers	A5, A16, A158, A161, A162, A164, A177, A182, A184, A193, A239, A259, A261, A263-A266, A269, A274, A276, A278, A279, A295, A305-A312, A319-A322, A324, A326-A329, A500, A503, A512, A517-A523, A530-A533, A540-A544, A546, A548, A550-A554 / 1005, 1016, 1158, 1161, 1162, 1164, 1177, 1182, 1184, 1193, 1239, 1259, 1261, 1263-1266*, 1269, 1274, 1276, 1278, 1279, 1295, 1305-1312*, 1319-1322, 1324, 1326-1329, 1500, 1503, 1512, 1517-1523, 1530-1533, 1540-1544, 1546, 1548, 1550-1554
BR numbers	31005, 31016, 31158, 31161, 31162, 31164, 31177, 31182, 31184, 31193, 31239, 31259, 31261, 31263, 31265, 31266, 31269, 31274, 31276, 31278, 31279, 31295, 31305-31311, 31319-31322, 31324, 31326-31329, 31500, 31503, 31512, 31517-31523, 31530-31533, 31540-31544, 31546, 31548, 31550-31554

*   Nos 1264 and 1312 withdrawn 1944

Below: *In pristine condition following a general overhaul and repaint at Ashford Locomotive Works, Class H 0-4-4T No 31500 stands on shed at Ashford on 7 July 1956. The shape of the cab roof and flared top to the bunker side gives this design its particular style. No 31500 was not push-pull-fitted.* Author

Below: *The last example of the 'H' class to remain in service was No 31263, which worked the Three Bridges– East Grinstead push-pull trains until the line's closure. This view, recorded at Three Bridges shed on 8 December 1962, shows the air pump for the push-pull system alongside the smokebox. This locomotive is now preserved.* Author

CLASS P

The story goes that Wainwright, realising how well the Stroudley Class A1 0-6-0Ts performed on the LBSCR, wanted to provide the SECR with similarly sized locomotives for branch-line working. The railway had had only limited success since 1905 with steam railmotors — single carriages incorporating a small four-wheeled locomotive at one end — and wanted to revert to locomotive haulage, but with push-pull operation using separate locomotives. A small 0-6-0T about the size of a 'Terrier' was seen as ideal for this work.

The 'P'-class 0-6-0T design was certainly a diminutive locomotive, weighing about the same as an 'A1', but stood higher in terms of the centre-line of its boiler and the height above rail level of the running plates and buffer-beams. The cab was the usual 'pagoda' style. From 1913 the class of eight moved on to become shunting locomotives, it having been proved that bigger locomotives such as the 'H'-class 0-4-4Ts were better suited to branch-line work. Maunsell decided that the 'P' class's boiler pressure of 180lb/sq in was unnecessarily high for shunting duties and had it reduced to 160lb/sq in.

In 1915 two 'Ps' went to France for war service, shunting at Boulogne, but returned following the end of hostilities; indeed, all eight locomotives survived to enter British Railways stock in 1948. Withdrawals began in 1955 as diesel shunters began to make their steam predecessors redundant. The last 'P' in BR service was No 31556, which was sold to Bowaters' paper mills at Sittingbourne in north Kent. Three others — Nos 31027, 31178 and 31323 — passed into preservation, taking up residence on the Bluebell Railway, while the Bowaters locomotive is now based on the Kent & East Sussex Railway with its original SECR number (753).

Class	P 0-6-0T
Engineer	H. S. Wainwright
Designed for	SECR
Built by	SECR Ashford
Number in class	8
Introduced	1909
BR power rating	0F
Cylinders (2 inside)	12in x 18in
Coupled wheels	3ft 9⅛in
Boiler pressure	160lb/sq in*
Tractive effort	7,830lb*
Weight	28 tons 10cwt
SR numbers	A27, A178, A323, A325, A555, A558, A753 (A556**), A754 (A557**) / 1027, 1178, 1323, 1325, 1555-1558
BR numbers	31027, 31178, 31323, 31325, 31555-31558

*   Reduced from 180lb/sq in from 1913, tractive effort being reduced from 8,810lb/sq in
**   Renumbered thus in 1913

Below: *The diminutive, almost cheeky appearance of the SECR Class P 0-6-0Ts is clear from this view of No 31325 at Eastleigh depot on 15 August 1958.* Author

The South Eastern Railway obtained its first 0-6-0Ts in 1888, under Locomotive Superintendent James Stirling, and over the next 10 years built a total of 25, these forming Class R. Intended for shunting duties, mainly away from the London area, the design had frames similar to those of the Class O 0-6-0 goods locomotive, while the boiler was the same as on the earlier Class Q. The 'Rs' were the only locomotives that Stirling had fitted with round-topped cabs.

From 1910 Wainwright had 13 of the 'R' class rebuilt as Class R1, with domed boilers and, in most cases, the Stirling round-topped cab replaced by the standard 'pagoda' type; they were also fitted with additional sandboxes for use on the very steep Folkestone Harbour branch. However, the need for locomotives to negotiate the tight confines of the Tyler Tunnel, on the former Canterbury & Whitstable route, saw three 'R1s' retain their round-topped cabs, being additionally given shorter chimneys and domes, which afforded them a particularly squat appearance. From 1938 three replacement boilers were provided that had Ross 'pop' safety valves. Subsequently boilers were switched between locomotives as overhauls took place, and it was possible to see combinations of low-profile cabs with full-height chimneys, squat chimneys with full-height domes, and so forth.

While the 'Rs' were all withdrawn before nationalisation, all 13 'R1s' entered BR stock in 1948. Their last duties included hauling heavy boat trains up the 1-in-30 gradient from Folkestone Harbour (the steepest on any main-line railway in the British Isles), their retention dictated by limited clearances. The heaviest trains required several locomotives — two or three at the front, with one or two banking at the rear — and the sound of up to five exhausts as they tackled the ascent had to be heard to be believed!

The 'R1s' on the Folkestone Harbour branch were finally displaced in 1959 by ex-Great Western '57xx' pannier tanks, and the last was withdrawn in 1960. None was retained for preservation.

Above: *Standard Class R1 0-6-0T No 31128 takes water outside the depot at Dover Marine on 26 July 1959. Note the large sandbox behind the buffer-beam below the running plate, to aid climbing away from Folkestone Harbour station; also the Wainwright cab of the 'pagoda' type.* Author

Above: *Pictured at Folkestone Junction depot on 26 July 1959, No 31010 shows its short Urie chimney and Stirling round-topped cab, both features enabling it to work the Canterbury & Whitstable route, which finally closed in 1953. The dome, however, is of full height, following a subsequent boiler change.* Author

Below: *'R1' 0-6-0T No 31174, also at Folkestone Junction depot, has leading splasher sandboxes and retains smokebox wing plates. This locomotive has acquired a boiler with a squat dome, originally intended for Canterbury & Whitstable-line locomotives!* Author

Class	R1 0-6-0T
Engineer	H. S. Wainwright*
Designed for	SECR
Rebuilt by	SECR Ashford
Number in class	13
Introduced	1910*
BR power rating	2F
Cylinders (2 inside)	18in x 26in
Coupled wheels	5ft 2in
Boiler pressure	160lb/sq in
Tractive effort	18,480lb
Weight	46 tons 15cwt**
SR numbers	A10**, A47**, A69, A107**, A127, A128, A147, A154, A174, A335, A337, A339, A340 / 1010**, 1047**, 1069, 1107**, 1127, 1128, 1147, 1154, 1174, 1335, 1337, 1339, 1340
BR numbers	31010**, 31047**, 31069, 31107**, 31127***, 31128, 31147, 31154, 31174, 31335, 31337, 31339, 31340

*   Rebuilt from Stirling Class R, of which 25 had been built by the SER from 1888
**   Locomotives with short chimneys and Stirling cabs weighed 46 tons 8cwt
***   Never carried this number

CLASS J

As a response to a perceived need for more powerful suburban passenger tank engines, Wainwright in 1913 introduced the 'J'-class 0-6-4Ts. To improve on the power of the Class H 0-4-4Ts the 'J' class had 19½in-diameter cylinders with 8in-diameter piston valves. The boiler had a Belpaire firebox, and was superheated from new. The side tanks were of small capacity, holding only 350 gallons each; a larger tank behind the cab and below the bunker held 1,300 gallons, giving 2,000 gallons of water in total. These measures would aid stability at speed. The cab roof demonstrated the 'pagoda' style of locomotive design that was seen on all SER and SECR tank-engine types but not on the tender engines.

Only five of the 'J' class were built, suggesting that the expected need had not significantly materialised. Even so, the SECR gave the five locomotives running numbers that were scattered between 129 and 614. In 1927 and 1928 the Southern Railway tidied things up by numbering them in a straight sequence, a task it did not undertake with other classes.

The 'J' class worked suburban trains in South London, to such destinations as Addiscombe and Oxted, until displaced by the Southern Railway's suburban electrification. They then gravitated to the Ashford area, where they found employment on stopping services. Regarded as non-standard, they were soon withdrawn by BR, all being condemned by the end of 1951. Unsurprisingly, none was retained for preservation.

Class	J 0-6-4T
Engineer	H. S. Wainwright
Designed for	SECR
Built by	SECR Ashford
Number in class	5
Introduced	1913
BR power rating	3MT
Cylinders (2 inside)	19½in x 26in
Coupled wheels	5ft 6in
Boiler pressure	160lb/sq in
Tractive effort	20,400lb
Weight	70 tons 14cwt
SR numbers*	A129, A207, A597, A611, A614 / A595-A599 / 1595-1599
BR number series	31595-31599

*   In 1927/8 the class was renumbered
     in a more logical sequence

Below: *Usually handsome is as handsome does, and the 0-6-4Ts of Wainwright's 'J' class were indeed handsome locomotives. In this 1930s view at Ashford No 1599 displays the headcode for the Maidstone East line, whence it has just arrived.* Ian Allan Library

When Richard Maunsell arrived at Ashford in 1913 to take up his rôle as Chief Mechanical Engineer a new, larger 4-4-0 than the 'D' and 'E' classes was already designed and waiting for authorisation for construction. This was Wainwright's 'L' class, designed with the heavy boat trains to Dover and Folkestone in mind. In many ways the 'L' was an enlarged Class E 4-4-0 that included the bigger cylinders used for the first two superheated 'Es', though the coupled wheels were of the 6ft 8in diameter used on the 'D' class. The low boiler pressure of 160lb/sq in (applied because in those days some engineers believed that superheated steam could be used as a means of lowering boiler pressure for the same amount of work at greater efficiency) meant that starting tractive effort was similar to that of an 'E'. However, the low pressure remained as standard throughout the lives of these locomotives.

Maunsell made a few changes to the design, including adjusting the valve events, before ordering construction of the 22 locomotives. They were needed for the 1914 summer services, and the locomotive-construction industry was asked to tender for the work. Only two companies — Beyer Peacock of Gorton, Manchester, and Borsig in Berlin — could meet the required delivery time, Borsig fitters being present at Ashford Works to supervise the assembly of the German-built components almost right up to the outbreak of World War 1!

The 'Ls' were steady and reliable performers but were inevitably later outclassed by the 'E1' and 'D1' types, which had the benefit of a wider source of engineering expertise. Among the Class L duties were passenger workings all over the Eastern Section. In BR days some were allocated to Brighton depot and occasionally appeared at Bournemouth on the daily through train between the two resorts.

When the last 'L' 4-4-0 had been withdrawn but not yet scrapped a proposal emerged within the Southern Region to overhaul and repaint a Class L and a 'T9' 4-4-0 in SECR grey and LSWR green respectively, to work on special trains while being used in regular traffic to justify the cost of retaining them. However, only the 'T9' was authorised and so treated, and the last 'L' was scrapped in 1961.

Class	L 4-4-0
Engineer	H. S. Wainwright
Designed for	SECR
Built by	Borsig (10) /
	Beyer Peacock (12)
Number in class	22
Introduced	1914
BR power rating	3P
Cylinders (2 inside)	20½in x 26in
Coupled wheels	6ft 8in
Boiler pressure	160lb/sq in
Tractive effort	18,575lb
Weight	57 tons 9cwt
SR number series	A760-A781 / 1760-1781
BR number series	31760-31781

Below: *Class L 4-4-0 No 31777 looks handsome enough at Bournemouth Central on 1 March 1958 as it waits to restart the daily through train to Brighton. The application of the BR-style red, cream and grey lining over the driving-wheel splashers lends an air of grace to an otherwise functional-looking locomotive.* Author

When R. E. L. Maunsell arrived at Ashford as the new CME he recruited some of the brightest design engineers from Swindon and Derby. Holcroft brought with him a clear understanding of Churchward principles of locomotive design, and Clayton, from Derby, appears to have been well ahead of his contemporaries on the Midland Railway. It was to be expected, therefore, that the first completely new locomotive design to emerge under Maunsell would represent a significant step forward. Delayed three years by the onset of World War 1, the Class N 2-6-0 emerged in 1917 and was to Ashford eyes an austere-looking machine. No 810 had a sharply tapered boiler of Swindon appearance, with top feed connected with a conventional dome. The two large outside cylinders had long-travel piston valves driven by outside Walschaerts valve gear, and all wheels and motion parts were easily accessible under a high, straight running plate. The cab and tender looked like Derby products. In all probability this was the most modern steam locomotive in Great Britain at that time.

So successful was the 'N' class that the Government decreed that 100 be built at Woolwich Arsenal during the slump in employment following the end of World War 1. The 'N' might have become a standard type for the nationalised railways, but politics soon determined that the railways should be grouped into four large companies rather than nationalised. The new Southern Railway, with Richard Maunsell as CME, ordered 50 of the Woolwich-built locomotives, leaving 50 to be sold elsewhere. Twenty-seven sets of parts went to the Midland Great Western and Great Southern Railways in Ireland to be re-gauged to 5ft 3in and assembled as 26 locomotives plus one set of spares (see *Locomotive Compendium: Ireland*). These became GSR Classes K1 (5ft 6in) and K1a (6ft) and worked express passenger and freight trains all over the GSR and, later, CIÉ network. They lasted until displaced by diesel locomotives and railcars in the 1950s.

Class	N 2-6-0
Engineer	R. E. L. Maunsell
Designed for	SECR
Built by	SECR and SR Ashford*
BR power rating	4P5F
Number in class	80
Introduced	1917
Cylinders (2 outside)	19in x 28in
Coupled wheels	5ft 6in
Boiler pressure	200lb/sq in
Grate area	25sq ft
Tractive effort	26,035lb
Weight	61 tons 4cwt
SR number series	A810-A821, A823-A875 / 1400-1414, 1810-1821, 1823-1875
BR number series	31400-31414, 31810-31821, 31823-31875

* Nos A826-A875 assembled at Ashford from parts fabricated at Woolwich Arsenal

Right: Grubby workhorse though it is, Class N 2-6-0 No 31847, at Exmouth Junction on 24 July 1960, shows clearly its tapered boiler, top feed and dome, its SR-style smoke-deflectors, Derby-style cab and its straight-sided 3,500gal tender. This locomotive is in close to its original condition technically, except that in early SR days the piston tail rods had been removed, while Bulleid had undertaken wholesale removal, from all SR locomotives so fitted, of the two snifting valves that used to sit either side of the smokebox behind and below the chimney. Author

Left: Photographed at Hither Green on 31 May 1958, No 31400 was the first of the final batch of 'N'-class 2-6-0s and as such had a 4,000gal tender with turned-in sides. This locomotive was one of those rebuilt by BR with new front frames, cylinders with outside steam pipes and a Standard Class 4 blastpipe and chimney. Note the curved tops to the frames behind the front buffer-beam. Author

Six sets of Woolwich Arsenal-built parts were turned into handsome 2-6-4Ts for Metropolitan Railway freight workings. In 1937 these became part of LNER stock as its Class L2 but, being regarded as non-standard, were withdrawn in 1947/8. Tales and rumours surround the remaining 17 Woolwich Arsenal locomotive kits, including disposal to Egypt or to Romania, neither of which appears to have substance. However, the SR's assembly at Ashford of many more 2-6-0s of the 'N' and other classes would have enabled most surplus parts to be used up, assuming the SR purchased them.

The 'Ns' were built without smoke-deflectors, but they had a rather soft exhaust beat when running lightly and exhaust drift could be a problem. They received smoke-deflectors from 1933 when Maunsell was fitting them to all the larger SR locomotives. The Maunsell Moguls remained the only 2-6-0s in the UK to be so adorned. Ireland did not follow suit with its Woolwich 2-6-0s.

The locomotives have been paired with at least three different tender types. The most common was the standard 3,500gal flat-sided tender. The last batch built, Nos 1400-14, had 4,000gal tenders with turned-in sides like the 'V' class after them. A number also received wider, flat-sided tenders. The overall width of the locomotives did not exceed 8ft 10in, giving them a wide route availability.

The performance of the Class N 2-6-0s met all expectations. Although considered by some observers to be under-boilered, in reality they steamed well and were very competent machines. The author saw 'N' and 'U' 2-6-0s handling trains of up to 10 carriages on the Salisbury–Portsmouth route with ease; most impressive was the sure-footed way a Woolwich Mogul could start such a load when the driver pushed over the regulator handle, confident in the knowledge that the locomotive would 'dig its heels in' and accelerate its load well.

Their area of work covered the whole of the Southern system, particularly the Eastern Section, but they were equally employed in the west. Duties were truly mixed traffic, from short stopping trains on main and secondary lines to heavy cross-country workings, heavy freights, and local pick-up goods trains.

The SR painted the Class N locomotives in Maunsell lined dark green. After World War 2 they joined the ranks of black locomotives with Bulleid 'sunshine' lettering and numerals shaded in green. BR painted them in standard mixed-traffic lined black, the livery that probably suited them best.

Under BR, when component renewals were needed, some but not all of the class received new cylinders and outside steam pipes with BR Class 4-style blastpipes and chimneys. The last 'N' 2-6-0 was withdrawn in 1966, and No 31874 is preserved on the Mid-Hants Railway.

Above: *Some 'Ns' received the BR exhaust and chimney but not the new cylinders and front frames, as apparent from this view of No 31826 at Stewarts Lane depot on 6 October 1962.* Author

Below: *One of the 27 kits of SR Mogul parts sold by Woolwich Arsenal to the railways in Ireland was used to create CIÉ Class K1 2-6-0 No 383, seen at Broadstone shed, Dublin, in July 1956.* Author

Below: *A further six sets of parts produced by Woolwich Arsenal were sold to the Metropolitan Railway and used to construct the latter's Class K 2-6-4Ts, including No 111 seen here.* Ian Allan Library

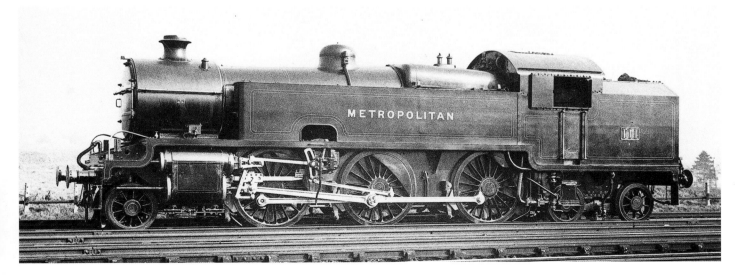

CLASS N1

At the time when Maunsell was building the 'N' class at Ashford he experimented on one locomotive by giving it three cylinders with the centre cylinder piston valve driven by the Holcroft derived gear from the outside cylinder Walschaerts valve gears. SECR No 822 was outshopped in this form late in 1922, just before the Grouping. The drive on each side to the derived gear was taken from the top of the combination lever, a long rod leading forwards past the upper side of the outside cylinder, which had the piston valve chest set inwards to accommodate this. The long rods drove a pair of horizontal levers across the front of the locomotive behind the structure above the buffer-beam, in turn actuating the inside cylinder's piston rod. This was somewhat similar to the Gresley conjugated gear except that in the latter the drive is taken from the front end of the outside cylinder piston valve rods. The smaller cylinder diameter enabled the class to fit the narrower loading-gauge of the Tonbridge–Hastings main line.

No 822 was coupled to a standard 3,500gal tender. A few years later the derived gear was replaced by an independent set of Walschaerts gear for the inside cylinder. Five more 'N1s' were built in 1930, and these had three sets of Walschaerts gear from the start. Even so, like all other Maunsell 2-6-0s and 2-6-4Ts with three cylinders the locomotives retained the inset piston valve chests and high structure above the front buffer-beam, giving them their somewhat grander appearance than the two-cylinder locomotives. The six 'N1s' had 4,000gal tenders, and to line up with the bottom of the cab each tender had a reverse bend in the lower side frames and valances. During their life span a number of the 'U' and 'U1' classes had similar tenders, some flat-sided and some with the sloping top raves.

The 'N1s' served mainly in the South Eastern Division of BR's Southern Region, in their last years working out of Hither Green depot in South London. All were withdrawn in late 1962, rendered surplus by the Kent electrification and 'dieselisation' schemes.

Class	N1 2-6-0
Engineer	R. E. L. Maunsell
Designed for	SECR
Built by	SECR and SR Ashford
BR power rating	4P5F
Number in class	6
Introduced	1922
Cylinders (3)	16in x 28in
Coupled wheels	5ft 6in
Boiler pressure	200lb/sq in
Grate area	25sq ft
Tractive effort	27,695lb
Weight	64 tons 5cwt
SR number series	A822, A876-A880 / 1822, 1876-1880
BR number series	31822, 31876-31880

Below: *Class N1 2-6-0 No 31878 rolls through Ashford station in Kent with a main-line goods. Note the inset piston-valve chests, giving the outside cylinders their sloping sides, and the high structure above the front buffer-beam, necessary to accommodate the derived valve gear for the inside cylinder. However, this locomotive never had derived gear, having been built with three sets of Walschaerts gear from new.* Author

Needing a more substantial shunting tank engine than the erstwhile 'R1' 0-6-0Ts (page 45) to meet a specialist requirement, Maunsell in 1917 had Ashford Works convert Class C 0-6-0 No 685 into a tank engine. Losing its tender, the locomotive gained a large saddle tank and a typical Maunsell-style cab, fully enclosed, with a small coal bunker behind it. Unlike the 'C'-class locomotive from which it had been rebuilt it had a smokebox door with clasp fixers around the rim, rather than the more usual centre handle and dart. In all other respects, however, it was essentially a Class C with more adhesion weight.

The locomotive was rebuilt specifically for employment at the Port of Richborough (then being developed by the War Department for shipping materials across the Channel to the Western Front), where it worked from 1917 to 1919.

Why the class was limited to this one locomotive is uncertain, for it should also have been useful in large goods yards such as Hither Green and Ashford. However, in reality the 'S' tank developed very little more tractive effort than the 'R1', though its adhesion weight was more than 15% greater, so it should have been, if anything, even more sure-footed. Nevertheless, it was useful enough to last 34 years in rebuilt form, working mainly from Bricklayers Arms depot. It was scrapped upon withdrawal in 1951.

Class	S 0-6-0ST
Engineer	R. E. L. Maunsell*
Designed for	SECR
Rebuilt by	SECR Ashford*
Number in class	1
Introduced	1917*
BR power rating	2F
Cylinders (2 inside)	18½in x 26in
Coupled wheels	5ft 2in
Boiler pressure	160lb/sq in
Tractive effort	19,520lb
Weight	53 tons 10cwt
SR number	A685 / 1685
BR number**	31685

*   Rebuilt from Wainwright Class C 0-6-0 No 685, built 1900 by Neilson Reid
**   Never carried

Below: *Maunsell's style of cab and bunker is evident in this view of the sole Class S 0-6-0ST, No A685. The locomotive is seen in the early Southern Railway period, sometime between 1923 and c1931, when its new number (1685) would have been applied.* Ian Allan Library

CLASS E1

A business decision by the SECR to concentrate all boat trains to be worked from Victoria over the LCDR route presented the motive-power department with a problem. The lighter axle load of this route compared with the original SER main line meant that heavier locomotives such as the 'N', 'K' and 'L' classes could not be used, and the biggest express locomotives that could be accommodated — the 'D' and 'E' classes — were insufficiently powerful for the heavier loads envisaged. In 1919 Maunsell had one of the Class E 4-4-0s rebuilt with two key objectives in mind: to increase the power and performance, and to keep the weight down. New cylinders were cast for the rebuild and given long-travel 10in-diameter piston valves with outside steam admission and thus a direct exhaust passage to the blastpipe. A new firebox was provided, with greater heating surface, married to the existing boiler barrel. Weight was kept down by eliminating all decoration and giving the locomotive a raised running plate over the coupled wheels. The Derby influence in the design office emerged with the straight-sided firebox cladding, the shape of the cab and the design of the extended smokebox and smokebox door, with edge clips and no centre dart handles. No 179 looked quite like a Midland Railway '2P' 4-4-0, but there the similarity ended. In traffic it performed exceptionally briskly and powerfully for a locomotive of such modest dimensions, completely eclipsing the 'E' class from which it had been derived. As a result of its success a further 10 Class E locomotives were rebuilt as 'E1s' from 1920.

The 'E1s' performed outstandingly on the Southern's Eastern Section main lines until bigger locomotives, in the form particularly of the 'Schools' class, ousted them from the top jobs. That did not reduce the demand for these versatile machines, which performed well on secondary stopping trains, on rush-hour commuter workings and on heavy seasonal holiday trains, right through until the first phase of the Kent Coast electrification scheme in 1959. Class E1 4-4-0s then began to appear on some Central Division services, and towards the end a few went to work local trains on the Salisbury–Bournemouth route until that line closed. The last was withdrawn for scrap in 1961; none has survived.

Class	E1 4-4-0
Engineer	R. E. L. Maunsell
Designed for	SECR
Rebuilt by	SECR Ashford (1), Beyer Peacock (10)
Number in class	11
Introduced	1919
BR power rating	3P
Cylinders (2 inside)	19in x 26in
Coupled wheels	6ft 6in
Boiler pressure	180lb/sq in
Tractive effort	18,410lb
Weight	53 tons 9cwt
SR numbers	A19, A67, A160, A163, A165, A179, A497, A504, A506, A507, A511 / 1019, 1067, 1160, 1163, 1165, 1179, 1497, 1504, 1506, 1507, 1511
BR numbers	31019, 31067, 31160, 31163*, 31165, 31179, 31497, 31504, 31506, 31507, 31511

*   Never carried this number

Below: *Displaced to the South Western Division by Kent-area electrification, Class E1 4-4-0 No 31507 stands to attention outside Eastleigh depot on 15 October 1959. Although the 'E1s' were rebuilt with top feeds to the side of the dome, the Southern Railway later moved the clack valves to the boiler barrel sides, making the boilers interchangeable with those of the 'D1s'.* Author

Following the success of the rebuilt Class E 4-4-0s Maunsell also redesigned the 'D' class to produce the 'D1' 4-4-0s. These received much the same treatment as the 'E1s', the new inside cylinder block being standard between the two classes. Twenty-one 'D1s' were produced by rebuilding 'Ds', and they enabled the acceleration of the Chatham-line business expresses — a route that included the long stretch of 1 in 100 of Sole Street Bank, up which they had to haul eight-coach commuter trains at reasonable speeds.

External the 'D1s' were difficult to distinguish from the 'E1s', being almost identical in appearance. The 2in difference in driving-wheel diameter was hardly discernible to the naked eye, nor was the 6in-longer wheelbase of the 'E1s'. The key visual difference was that the 'E1s' had fluted coupling rods, whereas the 'D1s' had plain, rectangular-section rods.

Like the 'E1' class, the 'D1' 4-4-0s performed outstandingly throughout their lives, being eclipsed only when the 'King Arthur' and 'Schools' locomotives were introduced by the Southern Railway on Eastern Section workings. In the late 1950s some were displaced to the Central and Western Divisions of BR's Southern Region to replace the last few Drummond 4-4-0s. The last Class 'D1' was withdrawn in 1961. All were scrapped.

Class	D1 4-4-0
Engineer	R. E. L. Maunsell
Designed for	SECR
Rebuilt by	SECR Ashford (11), Beyer Peacock (10)
Number in class	20 (plus 1 withdrawn before 1948)
Introduced	1921
BR power rating	3P
Cylinders (2 inside)	19in x 26in
Coupled wheels	6ft 8in
Boiler pressure	180lb/sq in
Tractive effort	17,950lb
Weight	52 tons 4cwt
SR numbers	A145, A246, A247, A470, A487, A489, A492, A494, A502, A505, A509, A545, A727, A735, A736, A739, A741, A743, A745, A747, A749 / 1145, 1246, 1247, 1470, 1487, 1489, 1492, 1494, 1502, 1505, 1509, 1545, 1727, 1735, 1736, 1739, 1741, 1743, 1745, 1747*, 1749
BR numbers	31145, 31246, 31247, 31470, 31487, 31489, 31492, 31494, 31502, 31505, 31509, 31545, 31727, 31735, 31736, 31739, 31741, 31743, 31745, 31749

* Withdrawn 1944

Below: *The 'D1' 4-4-0s looked similar to the 'E1s' except for their shorter coupled wheelbase and plain coupling rods (the 'E1' rods being fluted), as seen on No 31145 at Nine Elms on 16 August 1959.* Author

LONDON, BRIGHTON & SOUTH COAST RAILWAY

Sandwiched between the SER and the LSWR, the London, Brighton & South Coast Railway was quite a substantial concern even though its main lines were not over long. It was very much a passenger railway, used largely by commuters (even though the term 'commuter' had yet to enter the English language on this side of the Atlantic). Its suburban services ran on a dense network of lines south of the River Thames, which it crossed only to reach its London terminus, Victoria. Its main lines all served coastal towns or ports, from Hastings in the east to Portsmouth at its western extremity. Indeed, having been the first railway into Portsmouth, it sold to the LSWR access to the Harbour line by dint of running rights.

Of the LBSCR main lines that to Brighton, which originally started from the terminus platforms at London Bridge, was its most important. Both main lines out of London were four-track, joining at a major junction between Selhurst and East Croydon to form one southbound trunk route; this was four-track until beyond Haywards Heath, save for a stretch of double track through the cuttings and tunnels near Redhill (which the Southern Railway later by-passed with its Quarry line). Other main lines to Portsmouth and to Eastbourne peeled off at Three Bridges and Wivelsfield respectively. A group of secondary lines, bordering on the rural but effectively in outer-suburban territory, diverged at South Croydon and split further at Oxted to serve various towns and villages in Sussex, rejoining the Brighton and Eastbourne main lines at Haywards Heath and Lewes. The coast line — and branches off it — joined up all the settlements between Hastings and Portsmouth.

The main connection to the Continent was the Newhaven–Dieppe ferry, for which the LBSCR ran regular boat trains to Newhaven Harbour. Portsmouth Harbour also had cross-Channel links but was known primarily for its frequent steamers to and from the Isle of Wight.

In view of its operations it is not surprising that the LBSCR's passenger locomotives should have fallen largely into two categories — suburban tank engines and medium-distance express locomotives. To satisfy season-ticket-holders and holidaymakers alike these locomotives had to perform consistently well, and most did. William Stroudley introduced some of the mightiest midgets anywhere in the form of the Class A (later Class A1) 'Terrier' 0-6-0Ts, one of which lasted so long that for a time in rebuilt form that it had the honour of being British Railways' oldest locomotive!

At Stroudley's death in 1889 the LBSCR was probably unique in not having any locomotives with bogies, tender engines included; even its principal express locomotives were of the unusual 0-4-2 arrangement. Stroudley was succeeded by Robert John Billinton, who introduced some moderately successful 4-4-0 express locomotives and a fleet of solidly useful 0-6-0s and 0-6-2Ts for freight and lesser duties. However, it was Douglas Earle Marsh's tenure of the chief engineering role that brought the Brighton railway into the public eye, and his Atlantics and 4-6-2Ts are admired in retrospect to this day. Lawson Billinton, son of Robert, continued Marsh's work with his big and successful 4-6-4Ts, but his lighter 4-4-2Ts for the more rural lines were perhaps less popular, allegedly not always steaming well.

This section follows the varied careers of the LBSCR's interesting locomotives and brings their stories up to date.

Below: *A typical LBSCR local train formed by Stroudley Class D3 0-4-4T No 32390 with a push-pull set at Brighton. This may have been a railtour duty but could equally have been a service from Horsham via Shoreham.* E. R. Wethersett

Above: *The only surviving Class A1 0-6-0T in service in BR days was No DS680, the shunter at Lancing Carriage Works, where it was photographed on 11 April 1960. This locomotive had been LBSCR No 54 (later 654) and was sold in 1904 to the SECR, becoming the latter's No 751; following the Grouping it joined the SR's service stock as No 680S. It actually had a Class A1X boiler but retained its short smokebox, with Drummond LSWR-type chimney, hence its 'A1' classification. After withdrawal by BR in 1962 it would be sold for preservation in Canada and restored externally to its original Stroudley condition as No 54* Waddon. Author

The small 0-6-0Ts of Class A1 were designed for working suburban trains on the East London line between New Cross and Liverpool Street and also between London Bridge and Victoria on the South London line, with the ability also to haul trains on lightly laid branch lines. With an overall weight in working order of just 27 tons 11cwt the little 0-6-0Ts were indeed lightweights but were competent performers with an ability to accelerate trains from frequent stops with alacrity. So good were they that the class total reached 50 examples, built over the period from 1872 to 1880.

As larger locomotives came into use and early electrification advanced, the need for these locomotives in the London area disappeared; there was a heavy cull in the first three years of the 20th century, and three-quarters of the class were either sold or scrapped. Starting in 1911 Marsh was able to prolong the useful lives of the few that were needed thenceforth on branch-line and shunting service. He rebuilt 21 locomotives with new superheated boilers and cylindrical extended smokeboxes on saddles, and these locomotives became known as Class A1X. Only one Class A1 survived into BR service, this being No 680S, the Lancing Carriage Works shunting locomotive, and even this actually had an 'A1X' boiler. The only pure 'A1' surviving was preserved by the SR, and No 82 *Boxhill* remains safe in the National Collection, painted in Stroudley's 'improved engine green' — in fact a striking shade of yellow.

The 'A1X' class survived as a group because of their light weight and their sprightly performance, their duties including maintaining services on the Kemp Town and Hayling Island branches, shunting at Lancing and Brighton works and Shoreham and Newhaven harbours and working push-pull services on the Isle of Wight.

Those locomotives sent to the Isle of Wight were modified with extended coal bunkers. Their field of operation there included the Freshwater, Yarmouth & Newport line, the Bembridge branch and that from Merstone to Ventnor West. They were later displaced by Class

O2 0-4-4Ts (page 11) and returned to the mainland for further service, reverting to normal BR numbers. There they lasted until rendered redundant by line closures, the last being withdrawn in the early 1960s.

Significant numbers of 'Terriers' were sold by the LBSCR to other railways, including the LSWR (Nos 646 and 668 becoming LSWR Nos 734 and 735, the former being sold on to the Freshwater, Yarmouth & Newport Railway, eventually passing to the SR as No W2, the latter becoming SR No E735), SECR (No 654, becoming SECR No 751 and then SR No A751 — and, later, 680S) and the Isle of Wight Central Railway, whilst following the Grouping the SR sold two to the Weston, Clevedon & Portishead Railway. Most of these locomotives ultimately passed into to BR stock.

Preservation dealt kindly with the 'Terriers'. Besides the two surviving 'A1s' (the second being No 54 *Waddon*, which is now in Canada), eight of the 'A1X' class are also preserved, probably because their light weight reduced their value as scrap, and their performance is ideal for small railways. Examples of these locomotives can nowadays be found on the Bluebell Railway, the Kent & East Sussex Railway, the Isle of Wight Steam Railway (two each), the Spa Valley Railway and at Bressingham Steam Museum.

CLASS A1 / A1X 0-6-0T

Above: *Most 'A1Xs' had four coal rails added to the bunker tops. Seen at Eastleigh on 5 May 1959, No 32655 additionally retained its elegant Stroudley chimney. Note also the toolbox behind the bunker.* Author

Below: *No 32636, formerly LBSCR No 72* Fenchurch, *was sold in 1898 to the Newhaven Harbour Co and absorbed in 1927 by the SR, which numbered it B636 and, later, 2636. This locomotive, unusually, had no coal rails on its bunker. Built in 1872, it was for many years the oldest locomotive on BR and was still active when photographed at Lancing Works on 8 March 1960.* Author

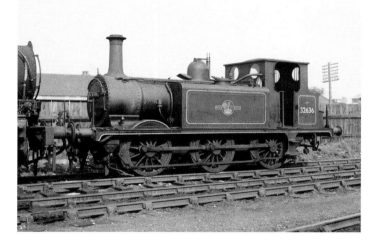

Below: *Those locomotives allocated for service on the Isle of Wight received extended coal bunkers (eliminating the toolbox), some with two coal rails above, and some without. No 32677 was one of the former and when photographed at Fratton depot on 29 April 1958 was resting between duties on the Hayling Island branch.* Author

Class	A1 / A1X 0-6-0T
Engineer	W. Stroudley
Designed for	LBSCR
Built by	LBSCR Brighton
BR power rating	0P
Number in class	15* (plus 35 withdrawn before 1948)
Introduced	1872
Cylinders (2 inside)	12in x 20in
Coupled wheels	4ft 0in
Boiler pressure	150lb/sq in
Grate area	10sq ft
Tractive effort	10,695lb
Weight	28 tons 5cwt
SR numbers	B635, B636, B643, B644, B646 (later W2), B647, B650 (later W9), B653, B655, B659, B661, B662, B677 (later W3 and then W13), B678 (later W4 and then W14), B682 (later 380S), A751 (later 680S), E735, W10, W11, W12
	735, 2635 (later 377S), 2636, 2644, 2646, 2647, 2650 (later 515S), 2653, 2655, 2659, 2661, 2662, W2 (later W8), W9 (later 515S), W10, W11 (later 2640), W12, W13, W14 (later 2678), 380S, 680S
BR numbers	32636, 32640, 32644, 32647**, 32655, 32659 (later DS681), 32661, 32662, 32670, 32678, W8 (later 32646), W13 (later 32677), DS377 (later 32635) DS515 (later 32650), DS680

* Total excludes Nos W10 and W12, withdrawn 1936 but not scrapped until 1949/50, and Nos 5 and 6 (formerly SR Nos B643 and 2653), which reached BR via the Weston, Clevedon & Portishead Railway and the GWR but were not taken into Southern Region stock

** Never carried its allocated BR number

Below: *Another oddity was No 32670, which had taller bunker sides after modification by the Kent & East Sussex Railway, on which it had worked as No 3* Bodiam *until absorbed by BR in 1948. It was photographed shunting Brighton Works yard on 25 July 1962.* Author

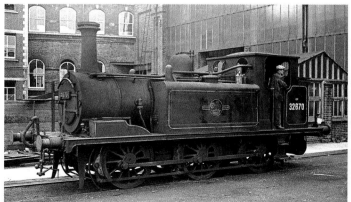

In 1874 William Stroudley produced the first of 79 Class E1 0-6-0Ts for freight work. These were considerably larger locomotives than the 'A1s', being in fact as large as the 'D1' 0-4-2Ts. Some were used for a time on passenger duties, for which the LBSCR painted them in passenger livery, but the majority spent their lives on goods and shunting work. The 'E1' was a straightforward, conventional 0-6-0T with typical LBSCR features such as the domed cab roof, copper chimney cap (later replaced by a cast-iron chimney) and the characteristic toolbox behind the bunker over the rear buffer-beam.

As the 'E1s' aged, successive engineers fitted them with new boilers. Like all Stroudley's locomotives they were never superheated. However, in 1911 Marsh rebuilt one (No 689) with a larger-diameter boiler and cylindrical smokebox on a saddle, and larger side tanks and bunker, the result being classified 'E1X'. In 1930, by which time the new boiler was worn out, the locomotive reverted to the form of a standard 'E1'. In the late 1920s Maunsell had 10 'E1s' rebuilt as 0-6-2Ts and reclassified 'E1/R', and these are described separately on page 85.

In 1932/3 four 'E1s' were sent to the Isle of Wight, where they were used on goods trains, in particular those serving Medina Wharf, Cowes. Those that stayed on the mainland remained on their regular goods and shunting duties, chiefly in the Central Division, but a number were used for many years in and around Southampton Docks, where they spent much of their time on freight transfers between the Eastern and Western Docks — a stretch that included some street running.

Ultimately all the 'E1s' were rendered surplus by yard rationalisation or by the introduction of new diesel shunting locomotives, the last being withdrawn in 1960. One of those sold by the SR for industrial use, No B110, survives in preservation at the East Somerset Railway.

Class	E1 0-6-0T
Engineer	W. Stroudley
Designed for	LBSCR
Built by	LBSCR Brighton
BR power rating	2F
Number in class	30 (plus 49 withdrawn before 1948)
Introduced	1874
Cylinders (2 inside)	17in x 24in
Coupled wheels	4ft 6in
Boiler pressure	170lb/sq in
Grate area	16sq ft
Tractive effort	18,560lb
Weight	44 tons 3cwt
SR numbers	B92, B94-B97, B110, B112 B113, B116, B120, B122-B129, B131-B133, B135-B145, B147, B150-B154, B156, B157, B159-B164, B606-B611, B685-B687, B689-B697 / 2112, 2113, 2122, 2127-2129, 2131 (later W4), 2133, 2136 (later W1), 2138, 2139, 2141-2145, 2147, 2151, 2152 (later W2), 2153, 2154 (later W3), 2156, 2160, 2162, 2164, 2606, 2609, 2689-2691, 2694
BR numbers	32097*, 32112*, 32113, 32122*, 32127*, 32128, 32129, 32133*, 32138, 32139, 32141*, 32142, 32145, 32147, 32151, 32153*, 32156*, 32160*, 32162*, 32164*, 32606, 32609*, 32689, 32690*, 32691*, 32694, W1-W4

* Never carried

Below: *Stroudley Class E1 0-6-0T No 32694 was originally LBSCR No 102* Cherbourg, *later renumbered 694. Built in 1875, it was photographed at Southampton Docks on 22 April 1961, by which date it was the last example in BR stock. The Drummond chimney was common on this class in later years.* Author

Below right: *Transferred to the Isle of Wight in 1932 and 1933, four Class E1 0-6-0Ts operated without modification to work goods trains, mainly centred on Cowes, Medina Wharf and Newport, as well as service and civil engineers' trains. The 'E1s' were renumbered in the Isle of Wight sequence, with 'W' prefix, and were named after locations on the island in common practice with the other classes there. No W4* Wroxall *is seen at Ryde St John's Road depot in 1960, its last year of operation.* Author

CLASS D1

In the year after the first Class A1 0-6-0T was delivered the LBSCR built its first Class D1 0-4-2T, aimed also at suburban trains and local services in Sussex and Hampshire but capable of hauling much heavier trains than could the 'A1s'. Interestingly Stroudley did not think it necessary to provide three coupled axles, regarding two as sufficient, presumably because the 'D1s' had an adhesion weight similar to that of the 'A1s'. The 'D1s' were significantly larger than the 'A1s' in all significant respects, weighing 16 tons more, and their coupled wheels, at 5ft 6in in diameter, were larger, rendering them more suitable for longer-distance running at speed. Of the 125 locomotives built 35 came from Neilson & Co of Glasgow, the rest from Brighton Works.

Interestingly the 'D1' class provided the basis for the first Stroudley 0-4-2 tender engine design for longer-distance passenger workings, namely the Class D2 of 1876. These 14 locomotives were successful enough to spawn the six examples of Class D3, which were 0-4-2s with 6ft 6in coupled wheels for express work, and the 36 examples of Class B1, which included No 214 *Gladstone*, now preserved. Apart from the Adams 'A12' 'Jubilees' no other large railway followed this lead. None of these tender engines lasted into BR days.

Under D. E. Marsh the 'D1' locomotives were re-boilered, some for the second time, and several acquired push-pull apparatus using compressed air to operate the regulator remotely from the driving cab of the carriage at the far end of the train. Marsh also rebuilt one locomotive, No 79A, with a bigger, higher-pitched boiler, raised cab floor and roof and the leading sandboxes repositioned under the running plate; this locomotive, known as Class D1X, was scrapped in 1934. Three 'D1s' were tried on the Lyme Regis branch, with reduced fuel capacity to lighten them, but were not successful. During World War 2 Class D1 locomotives ventured as far north as Ayr (No 2605), Inverness (2358) and Wick (2699).

Withdrawal of the 'D1s' began in 1903, larger numbers being condemned in the 1910s, '20s and '30s as suburban electrification spread. By the end of World War 2 only 27 remained in stock. During the war nine were temporarily modified to fight fires by means of a powerful steam-driven pump carried above the rear buffer-beam; this had a maximum output of one ton of water per minute pumping through four powerful jets, and the locomotives so equipped were known as Class D1/M. In 1947, as part of the drive for oil firing of steam locomotives, Nos 2244 and 2284 were used as oil-pumping locomotives at depots and given the service stock numbers 700S and 701S. They were retired in 1949 and 1951, by which time the remaining 18 members of the class had all been withdrawn by BR as non-standard. None survived to be preserved.

Class	D1 0-4-2T
Engineer	W. Stroudley
Designed for	LBSCR
Built by	LBSCR Brighton / Neilson & Co
BR power rating	1P
Number in class	20 (plus 105 withdrawn before 1948)
Introduced	1876
Cylinders (2 inside)	17in x 24in
Coupled wheels	5ft 6in
Boiler pressure	170lb/sq in
Grate area	15sq ft
Tractive effort	15,200lb
Weight	43 tons 10cwt
SR numbers	B214-B262, B264-B297, B299, B605, B612, B614-B617, B623-B629, B631, B633, B634, B684, B699 / 2214-2221, 2224, 2226-2229, 2231-2235, 2237, 2239-2241, 2244 (later 700S), 2247-2249, 2252-2256, 2259-2262, 2266, 2267, 2269, 2270, 2273-2276, 2279, 2282, 2283, 2284 (later 701S), 2286, 2288-2290, 2294-2297, 2355-2359, 2361, 2605, 2612, 2614-2616, 2623, 2625-2627, 2629, 2631, 2633, 2699
BR numbers**	32215, 32234, 32235, 32239, 32252, 32253, 32259, 32269, 32274, 32283, 32286, 32289, 32299, 32358, 32359, 32361, 32605, 32699, DS700, DS701

* In 1947 Nos 2244 and 2284 were numbered 700S and 701S respectively

** Never carried

Left: *The Class D1 0-4-2Ts were sizeable locomotives for their wheel arrangement and had a good turn of speed. No 2615 in SR Maunsell dark-green livery carries a LBSCR-style chimney. The toolbox behind the bunker is just visible.* Ian Allan Library

R. J. BILLINTON LOCOMOTIVES

CLASSES D3 AND D3X

R. J. Billinton had been Stroudley's assistant at Brighton, with specific responsibility for rolling-stock engineering, before he moved on to become Chief Draughtsman at Derby, on the Midland Railway. When Stroudley died in 1889 Billinton was doubtless keen to return to Brighton to take over the rôle of Locomotive, Carriage & Marine Superintendent of the LBSCR, which he duly did in 1890.

Billinton's first new design for the LBSCR was a class of 0-4-4Ts for hauling passenger trains on secondary and branch lines and for main-line stopping services. Something more powerful than the erstwhile 'D1' class was needed. Emerging from Brighton Works in 1892 was No 363, a handsome, well-proportioned locomotive that bore the hallmarks of a Brighton locomotive in the curved tops to the side tanks whilst having a simpler curved cab roof than the domed shape on Stroudley locomotives. Dimensionally the 'D3s' were bigger than the 'D1s' by dint of a larger boiler (with higher pressure) and cylinders with a longer piston stroke.

Given that Stroudley had left the LBSCR without any bogie locomotives, having preferred the rigid wheelbases of 0-4-2 and 0-6-0 types, a bogie tank was seen as an innovation, even though other railways already made much use of the principle. No 363 was followed by many more until the 'D3' class totalled 36 locomotives, delivered over a period of five years.

In 1909 two 'D3s' (Nos 396 and 397) were rebuilt by Marsh with larger-diameter boilers and cylindrical smokeboxes, becoming Class D3X. Although only two were converted, they were good enough to run alongside the rest of the class until withdrawal began in 1933. However, in that same year some 'D3s' began to displace older locomotives on branch services for which push-pull equipment was needed, and ultimately most examples were so fitted. One 'D3X' and 28 'D3s' lasted to become part of BR stock in 1948, the 'D3X' being withdrawn the following year and the final 'D3' in 1953, after a life of 60 years.

Class	D3 / D3X 0-4-4T
Engineer	R. J. Billinton / D. E. Marsh*
Designed for	LBSCR
Built by	LBSCR Brighton
BR power rating	1P
Number in class	29 (plus 7 withdrawn before 1948)
Introduced	1892 / 1909*
Cylinders (2 inside)	17½in x 26in
Coupled wheels	5ft 6in
Boiler pressure	170lb/sq in
Grate area	17sq ft
Tractive effort	17,430lb
Weight	52 tons 0cwt / 53 tons 0cwt*
SR number series	B363-B398 / 2363-2398**
BR numbers**	32364-32368, 32370-32374, 32376-32380, 32383-32391, 32393-32395, 32397, 32398

* Details refer to Class D3X locomotives Nos 396 and 397
** Nos 2363, 2369, 2375, 2381, 2382, 2392 and 2396 withdrawn 1933-47
*** Not all locomotives received their allocated BR numbers

Right: R. J. Billinton's first design for the LBSCR was the 'D3' 0-4-4T, which performed well and lasted into the BR era. No 32365 looks handsome in newly applied BR lined black at Ashford on 15 May 1950. R. H. Tunstall

Right: The 'D3X' 0-4-4Ts carried larger Marsh boilers, but rebuilding was not extended beyond two locomotives. No 2396 seen here would be withdrawn in 1937, but No 2397 survived to enter BR stock. Ian Allan Library

CLASS C2

R. J. Billinton led the design of his standard goods 0-6-0 that was introduced in 1893, 55 examples being built. Because of the pressure on Brighton Works' building capacity at that time, construction of all 55 locomotives was contracted to the Vulcan Foundry at Newton-le-Willows, with the result that the 'C2s' were nicknamed 'Vulcans'. Robust, simple locomotives, they had driving wheels of 5ft diameter — small enough for a reasonable though not exceptional tractive effort at the wheels, yet large enough for a reasonable turn of speed when occasionally called upon to work passenger trains or fast freight or van trains. The 'C2s' were fitted with air brakes, for working fitted trains, but these were later supplemented by vacuum brakes and provision for steam heating. Later in R. J. Billinton's tenure at Brighton some of the locomotives received new boilers. At the same time the cylinders were lined by half an inch, and the boiler pressure was increased — to 175lb/sq in, according to one source, though another quotes 170lb/sq in, which figure the author believes more likely in view of the widespread use of that pressure on the LBSCR.

From 1908 no fewer than 45 'C2s' were subjected to a thorough rebuild by D. E. Marsh (see page 69). Withdrawals of the other 10 (which continued to work on what, post-Grouping, became the SR's Central Section) began in 1935, seven having succumbed by the outbreak of World War 2. The remaining three survived to join BR stock in 1948, the last two being condemned in 1950. None was preserved.

Class	C2 0-6-0
Engineer	R. J. Billinton
Designed for	LBSCR
Built by	Vulcan Foundry
BR power rating	2F
Number in class	3 (plus 7 withdrawn before 1948 and a further 45 rebuilt 1908-40 as Class C2X
Introduced	1893
Cylinders (2 inside)	18in x 26in / 17½in x 26in*
Coupled wheels	5ft 0in
Boiler pressure	160lb/sq in
Grate area	19.32sq ft
Tractive effort	19,095lb / 18,050lb*
Weight	38 tons 0cwt
LBSCR No series	433-452, 521-555
SR numbers	B433, B435, B436, B439, B452, B526, B527, B530, B531, B533, B535, B542, B552, B555 / 2433, 2435, 2436, 2439, 2452, 2530, 2531, 2533, 2542, 2555
BR numbers**	32435, 32436, 32533

*   As modified by R. J. Billinton
**   Never carried

Note: The number series above shows only the numbers carried by unrebuilt 'C2s' during the currency of the individual number series

Below: *Class C2 0-6-0 No 2438 stands in line at Norwood Junction depot on 28 July 1945. Only three of this class would enter BR service, including this example, which was to last until in 1950.* H. C. Casserley

Above: *Although it had been withdrawn from service the previous October, Class E3 0-6-2T No 32167 was still extant alongside the former Longhedge Works on 18 February 1956. The dent at the rear of the tank side suggests the locomotive had been used by the breakdown gang for re-righting practice.* Author

The Class E3 0-6-2T was nominally an R. J. Billinton design. However, before his death Stroudley had laid down the designs for such a locomotive for freight and mixed-traffic work, and the first example emerged in 1891 as a Class E Special. So successful was this on freight duties along the Portsmouth–Brighton coast line that Billinton ordered a further 16 locomotives, which were delivered in 1894 and 1895. The 4ft 6in coupled wheels were the same as those on the earlier 'E1' class (page 57), but the cylinders had the longer, 26in stroke preferred by Billinton for all his designs, and the cylinder diameter was greater, at 18in (although replacement cylinders, when required, had a reduced diameter of 17½in). The rear of the locomotive was carried on a radial truck in which the axlebox cheek plates moved between curved horn guides to take up a position parallel to the rails on curved track. The boiler was considerably larger, with a slightly increased grate area and, indeed, was the same as used on Billinton's own 'D3' class (page 59) but with a cylindrical smokebox mounted on a saddle above the cylinder block. Like the 'D3' 0-4-4T, the 'E3' design featured a curved cab roof and rounded top edge to the side tanks.

As was regular practice on the LBSCR (until R. J. Billinton began to remove them), the 'E3s' had names painted (or transferred) on the tank sides, being named after locations in the railway's operating area.

The original 'E Special' 0-6-2T had been absorbed into Class E3 but was withdrawn as SR No 2158 in 1935 after 44 years of service.

Class	E3 0-6-2T
Engineer	R. J. Billinton*
Designed for	LBSCR
Built by	LBSCR Brighton
BR power rating	2F
Number in class	16 (plus 1 withdrawn before 1948)
Introduced	1891 / 1894*
Cylinders (2 inside)	17½in x 26in
Coupled wheels	4ft 6in
Boiler pressure	170lb/sq in
Grate area	17.35sq ft
Tractive effort	17,430lb
Weight	56 tons 10cwt
SR number series	B158, B165-B170, B453-B462/ 2158**, 2165-2170, 2453-2462
BR number series	32165-32170, 32453-32462***

* LBSCR No 158 (later SR No B158 / 2158) was built to a Stroudley design after his death; the class as a whole is credited to Billinton
** Withdrawn 1935
*** No 32457 never carried this number

All other 'E3s' ultimately joined BR stock: No 32457 was withdrawn in 1949, but the remainder lasted until at least 1955, the final example succumbing in 1959. None survives in preservation.

CLASSES E4 AND E4X

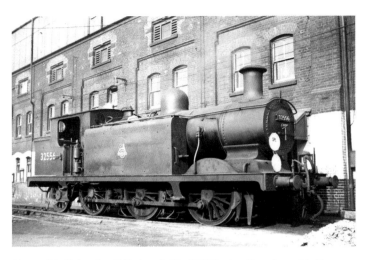

Above: *Typifying the 'E4' class is No 32556, standing alongside the offices at Eastleigh depot on 22 March 1953. The extended lamp irons at the side were an LBSCR alternative to the LSWR practice of affixing the middle irons to the smokebox door.* Author

Below: *Inevitably with a long-lived class (the 'E4s' lasted up to 67 years) there were detail differences. No 32491, seen at Eastleigh depot on 9 December 1958, had a cast smokebox door in place of the original pressed-dish type, and the safety valve casing is different from that in the previous photograph. This locomotive also has two extra coal rails on the bunker top.* Author

Following the success of the 'E3' class R. J. Billinton decided to develop the design to make it more suitable for working passenger trains by fitting coupled wheels that were 6in larger in diameter. Thus was born the 'E4' class, of which 75 examples were built in the period 1897-1903. These energetic locomotives were to be seen all over the LBSCR system, venturing further afield in SR and BR days. Several were allocated to Eastleigh depot when the author was based there in the 1950s, and among other duties they were used as the shed shunters, in which role they demonstrated a tendency to slip when starting heavy loads. However, crews in their native Sussex swore by their general usefulness, and during the Great War 12 locomotives had served in France. In 1947 No 32510 was shipped to the Isle of Wight for trials but was returned to the mainland in April 1949.

In his relentless quest for improving locomotives (not always successful) Marsh modified four 'E4s' with larger boilers pitched higher, the boilers in question being of the type used on his Class I2 4-4-2T. Apart from increasing their weight the change brought little improvement, and the 'E4X' class remained at just four locomotives.

With the exception of one wartime casualty (No 2483) the 'E4' and 'E4X' classes remained intact until 1955, and many locomotives survived until the early 1960s, the last being taken out of service in 1963. No 32473 was preserved on the Bluebell Railway and at the time of writing (December 2009) was about to emerge from overhaul in olive green as SR No B473. It is the sole Billinton locomotive to survive in preservation.

Class	E4 / E4X 0-6-2T
Engineer	R. J. Billinton
Designed for	LBSCR
Built by	LBSCR Brighton
BR power rating	2P2F
Number in class	74 (plus 1 withdrawn before 1948)
Introduced	1897 / 1909*
Cylinders (2 inside)	17½in x 26in
Coupled wheels	5ft 0in
Boiler pressure	170lb/sq in
Grate area	17.35sq ft
Tractive effort	19,175lb
Weight	57 tons 10cwt / 59 tons 5cwt*
SR number series	B463-B520, B556-B566, B577-B582 / 2463-2520**, 2556-2566, 2577-2582
BR number series	32463-32482, 32484-32520, 32556-32566, 32577-32582

*   Nos 466, 477, 478 and 489 rebuilt by Marsh as Class E4X
**   No 2483 withdrawn 1944

Left: *The bigger Marsh boiler, as fitted to the 'E4X' class of four locomotives, is readily apparent in this view of No 32466 at Norwood Junction on 31 May 1958.* Author

Thirty-three Class B4 4-4-0s were built from 1899 to 1902 as enlargements and improvements on the Billinton Classes B2 and B3 that preceded them. They had 6ft 9in coupled wheels, saturated boilers and slide valves and were elegant locomotives with flowing curves at each end of the side valances and tapered, graceful chimneys. Eight were built at Brighton, and the remaining 25 by Sharp, Stewart & Co in Glasgow. These locomotives were intended to work the heaviest expresses. In 1903 one hauled the down Pullman from Victoria to Brighton in 48 minutes 41 seconds, an outstanding achievement.

Nonetheless, when Billinton's son, Lawson, was nearing the end of his tenure of office in 1922 he ordered the 'rebuilding' of 12 of the B4s to produce a much more powerful locomotive. Using the superheated boiler designed for the 'K' class (page 72), larger cylinders of 20in diameter with piston valves, and extending the coupled wheelbase from 8ft 9in to 10ft 0in, the 'B4X' class was a useful improvement on the 'B4'. It has been suggested that, in practice, the locomotives were virtually new, all that was used from the old locomotives being the bogies, wheels and tenders. They handled secondary expresses well and lasted into BR days on services on the non-electrified lines around Brighton, including occasionally the through trains from that resort to Bournemouth and Salisbury (for Plymouth and Cardiff).

Seven of the 'B4s' and all 12 'B4Xs' entered BR stock in 1948 but were among the earliest 4-4-0s to be withdrawn by BR's Southern Region, all being condemned by late 1951. No 'B4' or 'B4X' survived to be preserved.

Classes	B4 and B4X 4-4-0
Engineer	R. J. Billinton / L. Billinton*
Designed for	LBSCR
Built by	LBSCR Brighton / Sharp, Stewart & Co
BR power rating	1P / 3P*
Number in class	19 (plus 15 withdrawn before 1948)
Introduced	1899 / 1922*
Cylinders (2 inside)	19in x 26in / 20in x 26in*
Coupled wheels	6ft 9in
Boiler pressure	180lb/sq in
Grate area	24sq ft / 25sq ft*
Tractive effort	17,700lb / 19,645lb*
Weight	51 tons 10cwt / 58 tons 1cwt
SR number series	B42-B74 / 2042-2074**
BR numbers***	32043-32045, 32050-32052, 32054-32056, 32060, 32062, 32063, 32067, 32068, 32070-32074

* Class B4X
** Nos 2042, 2046-2049, 2053, 2057-2059, 2061, 2064-2066, 2069 withdrawn 1934-47
*** Only Nos 32043, 32071 and 32072 carried their allocated BR numbers

Left: *R. J. Billinton's early 4-4-0s had disappointed by not surpassing the performance of Stroudley's 'B1' 0-4-2s, but his graceful 'B4s' salvaged his reputation, early examples being used to work the heaviest and fastest peak-hour expresses between London and Brighton. Pictured in early SR days, No B58 shows off the undulating splashers over its bogie wheels.* Ian Allan Library

Right: *Ostensibly rebuilds of his father's 'B4s', L. Billinton's 12 Class B4X 4-4-0s of 1922-4 were essentially new locomotives, with new, longer frames necessitated by the use of the 'K'-class boiler and firebox. Seen shortly after the Grouping, No B56 (later 2056) still has its top-feed clack valves, which the Southern Railway later moved to the boiler sides.* Ian Allan Library

CLASSES E5 AND E5X

In the years 1902-4 a third class of radial tank emerged from Brighton Works. The 30 'E5' 0-6-2Ts were intended for passenger trains only and represented a development of the 'E4' class with larger coupled wheels and bigger boilers. The 5ft 6in wheels gave them a potentially higher top speed, but they had a lower tractive effort than did the 'E4s'. In compensation the larger grate area of the 'E5' would have enabled it to be driven harder even though the cylinder diameter was the standard 17½in. Water-tank capacity was increased from the 1,410gal of the 'E4' class to a more useful 1,665gal, and the larger coal bunker held 3½ tons, an increase of 1 ton.

Faced with the expansion of SR electrification in their later years the 'E5s' found employment on the many secondary and branch lines in the Central Section. By the BR era they had also gravitated to goods work and could be found at sheds such as Norwood Junction and Three Bridges.

As was his wont, Marsh rebuilt four of the 'E5s' with larger boilers as used on the 'C3' 0-6-0 design; these locomotives were classified 'E5X'. No more were converted, although rebuilds lasted as long as their standard counterparts.

Apart from two locomotives withdrawn in 1936 and 1944, the 'E5' and 'E5X' classes remained intact until 1949, and the last four examples (including one 'E5X') survived until January 1956.

Class	E5 / E5X 0-6-2T
Engineer	R. J. Billinton
Designed for	LBSCR
Built by	LBSCR Brighton
BR power rating	2P2F
Number in class	28 (plus 2 withdrawn before 1948)
Introduced	1902 / 1911*
Cylinders (2 inside)	17½in x 26in (originally 18in x 26in)
Coupled wheels	5ft 6in
Boiler pressure	160lb/sq in / 170lb/sq in* / 175lb/sq in**
Grate area	19sq ft
Tractive effort	16,410lb/sq in / 17,435lb/sq in* / 17,945lb/sq in **
Weight	60 tons 0cwt / 64 tons 5cwt*
SR number series	B399-B406, B567-B576, B583-B594 / 2399-2406***, 2567-2576***, 2583-2594
BR number series****	32399-32402, 32404-32406, 32567, 32568, 32570 32576, 32583-32594

* Nos 401, 570, 576 and 586 rebuilt by Marsh as Class E5X
** Some 'E5s' had higher-pressure boilers
*** No 2403 withdrawn in 1944, No 2569 in 1936
**** Nos 32567, 32572 and 32589 never carried these numbers

Left: The 'E5' 0-6-2Ts had quite elegant chimneys placed forward on short smokeboxes, giving them a somewhat front-heavy look. No 32593 is seen in early BR condition, without power rating on the cabside. E. R. Wethersett

Left: The four Class E5X locomotives, rebuilt thus in 1911, looked businesslike with their larger-diameter boilers. No 32586 makes the point at Brighton on 5 October 1952. Note the cylindrical smokebox supported on a saddle (contrasting with the built-up smokebox on the original 'E5' design) and the helpful handrail partially surrounding the dome.
Ian Allan Library

Twelve more radial tanks appeared in 1904, the year after R. J. Billinton died. These were intended purely for freight traffic and were basically a goods version of the 'E5' class of 0-6-2T with 4ft 6in coupled wheels. However, their cylinder blocks were different in that they had the steam chests below the cylinders, as in the 'B4' 4-4-0s. Unlike the other radial 0-6-2Ts the 'E6s' did not have their cylinders reduced to 17½in diameter upon renewal, these remaining at 18in throughout.

The 'E6' class worked mainly out of depots such as Norwood Junction, in the heart of the LBSCR's freight-marshalling area. Indeed, Billinton had intended that the last two 'E6s' should be built as 0-8-0Ts for yard shunting, but Marsh cancelled this design development before the locomotives were built, and they emerged as standard 'E6s' save that their coupling rods were fluted rather than plain.

In 1911 Marsh rebuilt two of this class with larger boilers of the 'C3' type. As with the 'E4s' and 'E5s', the experiment was not pursued, but the two rebuilt locomotives continued to work alongside the unrebuilt examples. All survived to see BR service, being withdrawn in the period 1957-62.

Class	E6 / E6X 0-6-2T
Engineer	R. J. Billinton
Designed for	LBSCR
Built by	LBSCR Brighton
BR power rating	3F
Number in class	12
Introduced	1904 / 1911*
Cylinders (2 inside)	18in x 26in
Coupled wheels	4ft 6in
Boiler pressure	160lb/sq in / 170lb/sq in* / 175lb/sq in**
Grate area	19sq ft
Tractive effort	21,215lb / 22,540lb* / 23,205lb**
Weight	62 tons 0cwt / 67 tons 0cwt*
SR number series	B407-B418 / 2407-2418
BR number series	32407-32418

*   Nos 407 and 411 rebuilt by Marsh as Class E6X
**   Some 'E6s' had higher-pressure boilers

Above: *Class E6 0-6-2T No 32413 in store at Norwood Junction on Sunday 13 November 1954. The coupled wheels are smaller than those of an 'E5', and the water tanks higher.* Author

Right: *Class E6X 0-6-2T No 32411 trundles through the yards at Norwood Junction on 21 June 1951. This locomotive is carrying one of the two double-domed boilers used at various times on 'E4X', 'E5X' and 'E6X' locomotives. The dome handrail and the higher side tanks are also evident.* Brian Morrison

Douglas Earle Marsh had served for nine years at senior levels on the Great Northern Railway at Doncaster before being offered the senior engineering post at Brighton as successor to Robert Billinton. It came as no surprise therefore that the first new locomotive class he introduced on the LBSCR was closely based on a Doncaster type, his Class H1 4-4-2 looking very similar to a GNR 'Large Atlantic' with some detail differences. Where it was an improvement was in the higher boiler pressure and deeper firebox. Inherited from the GNR, the wide Wootton type of firebox was an innovation for any locomotive south of the Thames. The extra width allowed a grate area as large as 31sq ft — bigger than any current or subsequent LBSCR type apart from the second class of Atlantics, only the presence of the rear pony truck enabling provision of this feature. The locomotives were fitted with superheaters between 1925 and 1927.

Supplied by Kitson in 1905/6, the five 'H1s' were used on Brighton-line business expresses, Eastbourne-line services and on the South Coast line to Portsmouth. In later years they were used on secondary passenger work on non-electrified lines such as those via Oxted.

In SR days the Atlantics received names related to shoreland features of the South Coast, cast in brass on handsome plates curved to fit the rear coupled-wheel splashers. In Bulleid's time they received malachite-green livery.

In 1947 Bulleid selected No 2039 for experimental fitting with sleeve valves to gain experience for his forthcoming 'Leader' class. The locomotive had new cylinder castings that contained annular steam chests in which oscillated heavily lubricated cast-iron sleeve valves, the theory being that the sleeve valves would provide greater freedom for live and exhaust steam. The locomotive also had a five-jet Lemaître blastpipe and a wider, stovepipe chimney. The sleeve valves were not successful, and the locomotive was withdrawn in 1951 — albeit not the first to go, Nos 2040 and 2041 having already been condemned in 1944. The last two locomotives, Nos 32037/8, were also withdrawn in 1951. No Brighton Atlantic was saved for preservation.

Class	H1 4-4-2
Engineer	D. E. Marsh
Designed for	LBSCR
Built by	Kitson
BR power rating	3P
Number in class	3 (plus 2 withdrawn before 1948)
Introduced	1905
Cylinders (2 outside)	18½in x 26in
Coupled wheels	6ft 7½in
Boiler pressure	200lb/sq in
Grate area	30.95sq ft
Tractive effort	19,030lb
Weight	68 tons 5cwt
SR number series	B37-B41 / 2037-2041*
BR number series	32037-32039

* Nos 2040 and 2041 withdrawn 1944

Left: *Marsh's Class H1 4-4-2 design was very similar in basic shape to the GNR Ivatt 'Large Atlantic' except for the cab and tender and also the curves of the side running plates, which on the LBSCR locomotives rose up over the cylinders and coupled wheels. No 32037* Selsey Bill *was photographed at Brighton, probably in 1948 or 1949.* Walter Gilbert

Right: *When Bulleid needed an express locomotive on which to experiment with sleeve valves the only type made available to him by the operators was an 'H1' 4-4-2. Not a pretty sight in rebuilt form, No 32039* Hartland Point *also suffered significant unreliability, but probably too late for the lessons learned to be incorporated in the design of the 'Leader' 0-6-6-0T.* Ian Allan Library

The logical follow-on of the 'H1' 4-4-2 appeared in 1911 in the form of Class H2, which can be regarded as the final development of the wide-firebox 4-4-2 design that originated on the GNR under H. A. Ivatt. Unlike the 'H1s' the six 'H2s' were superheated from new and followed the contemporary — if, in hindsight, erroneous — practice of lower boiler pressure and larger cylinders. Thus the 'H2' boilers were pressed at 170lb/sq in (against the 200lb/sq in of the 'H1' class), and the cylinders were of 21in diameter (against 18½ or 19in) and were fed by piston valves. Another feature common to the 'H1s' was the provision of bogie-wheel brakes, though in later years these were removed. A proposal for the last two locomotives to have four cylinders appears to have been quietly dropped.

Under Maunsell the cabs were reshaped to fit in the SR composite loading-gauge, and the cab roofs extended back to provide greater protection for the crew. The other boiler mountings were also shortened, though not so much as to alter significantly the overall appearance of these fine-looking locomotives.

The Southern Railway applied brass nameplates to the 'H2s', as with the 'H1s' highlighting prominent features of the South of England coastline. The locomotives looked splendid in Maunsell's dark-green livery, although the author admired in particular the sight of malachite-green-liveried No 2423 *The Needles* when he saw it in Bournemouth c1949. The 'H2s' were employed on duties similar to those of the 'H1s', including the heavy Newhaven boat trains, and for much of their BR years they had a virtual monopoly of the daily through Brighton–Bournemouth train. By the 1950s they were recorded as having a boiler pressure of 200lb/sq in (though when the alteration was carried out is uncertain), justifying BR's '4P' power rating.

Apart from No 2423 *The Needles*, which was withdrawn in 1949, the 'H2' class outlived the 'H1s' by up to seven years. The last survivor was No 32424 *Beachy Head*, which had become very popular among travellers and enthusiasts alike, albeit insufficiently so to prevent its being cut up at Eastleigh Works in 1958.

Although no Brighton Atlantic is preserved, reference should be made to the project in hand at Sheffield Park, on the Bluebell Railway, to build a new, full size operational version of *Beachy Head*, using an Ivatt Atlantic boiler that was found in excellent condition in industrial ownership.

Class	H2 4-4-2
Engineer	D. E. Marsh
Designed for	LBSCR
Built by	LBSCR Brighton
BR power rating	4P
Number in class	6
Introduced	1911
Cylinders (2 outside)	21in x 26in
Coupled wheels	6ft 7½in
Boiler pressure	200lb/sq in*
Grate area	30.95sq ft
Tractive effort	24,520lb
Weight	68 tons 5cwt
SR number series	B421-B426 / 2421-2426
BR number series	32421-32426**

*   Originally 170lb/sq in
** No 32423 never carried this number

Below: *The Marsh 'H2' Atlantic was even more handsome than the 'H1', and neater in that the running plate rose only once to clear both the outside cylinders and the coupled wheels. This view features No 32425 Trevose Head, with the through Bournemouth–Brighton train, calling at Boscombe in 1955. The cab and boiler mountings were modified post-Grouping to fit the SR's composite loading-gauge.* Author

CLASS C3

Ten 0-6-0s to Marsh design were produced by Brighton Works in 1906. Intended as freight locomotives, they were dimensionally similar to R. J. Billinton's 'C2' class as modified by Marsh (Class C2X). The key feature of this class was its use of a new boiler design that became the standard for modifying other classes, being used on the 'B2X', 'C2X', 'E5X' and 'E6X' rebuilds. The 'C3s' were non-superheated and, unlike the other classes rebuilt with the standard boiler, never received extended smokeboxes. In effect the 'C3' was a 'C2X' with short, built-up smokebox. There were, however, other small differences, notably the use of outside brake rods which flanked the coupled wheels.

In service many of the 'C3s' were allocated to Horsham (gaining them the nickname 'Horsham goods'), where their duties would have included workings to Shoreham, Portsmouth, Brighton and Newhaven and up to the capital. However, being small in number, they were regarded by the SR as non-standard, and withdrawal began as early as 1936. BR inherited eight, but the last was withdrawn in January 1952. No Marsh-designed locomotive is preserved.

Class	C3 0-6-0
Engineer	D. E. Marsh
Designed for	LBSCR
Rebuilt by	LBSCR Brighton
BR power rating	3F
Number in class	8 (plus 2 withdrawn before 1948)
Introduced	1906
Cylinders (2 inside)	17½in x 26in
Coupled wheels	5ft 0in
Boiler pressure	170lb/sq in
Grate area	19.32sq ft
Tractive effort	19,175lb
Weight	47tons 10cwt
SR number series	B300-B309 / 2300-2309*
BR number series**	32300-32303, 32306-32309

*   No 2304 and 2305 withdrawn in 1936 and 1937 respectively
** Nos 32306-32309 never carried these numbers

Below: *One of the four 'C3s' to receive a BR number was No 32301, seen with the early style that still used SR 'sunshine' lettering and numerals. It was photographed* c*1950 at Brighton. W. Beckerlegge*

Douglas Earle Marsh was charged with making the 'C2' class more effective and in 1908 began rebuilding them at Brighton Works. The main component change involved replacement of the existing boiler with the more powerful type fitted to the 'C3' class (page 68), with an extended smokebox on a saddle. New 17½in-diameter cylinders were fitted, and an additional well tank was added to the tender, increasing water capacity from 2,835 to 2,985gal. Rebuilding was spread over many years, most locomotives being dealt with during the 1910s, but a few were treated in the 1920s and '30s. The last four to be rebuilt went to Ashford Works, emerging in 1939/40.

During L. B. Billinton's tenure at Brighton six of the rebuilds emerged with his top-feed apparatus, this time concealed by a second dome, which remained *in situ* even when, in later years, the top feed was replaced by side feed. These boilers were interchanged among several locomotives during their long lives, so many more than six were photographed at various times with two domes.

The 'C2Xs' were useful and competent locomotives, though rated by BR as no more than '2F' in its classification scheme; interestingly the larger boiler fitted on rebuilding did not result in any difference in the power rating of the 'C2' and 'C2X' classes. The 'C2Xs' worked throughout the Southern Region's Central Division, only occasionally venturing beyond its boundaries.

For whatever reason, 10 of the 'C2s' were never rebuilt, ensuring their earlier demise, but the 'C2X' class soldiered on for many more years; a few were withdrawn in the late 1950s, but the majority lasted until 1960 or 1961, the last two finally being taken out of stock early in 1962. Despite this, none survives in preservation.

Above: *Unusually outside the type's normal home territory, Class C2X 0-6-0 No 32549 poses at Eastleigh on 27 June 1956, at which time the locomotive was allocated to Fratton depot in Portsmouth.* Author

Below: *When photographed at Three Bridges depot on 26 July 1959 'C2X' No 32527 carried a double-domed boiler. The dome on the forward barrel ring originally covered the top feed fitted during rebuilding by L. Billinton but was not removed when this apparatus was replaced by conventional clack valves mounted on the boiler sides, as clearly seen here below the handrail.* Author

Class	C2X 0-6-0
Engineer	D. E. Marsh
Designed for	LBSCR
Rebuilt by	LBSCR and SR Brighton, SR Ashford
BR power rating	2F
Number in class	45
Introduced	1908
Cylinders (2 inside)	17½in x 26in
Coupled wheels	5ft 0in
Boiler pressure	170lb/sq in
Grate area	19.32sq ft
Tractive effort	19,175lb
Weight	45 tons 5cwt
SR numbers*	B434, B437, B438, B440-B451, B521-B525, B528, B529, B532, B534, B536-B541, B543-B551, B553, B554 / 2434, 2437, 2438, 2440-2451, 2521-2529, 2532, 2534-2541, 2543-2554
BR numbers	32434, 32437, 32438, 32440-32451, 32521-32529, 32532, 32534-32541, 32543-32554

* Locomotives not rebuilt as 'C2X' until after 1931 are not listed in the B-prefix series

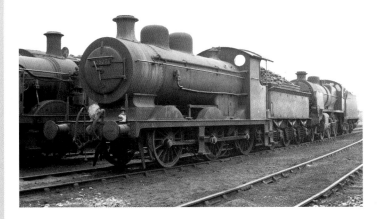

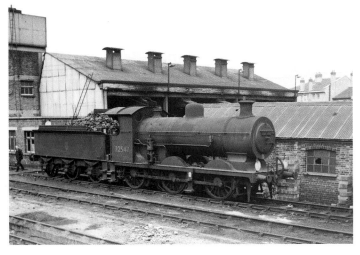

Right: *Pictured at Norwood Junction depot on 20 May 1961, Class C2X 0-6-0 No 32547 has a tender with an ex-LSWR body on top of LBSCR frames!* Author

CLASS I3

Marsh's second 4-4-2T design, Class I2, was no more successful than the original 'I1s', and all had been withdrawn by 1939. However, after experimenting in 1907 with No 21, a 4-4-2T version of the 'B4' 4-4-0, Marsh ordered further examples, the resultant 'I3' class eventually numbering 27 locomotives. These were very successful, being the first express locomotives in the UK to demonstrate beyond doubt the advantages of superheating the steam before it was expanded in the cylinders. This idea is credited to B. K. Field, who at the time was Chief Draughtsman at Brighton. Apart from No 21, which, like the 'B4s', had 6ft 9in coupled wheels, the 'I3s' were given wheels of 6ft 7½in diameter and cylinders of 20in (Nos 22-30 and 75-81) or 21in (82-91). For comparison purposes six of the 'I3s' were built with saturated boilers, but the fuel economy of the superheated locomotives was so convincing that these six were later converted. Trials showed that in traffic a superheated 'I3' would burn just 36lb of coal per mile, compared 40lb for an 'H1' and 42lb for a 'B4'. Moreover, the 'I3s' were economical with water, such that they haul the LBSCR's heaviest expresses from Clapham Junction to Portsmouth without taking on water *en route*, despite tanks' holding just 2,110 gallons.

The definitive demonstration of the superiority of superheating came when 'I3' No 23 (deputised on occasions by No 26) worked for several days the 'Sunny South Express' roster between Croydon and Rugby without taking on water *en route* and without having any coal loaded at Rugby before the return trip. The LNWR's 'Precursor' 4-4-0s, at the time regarded as good performers, could not match this economy.

Eventually the 'I3s' were relegated to secondary routes such as those via Oxted to the South Coast and to Tunbridge Wells. No 2024 was withdrawn in 1944, but the rest survived until taken out of BR service in the years 1950-2, having been displaced by LMS-designed (albeit Brighton-built) 2-6-4Ts.

For the sake of completeness mention should also be made here of the five superheated 4-4-2Ts of Class I4, introduced by Marsh from 1908 but withdrawn as surplus to requirements in the 1930s, the last going in 1940.

Regrettably none of the Brighton 4-4-2Ts was retained for preservation.

Class	I3 4-4-2T
Engineer	D. E. Marsh
Designed for	LBSCR
Built by	LBSCR Brighton
BR power rating	3P
Number in class	26 (plus 1 withdrawn before 1948)
Introduced	1907
Cylinders (2 inside)	19in x 26in* / 20in x 26in** / 21in x 26in****
Coupled wheels	6ft 7½in / 6ft 9in*
Boiler pressure	180lb/sq in
Grate area	23.75sq ft
Tractive effort	17,730lb* / 20,015lb** / 22,065lb***
Weight	76 tons 0cwt
SR number series	B21-B30, B75-B91 / 2021-2030****, 2075-2091
BR numbers*****	32021-32023, 32025-32030, 32075-32091

* No 32021
** Nos 32022, 32023, 32025-32030, 32075-32081
*** Nos 32082-32091
**** No 2024 withdrawn 1944
***** No 32025 never carried this number

Below: *Class I3 4-4-2T No 32089 in plain black with the early BR emblem at Ashurst in 1950. Despite their relatively small size the 'I3s' proved to be excellent performers and were the forerunners in Great Britain of all superheated express locomotives.* P. Ransome-Wallis

Right: *Class J1 4-6-2T No 32325, with Stephenson's inside valve gear, in early-BR condition — still in malachite green but with BR numbers and no emblem. Used latterly on local services around Tunbridge Wells and Oxted, it would be displaced by the arrival of new Fairburn 2-6-4Ts, being withdrawn in 1951. E. R. Wethersett*

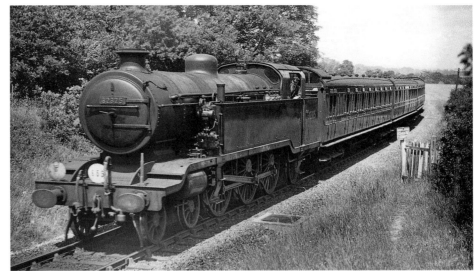

Right: *Class J2 No 32326, Marsh's second 4-6-2T, had Walschaerts outside valve gear. It is seen in the locomotive siding at Brighton station after gaining its BR number and lettering while retaining SR malachite green, the letters and numerals being in Bulleid's 'sunshine' style. Like No 32325, this locomotive would be withdrawn in 1951. Les Elsey*

Marsh is sometimes not given credit for producing some very good locomotives, mainly because of the poor performance of his original 4-4-2T classes. In fact he excelled in two important types, the Atlantics of Classes H1 and H2 (pages 66 and 67) and the two 4-6-2Ts that appeared in 1910 and 1912. The coupled wheels and cylinders were of the same key dimensions as those of the 4-4-2 express locomotives, but the boiler was slightly smaller, in terms of both diameter (5ft 3in) and length (6in shorter, at 15ft). Moreover, because of the six-coupled wheels the firebox was narrow and set in the traditional way between the frames, forcing use of a considerably smaller grate area. The large bunker held 3 tons of coal, and the water tanks of the first locomotive 2,300 gallons; the second locomotive's tanks were slightly smaller and held 1,989 gallons. It was reported that Marsh visited the drawing office many times during the progress of this design to pore over drawings and detail.

The first locomotive, Class J1 No 325, had the standard arrangement of Stephenson's valve gear between the frames. It was named *Abergavenny* after the Marquess of Abergavenny, a local landowner who had been a staunch supporter of the LBSCR. At the time of its introduction No 325 was notable as the first British express tank engine with the 4-6-2T wheel arrangement, as well as being the largest (if not the most powerful) locomotive the LBSCR had yet possessed. The second example, No 326 *Bessborough*, appeared in 1912 after Lawson Billinton had assumed the engineering chair. Besides its smaller side tanks this locomotive had outside Walschaerts valve gear, with rockers driving the valves (located between the frames), and was classified 'J2'. Both locomotives were superheated from new.

The LBSCR used its 4-6-2Ts on the heaviest Pullman trains, and they remained so employed until superseded by Maunsell 4-6-0s. In SR days they were painted green, entering the nationalised era in malachite. Displaced from the Brighton and Eastbourne lines by electrification in the 1930s, they spent their later years working from Tunbridge Wells depot on secondary-line passenger services and were withdrawn by BR for scrap in 1951.

Classes	J1 and J2 4-6-2T
Engineer	D. E. Marsh
Designed for	LBSCR
Built by	LBSCR Brighton
BR power rating	4P
Number in class	2
Introduced	1910
Cylinders (2 outside)	21in x 26in
Coupled wheels	6ft 7½in
Boiler pressure	170lb/sq in
Grate area	25.16sq ft
Tractive effort	20,800lb
Weight	89 tons 0cwt
SR numbers	B325, B326 / 2325, 2326
BR numbers	32325, 3232

Faced with a need for more powerful goods locomotives than the 'C2X' and 'C3' classes and to eliminate double-heading of London-area freights, L. B. Billinton drew up a design for a strong 2-6-0 with outside cylinders and inside Stephenson's valve gear driving the piston valves. It used standard 5ft 6in coupled wheels and 21in x 26in cylinders. The boiler was a new design and incorporated for the first time on the LBSCR a Belpaire-type firebox; this had the reasonable grate area of 24.8sq ft.

In 1914 the first five 'K'-class locomotives immediately proved useful in handling heavy munitions trains to Newhaven Harbour. The Government then authorised construction of five more, which emerged in 1916. The last seven locomotives could be built only after war restrictions had been lifted, emerging in 1920/1. At least one of the later build was reportedly intended to be a 2-6-2T, possibly called Class K2, but this did not materialise.

The 'Ks' were in many ways the LBSCR's most powerful locomotives and in the London area proved able to accelerate freights quickly to keep them ahead of suburban passenger workings. They also found employment on passenger trains, being free- and fast-running. Even in BR days it was not unusual to see a 'K' at the head of a holiday special to the coast, or on a train for seasonal workers. Indeed, BR regarded the 'Ks' as mixed-traffic locomotives, painting them in lined black, and also acknowledged their excellent performance by classifying them as 4P5F. However, electrification of the Kent main lines and 'dieselisation' of many freight services prompted their withdrawal *en bloc* at the end of 1962. None survives in preservation.

Class	K 2-6-0
Engineer	L. B. Billinton
Designed for	LBSCR
Rebuilt by	LBSCR Brighton
BR power rating	4P5F
Number in class	17
Introduced	1913
Cylinders (2 outside)	21in x 26in
Coupled wheels	5ft 6in
Boiler pressure	170lb/sq in
Grate area	24.8sq ft
Tractive effort	26,580lb
Weight	63 tons 15cwt
SR number series	B337-B353 / 2337-2353
BR number series	32337-32353

Below: *Regarded by many as the LBSCR's best locomotives, L. B. Billinton's Class K 2-6-0s were strong performers on both goods and passenger trains. No 32344 was photographed at Three Bridges depot on 26 July 1959.* Author

We read variously that the Class I2 boiler would not steam and also that it was used on other designs that did well! A case of the latter was L. B. Billinton's first design after taking the engineering chair at Brighton. The Class E2 0-6-0T was intended as a replacement for some of Stroudley's oldest 'E1' 0-6-0Ts. The design followed standard LBSCR principles, using existing components where possible. Wheels were the standard 4ft 6in, and cylinders, as on many other types, were 17½in x 26in. The 16ft wheelbase was marginally longer than that of the 'E1', and the 'E2' was also considerably heavier.

Five locomotives were built in 1913, followed from 1915 by five more to a slightly modified design. The second batch had side tanks extended forward, with a cut-out to allow crew easier access to the inside Stephenson's valve gear and motion. The extended tanks had a water capacity of 1,256 gallons compared with the originals, which carried 1,090 gallons.

As shunting tank engines the 'E2s' did the job for which they were designed and were not significantly modified during their long lives. In BR days, when the Southern Region needed larger shunting locomotives to handle inter-docks transfer freights at Southampton, three 'E2s' were allocated to Southampton Docks shed to support this work, the rest by now being at Stewarts Lane and Bricklayers Arms. All 10 were withdrawn by BR in the period 1961-3, the arrival at Southampton Docks in 1962 of 14 Ruston & Hornsby diesel shunters spelling the end for the last survivors. None is preserved.

Class	E2 0-6-0T
Engineer	L. B. Billinton
Designed for	LBSCR
Built by	LBSCR Brighton
BR power rating	3F
Number in class	10
Introduced	1913
Cylinders (2 inside)	17½in x 26in
Coupled wheels	4ft 6in
Boiler pressure	170lb/sq in
Grate area	17sq ft
Tractive effort	21,305lb
Weight	52 tons 15cwt / 53 tons 10cwt*
SR number series	B100-B109 / 2100-2109
BR number series	32100-32109

* Nos 32105-32109 had larger water tanks

Right: Looking rather forlorn on 15 April 1959 as it awaits entry to Eastleigh Works for overhaul, Class E2 0-6-0T No 32101 illustrates the style of the first five locomotives. Ahead of the tank is the Weir water-feed pump. Author

Below: No 32108 was one of the second batch of 'E2s', with extended side tanks, the forward part of the tanks being clear of the frames to allow access to the inside motion. This photograph was taken at Southampton Western Docks on 20 September 1958. Author

SOUTHERN RAILWAY

From its inception in 1923 to its absorption by BR in 1948, the Southern Railway was served by only two Chief Mechanical Engineers. R. E. L. Maunsell and O. V. S. Bulleid came from quite different backgrounds, but between them they provided the SR with several classes of effective locomotives. One can confidently state there were no duds among the SR-designed operating fleet.

Richard Maunsell came to the SR from the similar post on the SECR. While on the SECR he had managed the design and construction of some particularly modern locomotives starting with the Class N 2-6-0s and their larger-wheeled derivatives, the Class K 2-6-4 passenger tanks that were later named after rivers. He had also modernised two classes of old 4-4-0s into the 'D1' and 'E1' classes which were among the finest-performing 4-4-0s of their size anywhere in the country. The Sevenoaks derailment of a 'River' 2-6-4T at speed was said to have been caused by the high centre of gravity of the locomotive's side water tanks encouraging the locomotive to roll, while the inadequate track failed to restrain this near-resonant swaying. Responsibility for the accident was shared by Maunsell and the Chief Civil Engineer, G. Ellson, though admitted by neither. However, while Ellson set about the sizeable task of upgrading the track on SR main lines, Maunsell undertook the rebuilding of all the 'River' 2-6-4Ts as 2-6-0 tender engines.

To meet the need for greater power for express trains on the tightly gauged Hastings line Maunsell developed three-cylinder versions of both the 'N' and 'U' classes. The first of these had conjugated valve gear to drive the inside cylinder by a system of cross-levers driven from the inner ends of the outside cylinder valve rods. This explains the

high buffer-beam construction that provided the necessary forward space. Later, the 'N1' and 'U1' 2-6-0s received three sets of independent Walschaerts gear. When all the fuss about 2-6-4Ts had died down Maunsell introduced his 'W' class, intended for cross-London freights. To all intents and purposes these were a tank version of the 'N1' 2-6-0, and the SR always kept them off passenger workings. The other three-cylinder type that the SR introduced at this time were the eight beefy 0-8-0Ts of the 'Z' class, which went about their business of shunting marshalling yards quietly and efficiently.

Maunsell applied many of the techniques used in the successful Moguls and 4-4-0 rebuilds in developing his 'King Arthur' 4-6-0s. These had their genesis in the somewhat sluggish LSWR Urie 4-6-0s of Class N15 but had higher boiler pressure and large-diameter,

---

Below: *No 21C1* Channel Packet, *named after the Southern Railway's cross-Channel ferries, began life with a sharp, slightly pointed front to the roof of the overall casing. Note the smooth curve of the cab front and the way the tender sides curve over the coal bunker. This view also shows the casing enveloping all the space in front of the outside cylinders. The main cabside curve and that of the tender sides matched the curve of the sides of Bulleid coaching stock. To conform to the design weight, holes were cut in the frames; on locomotives from No 21C3 onwards front and cabside numbers and* 'SOUTHERN' *on the tender sides were applied as transfers in 'sunshine' lettering and figures.* Ian Allan Library

long-travel piston valves. The Maunsell two-cylinder 4-6-0s were strong and reliable performers. There were three classes of these: the 'N15s' were the express locomotives, with 6ft 7in coupled wheels; the 'H15s' were 6ft-wheeled mixed-traffic locomotives; the 'S15' 4-6-0s had 5ft 7in wheels and were intended for freight and parcels trains, though they were free-running enough to work passenger trains when required. Then came the 'Lord Nelson' four-cylinder 4-6-0s, designed to work 500-ton express trains at an average overall journey speed of 55mph. They proved that they could do this, but difficulty in firing the very long grate and thus in maintaining steam pressure plagued them until O. V. S. Bulleid modified them.

On the other hand the 'Schools' 4-4-0s, designed down to a weight and to a short length to fit 50ft turntables, immediately excelled, and no real improvement was detected when Bulleid modified some of them with multiple blastpipes. The 'Schools' 4-4-0s proved that they could match many of the fast running capabilities of the 'King Arthurs', even though their starting tractive effort was limited by their 42-ton adhesion weight. On medium-weight trains like the 'Bournemouth Limited' the 'Schools' were so economical that they could cover the 108 miles from Waterloo to Bournemouth non-stop with their relatively small tender tanks without replenishment. Remember that the SR, unlike the other 'Big Four' railways, had no water troughs for refilling tenders *en route*. The freight 0-6-0s of the 'Q' class were also good performers and very free-running for their type. Although Bulleid modified all the 'Qs' with multiple blastpipes, BR later replaced these with Standard Class 4 single blastpipes and chimneys, with no obvious detrimental effect.

Thus R. E. L. Maunsell provided the Southern with a fleet of generally excellent and straightforward steam locomotives. As already mentioned, there were no real 'duds' among them, though the 'Lord Nelsons' needed Bulleid's innovative touch to free them up.

Early in his tenure of the SR's CME position, which started in 1937, Bulleid rode the footplate of a 'Lord Nelson' from Victoria to Dover. He remarked that the locomotive performed well and ran quietly and smoothly, but he clearly believed that the class had greater potential. He modified all 16 'Nelsons' with five-jet blastpipes and wide chimneys, and 14 of the class also received new cylinders, outside steam pipes and extended smokeboxes. Their Achilles' heel remained the long grate. Bulleid also had Lemaître exhausts fitted to some of the Urie 'King Arthurs', which did help their steaming, but what they really needed was a better front end to help raise their upper running speeds.

O. V. S. Bulleid will always be best remembered for his Pacifics, the big 'Merchant Navy' locomotives and the only slightly smaller 'West Country' and 'Battle of Britain' class. The many novel features of these locomotives are described in the appropriate place in this Compendium. The drivers liked them because they were competent to haul any train to which they were attached, and their 'free running' at speed was legendary. The people responsible for maintaining them had distinctly less favourable views, despite Bulleid's intention that his innovations would make them need less maintenance!

Bulleid was certainly capable of producing a simple locomotive when specifically required, witness his 'Q1' freight 0-6-0. The 'Q1s' were Britain's most powerful 0-6-0s and were also very free-running locomotives, well able to haul passenger trains at up to 70mph when pressed. Their austere looks turned many opinions against them, which is a pity because they were most effective products of the wartime era.

It was not just steam traction that excited Bulleid's imagination. He was responsible for the mechanical parts design of the three Co-Co electric locomotives, for which Alfred Raworth specified the electrical equipment. Despite reports that the two men did not get on very well, the resulting locomotives were excellent and reliable machines that led busy lives on the Central Section of the Southern. 'OVB', as he was commonly known, was also at home designing diesels. The three 1Co-Co1s, Nos 10201-3, were pioneers built only just after the two LMS locomotives and worked mainly on the Western Section of the SR. They were joined by Nos 10000 and 10001, but later all five locomotives were transferred away, ending their days on the London Midland Region.

However, it is the 'Leader'-class experiment that courts the most controversy. With a view to replacing the multitude of smaller tank engines used for secondary-line and trip workings, Bulleid wanted to prove that a steam locomotive could be built that used all its weight for adhesion and which could perform just like a diesel. The story of the trials and tribulations of this pinnacle of innovation in steam locomotive design is taken up on the appropriate page in this Compendium. Was it a 'dud'? Opinions will always differ!

The rebuilding of 90 of the Bulleid 4-6-2s in BR days is an appropriate subject for pages in this book, as a means of completing the SR locomotive story. The result was some of the finest express locomotives in this country, and they were the last steam locomotives to work crack express trains on British Railways.

Above: *On Saturday 26 June 1954 Class N15 'Eastleigh Arthur' 4-6-0 No 30457* Sir Bedivere *calls at Bournemouth Central with an express for Waterloo. Externally it looks very similar to a 'Urie Arthur', except, perhaps, for its slightly smaller cylinders. The ex-LSWR Drummond tender came from a Class G14 4-6-0.* Author

Below: *From June 1955 No 30457 ran with the 5,200gal bogie tender from withdrawn Urie 'H15' 4-6-0 No 30490. Looking decidedly more handsome, it is seen stabled at Nine Elms depot on 24 October 1959.* Author

Above: *Withdrawal of Urie and Maunsell 'H15' and 'S15' 4-6-0s rendered surplus their Urie-type 5,000gal and 5,200gal bogie tenders, and from about 1957 some of these were transferred to the 'Eastleigh Arthurs', considerably improving the locomotives' appearance. One such locomotive was No 30454* Queen Guinevere, *seen attached to a 5,000gal tender at Salisbury in October 1957.* I. Davidson / Colour-Rail BRS1268

Though proved to be successful, the Urie design of Class N15 4-6-0s (page 29) was regarded by Maunsell as capable of further improvement. In 1925, having agreed with the SR Board to build 10 new locomotives rather than rebuild the Drummond 'G14' 4-6-0s, Maunsell saw his first 'N15' 4-6-0 emerge from Eastleigh Locomotive Works, basically a new locomotive incorporating just the tender and bogie of a 'G14'. The 'Eastleigh Arthurs', as these 10 locomotives soon became known, had smaller cylinders and higher boiler pressure than the Urie 'N15s' and incorporated a new steam passage layout devised by the Ashford drawing office. They were built with arched-roofed cabs of the true LSWR type and took the running numbers of the 'G14' 4-6-0s they were replacing, the first five being Nos 453-7 and the second five Nos 448-52. The ex-'G14' tenders were of the Drummond eight-wheeled type with inside axle bearings, commonly known as 'watercarts'; their antiquated appearance did little to impress the public with these otherwise quite modern locomotives.

In performance these locomotives were excellent and were put to work on the heavy expresses that had to tackle the steep gradients of the South Western main line west of Salisbury, on which route they were to remain for most of their working lives. They demonstrated the type's ability to run freely at reasonable speeds up to the 70s and to steam well enough to support strong pulling up long gradients.

Subsequent modifications were few. They shared with other Southern locomotives the removal by Bulleid of their snifting valves, originally intended as a means of preventing a vacuum forming in the cylinders when a locomotive is coasting. An instruction to drivers to coast with the regulator slightly open was said to obviate the need for these valves, which on the 'N15s' were located behind the chimney on the smokebox, feeding the ends of the superheater header.

In the years immediately following the Grouping the need for more express locomotives was becoming urgent, and before his first 10 'N15s' had entered service Maunsell ordered a further 30 from the North British Locomotive Co in Glasgow. The initial batch of 20 was ordered in December 1924, and the first locomotive delivered in May 1925 — probably a record short production time. Their Scottish

Class	N15 4-6-0
Engineer	R. E. L. Maunsell
Designed for	SR
Built by	SR Eastleigh / NBL Glasgow (E763-E792)
BR power rating	5P
Number in class	54
Introduced	1925
Cylinders (2 outside)	20½in x 28in
Coupled wheels	6ft 7in
Boiler pressure	200lb/sq in
Grate area	30sq ft
Tractive effort	25,320lb
Weight	79 tons 18cwt* / 80 tons 19cwt** / 81 tons 17cwt***
SR number series	E448-E457, E763-E806 / 448-457, 763-806
BR number series	30448-30457, 30763-30806

* Nos 30453-30457
** Nos 30448-30452, 30763-30792
*** Nos 30793-30806 (these originally had six-wheeled tenders)

construction earned them the grammatically incorrect nickname 'Scotch Arthurs'. Later locomotives were built at Eastleigh, bringing to 54 the total of Maunsell 'N15s'.

The later 'Arthurs' were dimensionally almost identical to the earlier build, the principal difference being that they had the more modern Ashford design of cab with continuous curve over the roof and which fitted within the SR composite loading-gauge. The last 14 locomotives also had six-wheeled tenders of a standard Ashford type in order to fit the smaller turntables at Central Section depots.

Both groups of Maunsell 'N15s' were good and reliable performers. They were used regularly on Bournemouth–London semi-fast trains loaded to about 12 carriages and also appeared on the South Western main line, at least as far as Exeter. Their duties on the Eastern Section took them to Ramsgate, while on the Brighton main line before the 1933 electrification the 'N15s' kept time with the fastest (51min) non-stop schedule then in force.

Bulleid could not resist the temptation to meddle and in 1940 fitted No 792 Sir Hervis de Revel with a Lemaître five-jet blastpipe and wide chimney, which it retained until 1952, thereafter reverting to the standard Maunsell single blastpipe and chimney. In the mid-1950s No 30784 Sir Nerovens sported an ugly fabricated chimney with an internal spark-arrestor, which aberration thankfully proved short-lived.

Withdrawals began in the mid-1950s and the class as a whole finished work in November 1962. No 30777 Sir Lamiel was chosen to be the National Collection's 'N15' for no other reason than that it was the locomotive which for many years held the record for the shortest journey time from Salisbury to Waterloo. It has since performed very well indeed on main-line steam workings in its preserved state.

Above: The 'King Arthur' locomotives were the first in Great Britain to be fitted with deflector plates to help lift exhaust smoke and steam clear of the driving cab at speed. No 30781 Sir Persant, fresh from a general overhaul at Eastleigh on 14 December 1957, looks very smart indeed in BR lined dark green. Note the rounded cab roof and the Urie-style bogie tender. Author

Right: The only 'Scotch Arthur' to be fitted with a Lemaître exhaust was No 792 Sir Hervis de Revel, seen thus equipped at Bournemouth Central during the summer of 1947. Author

Left: The spark-arrestor chimney fitted to No 30784 Sir Nerovens *was an ugly addition, as apparent from this view at Bournemouth Central on 28 August 1954. Author*

Below: No 30793 Sir Ontzlake *was one of 14 locomotives that were coupled to six-wheeled tenders for work in the Central Section of the SR. Because the design of the tender had higher side valances over the frames, the bottom of the cabside was truncated to finish higher above rail level that on the other 'N15s'. No 30793 still had this tender when photographed at Eastleigh depot on 23 June 1959. Author*

Bottom: By 21 July 1959 classmate No 30806 Sir Galleron *had received a bogie tender from one of the withdrawn 4-6-0s. This view at Eastleigh depot shows clearly the mismatch between the valance at the base of the cabside and that on the tender. Author*

Lawson Billinton followed the Marsh 'J1' and 'J2' 4-6-2Ts (page 71) with larger 4-6-4Ts of his own design, Class L. These were effectively enlargements of the 'J2' design, with outside Walschaerts valve gear, larger coupled wheels of 6ft 9in diameter and cylinders with the longer piston stroke of 28in, fed by piston valves. They performed well on the heaviest Brighton-line expresses.

When the Southern Railway electrified the London–Brighton main line in 1933 the seven large 4-6-4Ts became surplus. Some were transferred for a year or so to work expresses to Eastbourne, but electrification of that line in 1935 rendered them surplus, as they were too heavy for the secondary routes of the Central Section. In 1933 Maunsell had decided to rebuild them as 4-6-0s, which was done between 1934 and 1936. The locomotives were given Ashford-style cabs and vertical smoke-deflectors similar to those on the 'Schools' 4-4-0s. They received standard Urie 5,000gal bogie tenders. Transferred to Nine Elms depot, they started working on the Bournemouth and Salisbury main lines. No 2333 had been the LBSCR's memorial engine to the fallen of World War 1 and as such bore the name *Remembrance* and special plaques, which it retained as a 4-6-0. The other locomotives received the names of well-known locomotive engineers.

Had Maunsell followed the traditional reclassification method used by the LBSCR the rebuilds would have been Class LX. Instead, presumably to persuade Western Section operators that these locomotives were similar to 'King Arthurs', they were classified 'N15X', as if they were rebuilt 'N15s'! They were, however, inferior to the 'Arthurs' in terms of performance (BR's calculations giving them a power rating of 4P rather than the 5P of the 'N15s') and spent most

Class	N15X 4-6-0
Engineer	R. E. L. Maunsell*
Designed for	SR*
Built by	SR Eastleigh*
BR power rating	4P
Number in class	7
Introduced	1934*
Cylinders (2 outside)	21in x 28in
Coupled wheels	6ft 9in
Boiler pressure	180lb/sq in
Tractive effort	23,300lb
Weight	73 tons 12cwt
Grate area	26.7sq ft
SR number series	2327-2333
BR number series	32327-32333

* Rebuilt by Maunsell from L. Billinton 4-6-4Ts built LBSCR Brighton 1914-22

of their lives in rebuilt form on semi-fast and stopping trains and summer weekend extras. During the war they worked on the GWR as freight locomotives, and in later years they were transferred to Basingstoke depot, where they remained until displaced by BR Standard Class 4 4-6-0s, being withdrawn in the period 1955-7. None was preserved.

Right: Where they came from: Class L 4-6-4T No B333 Remembrance *shows off its handsome lines as drawn by L. B. Billinton.* Ian Allan Library

Below: Rebuilt by Maunsell, Class N15X 4-6-0 No 32329 Stephenson *stands at Eastleigh on 6 August 1950. Note the Maunsell cab, Urie tender and standard SR smoke-deflectors.* Walter Gilbert

CLASS LN 'LORD NELSON'

Above: *One of the two 'Lord Nelson' 4-6-0s that did not receive Bulleid's redesigned cylinders was No 30851* Sir Francis Drake, *seen at Southampton Central in 1956. The front end is distinguishable from modified locomotives by the small cover in front of the smokebox between the frames. The whole class had received Lemaître exhausts and large-diameter chimneys by the time they were absorbed into British Railways, and the SR had modified all the tenders with high sides and self-trimming coal bunkers before World War 2.* Author

The SR's traffic department having decided that it needed to run heavier trains, Richard Maunsell, the railway's first Chief Mechanical Engineer, was charged with producing a locomotive that could haul express trains of 500 tons at an average speed of 55mph. Maunsell decided to go for a four-cylinder design with the cylinders set outside and between the frames in line, not divided as on GWR 4-6-0s. He also, unusually, arranged the crank axle so that the cranks were at 135°. This gave eight exhaust beats per revolution of the coupled wheels and a very even torque applied to the rails on starting. The boiler was the largest yet used on the Southern Railway and had an impressively large Belpaire firebox with a fire grate that was 10ft 6in long. The grate was in two sections, the rear section being flat while the leading section was quite steeply inclined towards the front. Several firemen found this a difficult grate to manage with its potential for coal to build up at the back of the front section; when the heap of burning coal was then pushed forward it was possible to create a hole in the fire that could cause steam production to plummet. However, with an experienced fireman the boiler steamed well and the locomotives were reasonably competent.

Maunsell tried a number of experiments on these locomotives, most of which are described in the accompanying photograph captions. Not illustrated is No 857 which for a while had a unique round-topped boiler with an extended combustion chamber. The combustion chamber boiler was replaced by a standard 'LN' boiler at about the time of nationalisation. Also, Nos 862 (from 1934) and 865 (from 1938) ran with double Kylchap exhausts and chimneys until both were removed in 1939. No 862's chimney had a small capuchon.

Bulleid, on taking over from Maunsell in 1937, realised that the 'Lord Nelsons' were mechanically very sound. They kept their Walschaerts valve-gear settings very well between major overhauls, and they were acknowledged as running 'like sewing machines' except for a rather lively ride. Bulleid tackled their performance limitations from two angles. He had 14 of the class rebuilt with cylinders with 10in-diameter piston valves instead of the previous 8in, and with redesigned steam passages; these locomotives had smokeboxes extended forwards a few inches. He also significantly increased the draughting of all the locomotives by fitting a five-jet Lemaître blastpipe and wide, fabricated chimney. Only Nos 851 and 863 did not receive the new cylinders and extended smokebox.

The 'Nelsons' became surplus to requirements as electrification of the Kent lines displaced Bulleid Pacifics, BR Standard Class 5s and diesel locomotives to the South Western Division, and the last was withdrawn late in 1962. No 850 is preserved as part of the National Collection. It is in malachite green with yellow-and-black lining, but strangely the livery layout and lettering is appropriate for the prewar Maunsell era.

Above: *No 30855* Robert Blake *illustrates the condition of most of the 'Lord Nelson' class after fitting with new cylinders and extended smokebox. Its clean condition typical of Eastleigh depot, it is seen on 26 January 1959.* Author

Left: *Maunsell had No 859* Lord Hood *fitted with 6ft 3in-diameter coupled wheels to see if it performed any better on the gradients of the main line to Dover. Little difference was detected, but the locomotive remained non-standard for the rest of its life. It is seen at Bournemouth Central with an up semi-fast on 18 March 1956.* Author

Below: *The 'Lord Nelson' with a longer boiler barrel, No 30860* Lord Hawke *is seen at Bournemouth Central with an up express in 1955. The idea was to see if a greater heating surface was effective in improving steam production, but lengthening of the boiler barrel usually has the opposite effect, due to an increased resistance to gas flow, and No 30860 is said to have performed no better than the rest.* Author

Class	LN 4-6-0
Engineer	R. E. L. Maunsell
Designed for	SR
Built by	SR Eastleigh
BR power rating	7P
Number in class	16
Introduced	1926
Cylinders (4)	16½in x 26in
Coupled wheels	6ft 7in, 6ft 3in*
Boiler pressure	220lb/sq in
Grate area	33sq ft
Tractive effort	33,510lb, 35,300lb*
Weight	83 tons 10cwt, 84 tons 16cwt**
SR number series	E850-E865 / 850-865
BR number series	30850-30865

*   No 30859
** No 30860

Right: *A late attempt to improve draughting was made in 1960, when No 30852* Sir Walter Raleigh *received a cast-iron chimney and petticoat of the type used on rebuilt Bulleid Pacifics. The chimney may have been more elegant, but no further 'Nelsons' were so modified.* Author

CLASS L1

After the 1923 amalgamations there was a need for more express locomotives for the former South Eastern lines. Maunsell had already tinkered with the SECR Class L 4-4-0s, and by 1925 the urgency was such that the only practicable solution was to improve the existing design. Boiler pressure was raised from 160 to 180lb/sq in and an improved superheater was added. To compensate, the 'L1' inside cylinders were smaller than the 'L', with longer-travel valves and increased lap. The normal Maunsell cab and tender were added as well as a wider chimney.

Capacity for their construction was also a problem. The order was placed on the North British Locomotive Co of Glasgow, which responded by delivering all 15 locomotives in 1926. In traffic the changes made to the Class L design proved worthwhile. The 'L1s' were not dimensionally bigger than the 'L' class, yet their performance was more effective: they could haul the heavier expresses as required and met the immediate need. Later they would be totally eclipsed by the 'Schools' 4-4-0s, but that is another chapter in the SR's history.

The prestige duty for an 'L1' in BR days was piloting a Bulleid Pacific on the very heavy 'Night Ferry' train between Victoria and Dover. The 4-4-0 on duty was cleaned and equipped with a circular headboard of dark blue with a crescent moon symbol and the 'Night Ferry' motif. The consist included Wagon Lits sleeping and dining cars for Paris and Brussels.

Under BR the 'L1s' spent most of their time on South Eastern Division services, moving across to some Central Division routes as electrification began. For a short time a few ventured on Western Division metals, replacing 'T9' 4-4-0s on local trains, but their end came when the last was withdrawn in 1962. None is preserved.

Class	L1 4-4-0
Engineer	R. E. L. Maunsell
Designed for	SR
Built by	NBL Glasgow
BR power rating	3P
Number in class	15
Introduced	1926
Cylinders (2 inside)	19½in x 26in
Coupled wheels	6ft 8in
Boiler pressure	180lb/sq in
Grate area	22.5sq ft
Tractive effort	18,910lb
Weight	57 tons 16cwt
SR number series	1753-1759, 1782-1789
BR number series	31753-31759, 31782-31789

Below: *The Class L1 4-4-0 was a smart-looking locomotive, as apparent from this view of No 31786 at Robertsbridge in June 1961. It displays a marked similarity to an LMS 4-4-0 — hardly surprising, given that the Ashford draughtsmen responsible for its design included recruits from Derby.* S. M. Watkins / Colour-Rail BRS1239

Following on from Urie's successful design of goods 4-6-0 for the LSWR (page 30), Maunsell ordered 15 more for the SR. However, there were detail differences from the LSWR locomotives: the boiler pressure was raised to 200lb/sq in and the cylinders lined up to a 20½in diameter, as on the Maunsell 'N15s', while the boilers were pitched higher, at the same 9ft above rail level as the 'N15s', and the Urie cab was replaced by the standard Ashford curved-top design. Most of the class received flat-sided Maunsell bogie tenders with raised side raves, but from 1936 five locomotives, Nos 833-7, were coupled to flat-sided, six-wheeled tenders so that they could work on Central Section lines. Another 10 'S15s' were ordered and delivered from 1936, bringing the class total (including the 20 Urie locomotives) to 45.

The Maunsell 'S15s' were employed mainly on goods work and were particularly at home on the heavy freights carrying imported goods from Southampton Docks to Nine Elms or Feltham yards in London, for onward distribution. Their 5ft 7in-diameter coupled wheels limited their top speed to the mid-60s, but this was adequate for their use on stopping passenger trains and parcels trains as well as on summer-weekend holiday specials.

As with the 'King Arthur' 4-6-0s, in the mid- to late 1950s some tender swapping took place. A few 'S15s' received Urie bogie tenders to replace their Maunsell examples, making them even more like their 'N15' siblings, while the six-wheeled tenders on Nos 30833 and 30837 were replaced in 1962 by tenders from 'Schools' 4-4-0s.

One or two of the 'S15s' outlived all other Maunsell locomotives by quite a margin, the last one being withdrawn officially in 1965, though stored for an enthusiast special train which it worked in 1966! There are five preserved examples of Maunsell 'S15s', though one is used as a source of spares; the other four can be found on the Mid-Hants, Bluebell and North Yorkshire Moors railways.

Class	S15 4-6-0
Engineer	R. E. L. Maunsell
Designed for	SR
Built by	SR Eastleigh
BR power rating	6F
Number in class	25
Introduced	1927
Cylinders (2 outside)	20½in x 28in
Coupled wheels	5ft 7in
Boiler pressure	200lb/sq in
Grate area	28sq ft
Tractive effort	29,855lb
Weight	80 tons 14cwt*/ 79 tons 5cwt**
SR number series	E823-E847 / 823-847
BR number series	30823-30847

* Nos 30823-30837
** Nos 30838-30847
Note: Nos 30833-30837 had six-wheeled tenders

Above: *As Maunsell designed it but by now in BR black livery, 'S15' 4-6-0 No 30839 leaves Eastleigh with a stopping passenger train on 21 June 1955. Note the handsome bogie tender.* Author

Above: *During the 1950s some locomotives lost their Maunsell tenders due to worn tanks, gaining replacements from other locomotives. Seen at Eastleigh depot on 27 April 1959, No 30829 has a Urie tender, probably from an 'H15' 4-6-0.* Author

Above right: *No 30833, seen at Eastleigh depot on 13 March 1959, was one of five Maunsell 'S15s' coupled to six-wheeled tenders for working on the Central Section.* Author

Right: *In 1962 Class S15 4-6-0s Nos 30833 and 30837 (at least) received 'Schools' tenders with sloping top raves. This is No 30837.* Ken Cole

CLASS I1X

The origin of this class was Marsh's first 4-4-2T design, which the LBSCR classified 'I1'. This was intended for outer-suburban work and had 5ft 6in coupled wheels for brisk acceleration. The boiler was of similar dimensions to that used on the Class D3 0-4-4Ts and had a grate area of 17.35sq ft; it is thus not too surprising that the 'I1s' were limited in their ability to generate enough steam for the heavier trains of the day, and they quickly became unpopular with their crews.

The first batch had a coupled wheelbase of 8ft 9in. The second batch, somewhat confusingly numbered by the LBSCR as 1-10, utilised the coupled wheels, coupling rods and valve-gear components from earlier Class D1 and D2 0-4-2 mixed-traffic locomotives and thus had a shorter coupled wheelbase of 7ft 7in.

Despite their limitations the 'I1s' soldiered on until Maunsell, as Chief Mechanical Engineer of the Southern Railway, took the class in hand and re-boilered them. The chosen boiler was the type that was becoming available due to the re-boilering of the old Class B4 4-4-0s, express locomotives that had performed well and were to be upgraded as 'B4Xs' (see page 63). Adequate for express passenger work, the boilers from the 'B4s' were more than adequate for suburban work. Fitted with these boilers and with cylindrical smokeboxes on saddles the redesignated 'I1X' class, with their 23.75sq ft grates, were transformed into successful locomotives. All 20 'I1s' were rebuilt. They received modified cabs with curved tops to conform with the SR composite loading-gauge, and reduced-height boiler mountings to suit.

Below: *Wearing early SR livery, Class I1X 4-4-2T No B604 stands on a turntable in London, with LBSCR overhead electrification equipment visible in the background. Note that the smokebox door has no centre dart but is held by six bolted catches around the circumference. Maunsell's influence in the cab shape is also evident.* Hugh Ballantyne collection

After electrification of the main suburban routes the Brighton 4-4-2Ts were moved on to secondary passenger and branch-line work. All but two reached BR service, but withdrawals began then in earnest, and the last 'I1X' was taken out of traffic in the summer of 1951. Only one, No 32005, received its BR number.

Class	I1X 4-4-2T
Engineer	R. E. L. Maunsell*
Designed for	SR
Built by	SR Brighton
BR power rating	2P
Number in class	18 (plus 2 withdrawn before 1948)
Introduced	1925*
Cylinders (2 inside)	17½in x 26in
Coupled wheels	5ft 6in
Boiler pressure	180lb/sq in
Grate area	17.35sq ft
Tractive effort	18,460lb
Weight	71 tons 18cwt
SR number series	B1-B10, B595-B604 / 2001-2010, 2595-2604**
BR numbers***	32001-32010, 32595, 32596, 32598, 32599, 32601-32604

* Rebuilt by Maunsell from Marsh Class I1 locomotives introduced by the LBSCR in 1906
** Nos 2597 and 2600 withdrawn in 1946 and 1944 respectively
*** Only No 32005 received its allocated BR number

Above: *Class E1/R 0-6-2T No 32697 stands at Exeter Central in the summer of 1957, having banked a passenger train up the hill from St Davids. Originally 'E1' 0-6-0T No 105* Morlaix, *this locomotive was renumbered by the LBSCR as 697; following the Grouping it became SR No B697, then 2697 from c1931. Maunsell rebuilt this and nine other 'E1s' as 0-6-2Ts with extended rear frames carrying a larger bunker and water tank and supported by a radial truck. Note the Ashford-style cab and very plain bunker shape.* Author

In the mid-1920s the Southern Railway needed small but reasonably powerful tank engines for service in the West Country, in particular on the lightly laid Halwill–Torrington line and also for banking trains up the steep gradient between Exeter's two main stations. To fulfil this requirement Maunsell had 10 'E1s' rebuilt with bigger water tanks and longer frames and bunkers. At the rear of the elongated locomotive was a larger, round-topped cab of Maunsell 'Ashford' style and a very plain coal bunker. The rear of the lengthened frames was supported by the addition of a radial truck; this gave the impetus to classify these locomotives as 'E1/R' (or 'E1 radial'). No significant changes were made to the boilers or cylinders, the locomotives' principal dimensions remaining unchanged except for their overall length and weight.

In service, allocated to Exmouth Junction depot in Exeter, the 'E1/Rs' proved most effective as bankers for the 1-in-37 incline up from Exeter St Davids to Exeter Central; any full-length trains, such as the heavier freights or the 'Atlantic Coast Express', needed two of these sturdy locomotives at the rear as bankers. The 'E1/Rs' spent the whole of their lives from 1927 to their withdrawal by the end of 1959 working in the West Country, though their duties on branch passenger and goods services had by then already been taken over by BR-built Ivatt 2-6-2Ts.

Class	E1/R 0-6-2T
Engineer	R. E. L. Maunsell*
Designed for	SR
Rebuilt by	SR Brighton
BR power rating	1P2F
Number in class	10
Introduced	1927*
Cylinders (2 inside)	17in x 24in
Coupled wheels	4ft 6in
Boiler pressure	170lb/sq in
Grate area	16sq ft
Tractive effort	18,560lb
Weight	50 tons 5cwt
SR numbers	B94-B96, B124, B135, B608, B610, B695-B697 / 2094-2096, 2124, 2135, 2608, 2610, 2695-2697
BR numbers	32094-32096, 32124, 32135, 32608, 32610, 32695-32697

* Rebuilt from Stroudley Class E1 0-6-0Ts built LBSCR Brighton 1874-83

When it became uneconomic to submit the 'E1/Rs' for further overhauls at main works BR's Southern Region decided to replace them on the banking duties at Exeter with Class Z 0-8-0Ts, which settled easily into that rôle.

CLASS U

Back in 1917 R. E. L. Maunsell, as Chief Mechanical Engineer of the SECR, had introduced the Class K 2-6-4T for express passenger service. This was developed concurrently with his Class N mixed-traffic 2-6-0s and was very similar except for its 6ft coupled wheels (those on the 'Ns' being 5ft 6in) and for the coupled wheelbase, which on the 'K' was reduced to fit the form of a tank engine. Both were essentially very modern designs for the second decade of the 20th century, featuring outside cylinders and accessible Walschaerts outside valve gear, sharply tapered boilers and large Belpaire fireboxes.

The SECR had high hopes for the 2-6-4T, and the Southern Railway pursued this by ordering a further 20 examples, naming them (after rivers) and employing them on express trains on the former SER main line. However, it was on this type of duty that they exhibited a major problem — a tendency to sway and roll at speed, due largely, it was thought at the time, to their high water tanks and the likelihood that water was surging within them. Maunsell blamed the track and had one tested on the LNER main line out of King's Cross, on which it rode satisfactorily. However, in 1927 No A800 *River Cray* in charge of an express train derailed at speed near Sevenoaks, with serious loss of life. Mechanical and civil engineers blamed each other, and general management instructed both to make improvements; that demanded of Maunsell was that the 'K' class be rebuilt as tender engines. This was duly done, and thus was born the Class U 2-6-0. So successful were they that 30 more locomotives were built in subsequent years. All the names were, however, removed.

The Class U duties spread them over the whole Southern Railway system and all survived into BR days. They worked as far west as the SR's Cornish lines, and were common around Bournemouth as well as on the Hampshire and Sussex secondary routes. The last was withdrawn in 1966. There are four preserved examples, though none is to be found in the National Collection. Both the Bluebell Railway and Mid-Hants Railway have operated 'U-Boats' in service.

Above: *SR No A807 in original condition as Class K 2-6-4T* River Axe. *In common with the rest of its class it would be rebuilt as a direct result of the Sevenoaks disaster, in 1928 becoming a Class U Mogul.*
Ian Allan Library

Below: *Class U 2-6-0 No 31790 was the rebuild of the first 'River' 2-6-4T, No 790* River Avon. *The rebuilt locomotives are distinguishable from the later 'U' class by their lower valances and bigger splashers, different cab profile and the additional circular windows in the cab front. The buffer-beam ends are also different. Ex works at Ashford depot on 26 May 1959, No 31790 still retains its Maunsell chimney.* Author

Class	U 2-6-0
Engineer	R. E. L. Maunsell
Designed for	SR*
Built/rebuilt by	SR Ashford (A620-A639) / SR Eastleigh (A790-A796) / SR Brighton (remainder)
BR power rating	4P3F
Number in class	50
Introduced	1928*
Cylinders (2 outside)	19in x 28in
Coupled wheels	6ft 0in
Boiler pressure	200lb/sq in
Grate area	25sq ft
Tractive effort	23,865lb
Weight	63 tons 0cwt*, 62 tons 6cwt
SR number series	A790-A809, A610-A639 / 1790-1809, 1610-1639
BR number series	31790-31809*, 31610-31639**

* Nos A790-A809 converted from Class K 2-6-4Ts built SECR Ashford in 1917 (A790) or Armstrong Whitworth in 1925 (A791-A809)

Above: *No 31625, as seen at Eastleigh on 15 April 1959, was built new as a 2-6-0 and so had a higher running plate and smaller splashers. This was one of the locomotives modified by British Railways with new cylinders and a BR Standard Class 4 exhaust and chimney. Note also that the layout of the Walschaerts valve gear on all the Maunsell Moguls was unusual for a British design, the return crank driving the eccentric rod being set to lead the main crank by 90° rather than to trail it (when running forwards), with the result that the radius rod had to be raised for forward gear, whereas on more conventional Walschaerts layouts it is lowered.* Author

The last locomotive of the SR order for 20 2-6-4Ts was redesigned to be a three-cylinder locomotive with Holcroft derived gear for the inside-cylinder piston valve. The drive for this was taken forward from the outside valve gear on each side by a long rod. This passed to the side of the outside cylinder valve chest, which was set inwards at an angle to accommodate this. The long rods drove the conjugated levers in front of the cylinders and behind the specially heightened front buffer-beam. Later in the locomotive's life the derived gear was replaced by a full set of inside Walschaerts valve gear. However, on all the Ashford-inspired three-cylinder locomotives except the 'Schools' the features of the inward-inclined cylinders and high front buffer-beam were retained. Most also had a raised section of running plate over the cylinders. No A890 *River Frome* was delivered in 1925.

On a test run with the three-cylinder 2-6-4T, known then as Class K1, an observer stated that it ran more smoothly than the two-cylinder variety and pulled better; other opinions were that it was less stable than the two-cylinder locomotives at speed, and indeed it did derail on two occasions. Thus, just as with the 'K' class, the SR decided to convert the 'K1' into a tender engine, which was duly done at Ashford in 1928, No A890 becoming the first Class U1 2-6-0. Twenty other 'U1s' were built at Eastleigh Locomotive Works in 1931, these with detail differences from the prototype. Whereas the rebuilt locomotive had a raised section of the running plate over the outside cylinder on each side, the new build had high straight running plates with smaller splashers. They also had a different cab design, and they were given 3,500gal tenders with sloping top raves and a short raised section in the valances to line up with the cab bottom.

The 'U1s' worked initially in the West Country and on expresses on the Portsmouth Direct line but, having been displaced by 'Schools' 4-4-0s, spent the rest of their lives on the Central and Eastern Sections. Their haulage ability and turn of speed made them popular locomotives. The last were withdrawn in 1963 following the Kent electrification and 'dieselisation' of the Central lines. None is preserved.

Class	U1 2-6-0
Engineer	R. E. L. Maunsell
Designed for	SR
Built/rebuilt by	SR Ashford (A890) / SR Eastleigh (remainder)
BR power rating	4P3F
Number in class	21
Introduced	1928*, 1931
Cylinders (3)	16in x 28in
Coupled wheels	6ft 0in
Boiler pressure	200lb/sq in
Grate area	25sq ft
Tractive effort	25,385lb
Weight	65 tons 6cwt
SR number series	A890-A900 / 1890-1910
BR number series	31890-31910

* No A890, built SR Ashford as Class K1 2-6-4T in 1925

Below: *Class U1 2-6-0 No 31907 rolls into Stewarts Lane depot on 31 May 1958. Note the straight running plate, the turned-in top to the 4,000gal tender side and the slight kink in the tender valance, to line up with that under the cab.* Author

Above: *The prototype 'U1' 2-6-0, rebuilt from a 2-6-4T, was No 31890, seen at Bricklayers Arms depot on 4 April 1959. Note the sloping sides to the outside cylinders that made space for the rod drive to the former derived valve gear, and the high structure above the buffer-beam to accommodate the conjugated drive. This locomotive was distinguished by the raised section of running plate over the cylinders and its straight-sided 3,500gal tender, while the cabsides also differed from those of the production batch.* Author

CLASS V 'SCHOOLS'

Two special criteria governed the overall size and dimensions of the next express class to be produced during R. E. L. Maunsell's tenure as CME. The locomotives had to be narrow enough to pass through the tight loading-gauge of Mountfield Tunnel, on the Hastings main line; and each locomotive plus tender had to fit on the short turntables that were still in use around the Eastern Section of the SR, such as the one at Hastings. There was also a need to develop as much power as a 'King Arthur', a class that did not meet either of these demands. The resulting design bordered on genius!

Standard 6ft 7in coupled wheels were married to three cylinders so that the outside pair could fit within the Hastings gauge, being smaller than two cylinders would have had to be. To shrink the locomotive to the required length a 4-4-0 wheel arrangement was chosen, a 2-6-0 being deemed unsuitable for the speeds envisaged. A six-wheeled tender enabled the combined wheelbase to be no more than 48ft 7¼in. The use of three cylinders reduced hammerblow, and satisfied the Chief Civil Engineer that his track could withstand a locomotive with a 21-ton axle load running at speed. Even then, 42 tons' adhesion weight is not a lot for a locomotive expected to haul 10-coach expresses up steep inclines such as Sole Street Bank and the one out of Tonbridge on the Hastings line. The boiler was a shortened version of the free-steaming 'N15' type with a round firebox, chosen to give a better view forward from the narrow cab.

On the road the 'Schools' 4-4-0s performed outstandingly and very economically. When some were moved to the Bournemouth line in the late 1930s, their economic operation enabled non-stop working of trains from Waterloo to Bournemouth Central, 108 miles with no water, even with just a 4,000gal tender.

Class	V 4-4-0
Engineer	R. E. L. Maunsell
Designed for	SR
Built by	SR Eastleigh
BR power rating	5P
Number in class	40
Introduced	1930
Cylinders (3)	16½in x 26in
Coupled wheels	6ft 7in
Grate area	28.3sq ft
Boiler pressure	220lb/sq in
Tractive effort	25,135lb
Weight	67 tons 2cwt
SR number series	E900-E909 / 900-939
BR number series	30900-30939

Below: *'Schools' 4-4-0 No 30905* Tonbridge *calls at Bournemouth Central* on 18 August 1957 *with an up express. The locomotive has the lower cabside windows as fitted only to the first 10, while the tender, one of five transferred second-hand from 4-6-0s, had narrower footstep-backing plates than did the tenders of the other 35 Class V locomotives.* Author

Bulleid, always hopeful that he could improve any locomotive, modified 20 of the 'Schools' class with Lemaître five-jet blastpipes and wide chimneys. The 20 modified locomotives were said to have been slightly freer-running, but they invited being driven harder and made no measurable fuel economy, so the remaining 20 locomotives were left unchanged.

The 'Schools' class spent the 1930s and '40s mainly on the Eastern Section, where they generally remained until the Kent Coast electrification in 1959 and 1962 shifted them westwards to the Central and Western Divisions of BR's Southern Region. The last was withdrawn from service in 1962, 18 of them being condemned as surplus to requirements in December of that year.

Happily, on withdrawal three of the lowest-mileage Class V 4-4-0s were selected for preservation. These were No 30925 *Cheltenham*, for addition to the National Collection, and Nos 30926 *Repton* and 30928 *Stowe*, which were purchased privately. No 30926 went to Canada, where it stayed for 23 years before being repatriated to the UK, and now is on the North Yorkshire Moors Railway, where its surprising ability to haul eight carriages up a 1-in-52 gradient has earned it unique respect. No 30928 was displayed in the grounds of Lord Montague's estate at Beaulieu, in the New Forest, before moving to the Bluebell Railway, where it has seen active service. No 30925 was steamed in 1980 for the Rainhill Cavalcade celebrating 150 years of the Liverpool & Manchester Railway but ever since has remained as a handsome static exhibit in the Peter Allen building at the National Railway Museum, York.

Above: *Pictured at Eastleigh on 30 August 1955, No 30901* Winchester *was one of the 20 Class V locomotives given wide chimneys and Lemaître exhausts.* Author

Below: *For most of its career No 30932* Blundell's *ran with a high-sided self-trimming tender, but this was mistakenly repainted green in Ashford Works in 1958 and had to be coupled to a green locomotive. No 30905* Tonbridge *was chosen, being seen at Bournemouth on 19 July 1959 at the head of an up express.* Author

Class V 4-4-0s with Lemaître chimneys

30900	30915	30921	30933
30901	30917	30924	30934
30907	30918	30929	30937
30909	30919	30930	30938
30914	30920	30931	30939

Above: *Near the end of their lives, after transfer to Nine Elms depot, two 'V'-class 4-4-0s received bogie tenders from withdrawn 'Lord Nelson' locomotives. No 30912* Downside *had the tender from No 30865, and No 30921* Shrewsbury — *posing at Nine Elms on 6 October 1962, shortly before withdrawal — that from No 30854. The picture also shows the higher cabside windows fitted to the final 30 'Schools' locomotives.* Author

Right: *Following withdrawal No 926* Repton *was exported to North America and ended up on a preserved railway in the Lackawanna region of New York State, where it was subjected to various alterations to suit local operating conditions; most notably its tender was rebuilt with higher sides, as seen in this 1986 photograph. Repatriated to the UK, the locomotive now runs on the North Yorkshire Moors Railway as No 30926 but retains its high-sided tender.* George A. Forero Jr

For a fleet of additional shunting locomotives Maunsell decided not to repeat or develop the successful but heavy Urie 4-8-0Ts of Class G16 (see page 31) but to produce a new design. He chose the 0-8-0T arrangement with all the locomotive weight for adhesion and braking. The design used the same three-cylinder layout as on the 'N1', 'U1' and 'W' classes, with two sets of outside Walschaerts gear. The inside cylinder used Marshall's gear. The inside cylinder was inclined at 8° and drove on the second coupled axle; the outside cylinders drove through long connecting rods to the third wheel pair.

An existing type of boiler was selected, being one of the former LBSCR types of sufficient capacity but not superheated, similar to that used on the Class E6X 0-6-2T. The idea was that a superheated locomotive in shunting conditions would be more difficult to control with regards to wheel slip, having to allow for the superheated steam to expand before slipping could cease, and a higher-pressure boiler with occasional blowing off would also cause disturbance to residents of houses near the marshalling yards. The saturated boiler would in effect act as a steam reservoir for the short bursts of activity that shunting required. These decisions were proved to be correct, as the Class Z 0-8-0Ts performed their duties quietly and effectively. The steeply angled tank tops were to enable the crew to see the shunter's hand signals.

Only eight locomotives were built, an order for a further 10 being cancelled in 1931.

The 'Zs' were used at major yards around the railway, being allocated to places such as Ashford, Hither Green, Eastleigh and Salisbury, until displaced by diesel shunting locomotives. Then in 1961 five of them were transferred to Exmouth Junction depot to replace the Class E1/R 0-6-2Ts (page 85) on banking duties up the

Above: *The Class Z 0-8-0Ts were chunky yet handsome locomotives, as apparent from this view of No 30955 fresh from overhaul at Eastleigh on 10 September 1959.* Author

steep grade from Exeter St Davids to Central. One of the 'Zs' shuttled passenger trains between Templecombe station and the S&DJR main line. All were withdrawn in 1962, Class Ws being used at Exeter for a short time until dieselisation eliminated the need for banking there. No 'Z' is preserved.

Class	Z 0-8-0T
Engineer	R. E. L. Maunsell
Designed for	SR
Built by	SR Brighton
BR power rating	6F
Number in class	8
Introduced	1929
Cylinders (3)	16in x 28in
Coupled wheels	4ft 8in
Boiler pressure	180lb/sq in
Grate area	18.6sq ft
Tractive effort	29,380lb
Weight	71 tons 12cwt
SR number series	950-957
BR number series	30950-30957

Emerging from Eastleigh Locomotive Works in 1932 and Ashford in 1935 came two batches of five and 10 2-6-4Ts respectively, intended for cross-London freight workings. These were basically tank versions of the former SECR Class N1 2-6-0 (see page 50) and were identical to them in main details except that their cylinders were bored out to 16½in diameter. They had a high brake force applied to their coupled wheels and their rear bogies also had the wheels braked, unusual on the British tank engine. This was to enable them to control the many non-brake-fitted goods trains that were entrusted to them.

The 'W' class used redundant parts such as the side tanks and bogies that had been discarded when the 'River'-class locomotives were rebuilt into tender engines, and so were a good economic proposition for the SR. However, their bogie and pony truck suspension design was updated. There were detail differences between the Ashford and Eastleigh batches. The Eastleigh locomotives were built with a right-hand driving position and had gravity sanding, whereas the Ashford locomotives were left-hand-drive with steam sanding. Steam sanding was fitted to the others from 1959. Otherwise they remained more or less as built right through to their last days.

The locomotives spent most of their lives in the London area competently handling inter-Regional freight trains on London's tortuous and mysterious connecting routes. When displaced from these duties by the advent of the Type 3 Bo-Bo diesel-electrics they were redeployed for a time on Fawley–Southampton oil trains and also to Exeter for banking passenger trains up the steep incline from St Davids station to Exeter Central. They were withdrawn in 1963 and 1964.

Above: The Class W 2-6-4Ts were powerful and handsome locomotives. No 31918 manœuvres at Bricklayers Arms depot on 28 October 1961. Author

Class	W 2-6-4T
Engineer	R. E. L. Maunsell
Designed for	SR
Built by	SR Eastleigh (1911-1915) / SR Ashford (1916-1925)
BR power rating	6F
Number in class	15
Introduced	1932
Cylinders (3)	16½in x 28in
Coupled wheels	5ft 6in
Boiler pressure	200lb/sq in
Grate area	25sq ft
Tractive effort	29,450lb
Weight	90 tons 14cwt
SR number series	1911-1925
BR number series	31911-31925

CLASS Q

As the use of Maunsell's mixed-traffic 2-6-0s spread across the railway, the SR still had a large fleet of ancient goods locomotives of the 0-6-0 wheel arrangement. To begin the replacement of some of these Maunsell supervised the design of a small fleet of 20 new 0-6-0 goods locomotives. They actually emerged from Eastleigh Locomotive Works in 1938 and 1939, after Maunsell had retired.

The inside-cylinder arrangement was the one that had proved so successful in the 'D1' and 'E1' 4-4-0 rebuilds, with outside-admission piston valves that enabled the exhaust to escape unhindered to the blastpipe. The locomotives had Stephenson's valve gear which is recognised as being fine for heavy slogging work such as freight locomotives endured. The boiler was a new design, based largely on that of the Class L1 4-4-0, though slightly smaller in most dimensions. A standard Ashford-type cab complemented the usual 3,500gal flat-sided six-wheeled tender, though several locomotives had 4,000gal tenders with little difference in overall appearance. Maunsell's 'Q' had a steam reverser for ease of use when shunting. The locomotive looked a bit like a modern LMS '4F', and BR gave it the power rating '4F', but there the similarity with a Midland '4F' ends.

O. V. S. Bulleid was a bit scathing about such an orthodox and medium-sized machine being built. As usual, he tried to improve it with the Lemaître exhaust arrangement, and all 20 locomotives were so modified, to the detriment of their appearance. He did of course later develop the design into his own 'Q1' (page 93).

In terms of performance the 'Qs' were excellent locomotives. They were lively, good steamers and, when called upon, could pull passenger trains at speeds which made their 5ft 1in driving wheels spin quite fast, 60mph being common. BR thought the five-jet blastpipe and wide chimney unnecessary for such a modest locomotive and duly fitted the 'Qs' with BR Standard Class 4 single blastpipes and cast chimneys, which improved their appearance. The class was withdrawn between 1962 and 1965. No 30541 is preserved on the Bluebell Railway.

Class	Q 0-6-0
Engineer	R. E. L. Maunsell
Designed for	SR
Built by	SR Eastleigh
BR power rating	4F
Number in class	20
Introduced	1938
Cylinders (2 inside)	19in x 26in
Coupled wheels	5ft 1in
Boiler pressure	200lb/sq in
Grate area	21.9sq ft
Tractive effort	26,160lb
Weight	49 tons 10cwt
SR number series	530-549
BR number series	30530-30549

Above: *By the time they were absorbed into British Railways stock the Maunsell Class Q 0-6-0s had been modified by Bulleid with Lemaître exhausts and wide chimneys. No 30531 is seen at Eastleigh shed on 23 March 1959.* Author

Right: *Before embarking on wholesale replacement of the exhaust systems of the 'Q' class BR experimented with a single blastpipe and stovepipe chimney on No 30549, seen at Bournemouth Central on 28 August 1958. Note the steam-reverser cylinders above the middle splasher on the driver's side.* Author

Right: *No 30545 was one of the 'Qs' modified with a BR Class 4 single chimney and looked fine so fitted. It was photographed at Eastleigh depot on 13 December 1958.* Author

An urgent need for additional freight locomotives was created by World War 2, and the SR's new CME, O. V. S. Bulleid, rose to the occasion by designing a simple 0-6-0 that was essentially an enlargement of Maunsell's successful 'Q' class. The aim was to provide a more powerful locomotive within quite severe weight restrictions. The 'Lord Nelson' design boiler was chosen as the basis, but in considerably shortened form; this is often a good thing because shorter boiler barrels provide less resistance to the passage of flue gases, and, usually, a freer-steaming boiler results. This was indeed the case with the 'Q1s'.

Weight-saving went almost to extremes with this design. The obvious missing parts were the lack of running side plates and valances. The boiler lagging followed similar lines to the Pacifics, but was adapted to the shape of the narrow firebox. B-F-B wheels, as with all Bulleid's locomotives, helped to keep the weight down. The locomotive was thoroughly conventional in that it had two inside cylinders driving the centre coupled axle, and two sets of inside valve gear. However, use of outside admission cylinders gave them particularly direct exhaust passages, and the Stephenson's valve gear was better suited to the hard slogging that a freight locomotive had to do.

Because this was quite a powerful locomotive design, indeed the most powerful 0-6-0 in the country if not in Europe, the 'Q1s' had five-jet Lemaître exhausts and plain wide fabricated chimneys. Even the dome cover was fabricated out of plate rather than being a conventional iron casting. The locomotives having three axles, Bulleid numbered them from C1 to C40. That initial letter was the inspiration for their nickname, the 'Charlies'.

In traffic the 'Q1s' were well respected for their haulage capacity, but their modest weight was a disadvantage when stopping long unbraked trains, probably their only significant limitation. The 'Q1s' were very free-running locomotives and were quite at home hauling passenger trains when called upon. One of their summer duties was to

Class	Q1 0-6-0
Engineer	O. V. S. Bulleid
Designed for	SR
Built by	SR Brighton (20) / BR Ashford (20)
BR power rating	5F
Number in class	40
Introduced	1942
Cylinders (2 inside)	19in x 26in
Coupled wheels	5ft 1in
Boiler pressure	230lb/sq in
Grate area	27sq ft
Tractive effort	30,080lb
Weight	49 tons 10cwt
SR number series	C1-C40
BR number series	33001-33040

share with the local 'Q' class the job of taking 10-coach Lymington boat trains along the branch line from Brockenhurst. They also played a part in moving hop-pickers' specials to Kent.

The Southern Region's BRCW Type 3 Bo-Bo diesels, introduced in the early 1960s, eventually displaced all the Southern types of 0-6-0, the last 'Q1' being withdrawn in 1966. No 33001 (formerly C1) was set aside for preservation as part of the National Collection.

Below: *Shiny after general overhaul, Bulleid 'Q1' 0-6-0 No 33010 stands at Hither Green depot, in South London, on 16 August 1959. Author*

CLASS MN 'MERCHANT NAVY'

The year 1941 was an odd time to be producing new express passenger locomotives, when the traffic demand was for more freight locomotives. But SR CME Oliver Bulleid was persuasive and convinced the SR Board that these were to be mixed-traffic locomotives on account of their 6ft 2in coupled wheels. The design criteria were, however, aimed at their postwar use as high-speed machines. To satisfy the Chief Civil Engineer's requirement to reduce track forces as much as possible, Bulleid's first inclination to offer a 2-8-2 with a Krauss-Helmholtz front truck was rejected in favour of a conventional 4-6-2 format, albeit with unconventional details throughout. The three-cylinder layout enabled balancing of rotating parts to be eliminated, and only a small portion of the reciprocating weights was balanced. Because of this low balancing and because the three sets of Bulleid chain-driven valve gear located between the frames were of very light weight, these locomotives could run at speed with virtually no hammer-blow to the track. The oil for lubricating the inside big ends and the valve gear was contained in a large sump between the locomotive frames. The oil sump was not an oil bath in the sense that the inside big end and the valve gear were not immersed in oil, the oil being pumped to the oiling points.

The long casing over the smokebox and boiler was another weight-saving device that in this case also gave the locomotives their impressive 'air-smoothed' look. A number of the first 10 locomotives initially had casings made of lightweight composite material, but this was generally replaced by thin gauge steel plate. The wheel centres were the patented Bulleid-Firth-Brown (B-F-B) design, in effect corrugated plate wheels with weight-saving holes that gave them their somewhat American appearance.

An initial problem caused by the soft exhaust from the Lemaître chimney was of drifting steam and smoke blocking the driver's forward view. Smoke-deflectors of increasing size and different shapes were tried, and a cowl replaced the original sharp edge at the front of the casing above the smokebox. Meanwhile the front cab windows were moved back, so that they could be reached and cleaned by the driver and fireman, and the lower plating was removed from in front of the cylinders to improve access for servicing.

Class	MN 4-6-2
Engineer	O. V. S. Bulleid
Designed for	SR
Built by	SR and BR Eastleigh
BR power rating	8P
Number in class	30
Introduced	1941
Cylinders (3)	18in x 24in
Coupled wheels	6ft 2in
Boiler pressure	280lb/sq in*
Grate area	49.5sq ft
Tractive effort	37,500lb
Weight	94 tons 15cwt
SR number series	21C1-21C20
BR number series	35001-35030

*   Boiler pressure was reduced in the early 1950s to 250lb/sq in, giving a tractive effort of 33,480lb

Left: *No 21C1* Channel Packet, *at Exmouth Junction depot in June 1949, looks a little worn after its years of wartime service! It has its full-size smoke-deflectors and the cowl at the front of the casing top. Part of the casing in front of the outside cylinders has been removed.* W. H. G. Boot / Colour-Rail SR15

Left: *The first 10 locomotives were always distinguishable from the later batches of 'MNs' by dint of the narrower angle of the front of the main casing, the curved valances over the coupled wheels and the shape of the tenders. In this photograph taken c1952 at Eastleigh depot No 35002* Union Castle *shows the effect of removing the plating in front of the outside cylinders.* J. Davenport

Right: *Second-batch 'Merchant Navy' Pacific No 21C11* General Steam Navigation *heads the down 'Devon Belle' past Clapham Junction in July 1949. Although in near-original condition, it is seen here with deep plates enveloping the area in front of the cylinders and other detail differences as outlined in the text. Note signs of incomplete combustion in the black smoke emerging from the wide Lemaître chimney.*
H. N. James / Colour-Rail SR3

From 1945 the second batch of 10 'Merchant Navy' 4-6-2s began to emerge from Eastleigh Locomotive Works. These differed visually from the first 10 in a number of ways. Most noticeable was the wider appearance of the main casing at the front, which curved quite sharply to meet the ends of the buffer-beam. The side valances over the coupled wheels were angular and the cab front was vertical when viewed from the side. The tender side raves were not extended so far up as were those of the first-batch locomotives. The plating in front of the cylinders was progressively removed, No 21C11 being the only second-batch locomotive to have full-depth plates; Nos 21C12-20 did not have the curved plates encasing the cylinder fronts.

Cab fronts were modified in the same way as those of the first batch to improve the forward view. From the mid-1950s the tender side raves began to be cut down to improve the crews' rearward view, although few if any of the first-batch tenders were so modified before the locomotives were rebuilt more extensively (see page 96). The third batch, built at Eastleigh from 1949 (in BR's time), were identical to the second with the aforementioned modifications applied from new. The last five ran for some months with tenders intended for Light Pacifics until their own tenders were ready.

Performance of the 'Merchant Navy' class met all the requirements for train haulage and speeds. The locomotives were very popular with their crews; they steamed well, and they pulled well, running freely at high speeds. However, the locomotives proved to be heavy on coal and water, due mainly to their erratic valve events, proven when measured at the Rugby test plant and with dynamometer cars. They were also expensive in maintenance and in use of lubricating oil. Oil consumption was about 1 gallon per 100 miles running, much of it thrown out of the

Above left: *How the second- and third-batch 'Merchant Navy' locomotives looked in BR service. Pictured on 7 April 1956, No 35011* General Steam Navigation *has had its cab-front windows moved back and the plates in front of the outside cylinders removed for better servicing access. The narrow bars just below the top of the smoke-deflectors were to carry the side nameplates when hauling the 'Devon Belle' (see previous picture of No 21C11). The livery is BR Brunswick green lined in black and orange, the scheme that replaced the short-lived Prussian blue with black-and-white lining, introduced in 1949.* Author

Above: *Sporting the longer smoke-deflectors fitted in preparation for the 1948 Locomotive Exchanges, No 35020* Bibby Line *calls at Bournemouth Central in September 1954. The locomotive has a 6,000gal tender, cut down to improve the rear view from the cab.* Author

sump when the locomotives were running at speed. Getting oil splashed on to coupled wheel treads did nothing to help adhesion on starting!

The 'Merchant Navy' class worked mainly on the Western Section main lines from Waterloo to Exeter and Weymouth, though a small number was kept on the Eastern Section for many years to work the 'Golden Arrow' and other heavy trains.

Experimentally, No 35019 worked for a couple or so years with a single blastpipe and chimney but did not perform quite as well. Another 'MN' worked for a short time with a mechanical stoker, but this was not pursued.

CLASS MNX — REBUILT 'MERCHANT NAVY'

The perceived high cost of maintaining the Bulleid Pacifics led to the programme for their rebuilding. This was at the SR's Brighton drawing office under the design supervision of Ron Jarvis, a former LMS man who had led the Brighton team in designing three of the BR Standard locomotive classes.

To reduce coal and water consumption the Bulleid valve gear was replaced by three independent sets of conventional Walschaerts valve gear. To accommodate the off-centre-piston valve drive it was necessary to cast a new-design inside cylinder; this had inside steam admission. However, the retained outside cylinders had outside steam admission, ensuring the slightly off-beat exhaust sound of a rebuild. The oil sump between the frames was removed. The locomotives lost their Bulleid steam reversers in favour of standard screw reversers, to help drivers control steam cut-off more accurately. To strengthen the front frames, a large fabricated box stretcher was bolted between the frames in front of the inside cylinder; this stretcher also formed part of the smokebox saddle.

For more complete coal combustion each locomotive received a new, longer, cylindrical smokebox. The original, crudely fabricated petticoat and chimney were replaced by better-proportioned cast-iron ones.

The boiler was largely unchanged, except for repositioning the safety valves from their forward position on the boiler barrel to a more conventional place further back. The steam operation of the firehole door was removed. Boiler insulation was fibreglass matting retained by standard steel cladding. BR-style running plates and valances, set lower than on most BR locomotives, were complemented by smoke-deflectors similar to those on the 'Britannia' Pacifics. All tenders were cut down to improve rearward vision, and the cabs were standardised across the breed. After rebuilding there was no discernible difference between the locomotives of the three batches,

Class	MNX 4-6-2
Engineer	R. G. Jarvis
Designed for	BR
Rebuilt by	BR Eastleigh
BR power rating	8P
Number in class	30
Introduced	1956
Cylinders (3)	18in x 24in
Coupled wheels	6ft 2in
Boiler pressure	250lb/sq in
Grate area	49.5sq ft
Tractive effort	33,480lb
Weight	97 tons 18cwt
BR number series	35001-35030

except for the carrying capacities of the tenders, though tenders did move between locomotives of the different series.

Because the new valve gear kept the cut-offs stable, drivers claimed at first that the rebuilt locomotives did not run as freely at speed as previously. However, once they got used to opening the regulators wider to attain the same speed levels, the performance of these locomotives in traffic was sustained at an excellent level with useful and proven fuel economy. When all the class had been rebuilt the class designation reverted from 'MNX' to the original 'MN'.

All 'Merchant Navy' 4-6-2s were withdrawn in the years 1964-7. Eleven are now preserved or awaiting restoration.

Left: *Just after rebuilding, No 35013 Blue Funnel Certum Pete Finem stands at Southampton Central on a running-in turn from Eastleigh. Its appearance is common to all the rebuilt locomotives, with one minor exception: on the first locomotive to be rebuilt, No 35018, the twin pipes carrying steam for the blower and from the vacuum ejector that ran along the driver's side of the boiler barrel curved down with a bend just in front of the nameplate, whereas on No 35013 and the rest of the class the dog-leg curve was alongside the back of the smokebox, as seen here. No 35013 had an original 5,250gal tender. Note also the projection of the firebox cladding to embrace the steam-manifold valve, the handle for which is alongside the dome on the driver's side of the boiler.* Author

Left: *One of the 'Merchant Navy' tenders had a self-weighing coal bunker. In earlier years this was coupled to No 35014, but during rebuilding of that locomotive it was transferred to rebuilt No 35024* East Asiatic Company, *seen at Eastleigh depot late in 1959. This view shows clearly the two clack valves fixed to the right-hand side of the boiler barrel for supplying water from the two live steam injectors under the fireman's side of the cab.* Author

CLASS WC 'WEST COUNTRY' / BB 'BATTLE OF BRITAIN'

For mixed-traffic use on main lines and secondary routes the SR launched its Light Pacifics, initially known as the 'West Country' class. These were a smaller version of the 'Merchant Navy', with the same design features but with smaller fire grates, shorter boiler barrels, smaller-diameter cylinders and narrower cabs and tenders, this last feature so that they could work (if required) on the Hastings main line. So successful were these locomotives that they often deputised for 'Merchant Navy'-class locomotives on the heaviest trains such as the 'Bournemouth Belle'. Their wider route availability enabled them to run over all Eastern and Central Section main lines as well as Western Section main and secondary routes. Their field of operation extended as far west as Padstow in Cornwall and as far east as Ramsgate.

Their popularity and success gave the Southern Railway / Region the impetus to build a total of 110 examples. There being, in practice, no need for them to work between Tonbridge and Hastings, from No 34071 all locomotives were built with full-width cabs and wider tenders.

With several locomotives working on the South Eastern Section of the Southern Railway, management concluded that West Country names were somewhat inappropriate. Kent and Sussex having borne the brunt of the Battle of Britain during World War 2, locomotives numbered from 21C149 (later renumbered 34049) to 34090 and Nos 34109 and 34110 were named variously after the men, machines and airfields that participated, being classified 'Battle of Britain', though technically these locomotives were identical to their 'West Country' siblings.

Above: *In its original form, 'West Country' Pacific No 21C121 (later to be named* Dartmoor*) shows off its Southern malachite-green livery and 'sunshine' yellow stripes. The locomotive has its original short smoke-deflectors. One of the first 70 locomotives, it has a narrow cab on which the bottom sides blend with the lower part of the firebox casing. The early 'West Country' Pacifics were built with side plating shielding the outside cylinders, although this was later removed to allow better access for maintenance. The circular 'Southern' plate on the smokebox door records, in the bottom segment, the place and year of construction — Brighton Works, 1946.* Ian Allan Library

Class	WC and BB 4-6-2
Engineer	O. V. S. Bulleid
Designed for	SR
Built by	SR and BR Brighton*
BR power rating	7P5FA
Number in class	110
Introduced	1945
Cylinders (3)	16⅜in x 24in
Coupled wheels	6ft 2in
Boiler pressure	280lb/sq in**
Grate area	38.25sq ft
Tractive effort	31,040lb
Weight	86 tons 0cwt
SR number series	21C101-21C170
BR number series	34001-34110

*   Six locomotives (Nos 34095, 34097, 34099, 34101, 34102 and 34104) built by BR at Eastleigh, the remainder at Brighton
**   Boiler pressure reduced in the early 1950s to 250lb/sq in, giving tractive effort of 27,715lb

Below: *No 34009* Lyme Regis *stands at Nine Elms depot on 4 April 1959 in BR condition, painted Brunswick green with black-and-orange lining. The tender is a 4,250gal example and already shows signs of weakening of the upper side plates, leading to the corrosion that necessitated replacement. BR policy saw the elegant 'West Country' nameplates backed in black paint, but local opinion soon persuaded the works to repaint them red at the next overhaul.* Author

Right: *As one of the last 40 locomotives 'Battle of Britain' Pacific No 34078* 222 Squadron *had a wide cab, with the result that the bottom of the cabsides did not blend with the 'air-smoothed' casing. Pictured at Exmouth Junction on 29 July 1961, this locomotive has a 5,250gal tender. On the 'Battle of Britain' class only the nameplates were backed in Air Force blue, though black was used in early BR days. The yellow disc (later to be replaced by a yellow triangle) painted under the cabside number indicates that the tender is fitted for briquette water treatment. Above the buffer-beam is the battery box for the automatic warning system (AWS), fitted as standard to most locomotives from the early 1960s.* Author

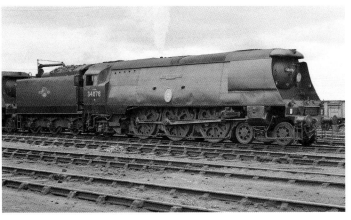

Above: *Pictured at Bournemouth depot on 10 October 1954, 'West Country' Pacific No 34005* Barnstaple *has had its smoke-deflectors extended backwards. The front cab windows have been moved back, as was done with the 'Merchant Navy' class, while the plating ahead of the outside cylinders, originally similar to that on a second-batch 'Merchant Navy', has been removed. The tender is of the 4,250gal variety.* Author

During the 1948 Locomotive Exchanges three 'West Country' 4-6-2s were selected and were temporarily coupled to Stanier (LMS) tenders which had water trough pick-up apparatus; these three, Nos 34004 *Yeovil*, 34005 *Barnstaple* and 34006 *Bude*, were given smoke-deflectors extended to the rear, similar to those on 'Merchant Navy' No 35020 (page 95). Later No 34039 *Boscastle* was given smoke-deflectors that were extended forwards, giving that locomotive a unique appearance which it retained until rebuilding. Further experiments in revised smoke-deflectors took place at Eastleigh in 1960 on Nos 34035 and 34049, but no more were modified.

An interesting experiment in the early 1960s saw No 34064 *Fighter Command* equipped with a Giesl oblong ejector. This performed well, taking the exhaust steam high above the train and reducing spark emissions, but no further locomotives were modified by BR, the improvement in traffic being deemed insufficient to justify the cost. However, the preserved No 34092 *City of Wells* ran with a Giesl ejector in the 1980s and 1990s and performed well on the main line.

Withdrawal of Light Pacifics that had not been rebuilt began in 1963. Oddly the last few non-rebuilt examples were to survive almost until the final demise of Southern steam, the last in service, No 34102 *Lapford*, running virtually to the end in July 1967.

Above: *No 34039* Boscastle *had smoke-deflectors extended forwards as part of an experiment to reduce smoke drift, being seen thus at Southampton Central on 22 November 1955 in charge of the Brighton–Plymouth through train.* Author

Above: *Nos 34035 and 34049 were subjected to further smoke-deflection experiments at Eastleigh during 1960, but these were not pursued. Attached to a cut-down 4,250gal tender, No 34049* Anti-Aircraft Command *looked rather odd when photographed at Eastleigh depot on 26 February.* Author

Above: *When, in the early 1960s, the self-weighing 'Merchant Navy' tender that had previously been coupled with No 35014 and then No 35024 (see page 96) required a new tank, a 6,000gal version of similar style to the new 5,250gal tanks was fitted to its longer underframe. This tender later passed into preservation, being coupled to non-rebuilt 'West Country' Pacific No 34105* Swanage *on the Mid-Hants Railway.* Stephen Leek

Above: *A subsequent modification to the 6,000gal tender of No 34105 saw it fitted with upper side extensions to resemble an original tender, in which condition it is pictured during a visit to the East Somerset Railway in 1994.* Brian Scales

CLASS WCX / BBX — REBUILT 'WEST COUNTRY' / 'BATTLE OF BRITAIN'

Sixty Light Pacifics were rebuilt at Eastleigh Locomotive Works before a stop was called on the grounds that the end of steam working was foreseen to be reached in the late 1960s. The design was based on exactly the same principles as was the rebuilding of the 'Merchant Navy' 4-6-2s. This entailed replacement of the three sets of chain-driven Bulleid valve gear by three independent sets of Walschaerts gear, with a new inside-admission middle cylinder and box stretcher both being placed under the new, extended smokebox. As with the bigger Pacifics, the Light Pacifics gained conventional boiler lagging and side valances, their outward appearance being little different from the rebuilt 'MNs'. The opportunity was taken to widen the cabs of those locomotives that had been built with narrower cabs because they would never be required to work to Hastings. Thus all 60 of the rebuilt 'West Country'/'Battle of Britain' locomotives ended up in an identical condition, apart from the inevitable differences between the three types of tenders; those of 4,250gal and 5,250gal were being cut down already for improved rearward view from the footplate. No 34039 *Boscastle* received one of the seven new 5,250gal tender tanks. Another 'WCX' locomotive received the former self-weighing tender (previously attached to No 35024) that had been rebuilt with a new 6,000gal tank of the same style as the 5,250gal replacement tanks.

Withdrawal of rebuilt Light Pacifics started in 1964 when their next major overhauls were due. Some were still in service at the end of SR steam on 9 July 1967. Fortunately, most of the later withdrawals went to Woodham's scrapyard at Barry, from where many locomotives were purchased for preservation. Twenty Light Pacifics are now restored or awaiting preservation — 10 rebuilt and 10 of the non-rebuilt variety.

Class	WCX and BBX 4-6-2
Engineer	R. G. Jarvis
Designed for	SR, BR
Rebuilt by	BR Eastleigh
BR power rating	7P5FA
Number in class	60
Introduced	1957
Cylinders (3)	16⅜in x 24in
Coupled wheels	6ft 2in
Boiler pressure	250lb/sq in
Grate area	38.25sq ft
Tractive effort	27,715lb
Weight	90 tons 1cwt
BR numbers	34001, 34003-34005, 34008-34010, 34012-34014, 34016-34018, 34021, 34022, 34024-34029, 34031, 34032, 34034, 34036, 34037, 34039, 34040, 34042, 34044-34048, 34050, 34052, 34053, 34056, 34058-34060, 34062, 34071, 34077, 34082, 34085, 34087-34090, 34093, 34095-34098, 34100, 34101, 34104, 34108, 34109

Right: *Fresh from rebuilding, No 34062 17 Squadron stands in Eastleigh Works yard on 2 April 1959. As with the rebuilt 'West Country' locomotives, the 'Battle of Britain' nameplates were placed below their badges on a bracket mounted on the running plate above the centre coupled wheels. This locomotive has a cut-down 5,250gal tender.* Author

Right: *The tender coupled to No 34039 Boscastle when the locomotive was rebuilt received one of the new 5,250gal tanks. It is seen at Eastleigh depot on 26 January 1959.* Author

CLASS LEADER

As the postwar Southern Railway faced the opportunity for further electrification of main lines and was building enough 4-6-2 locomotives to handle the more important steam-hauled passenger trains, there remained the need to replace a number of its oldest tank engines, in particular the 'M7' 0-4-4Ts. Early proposals included a four-axle steam locomotive type on two four-wheeled bogies. The locomotive would exhibit characteristics of diesel and electric locomotives in that its whole weight would be available for traction adhesion and the locomotive would be bi-directional. It proved difficult to produce such a design with less than a 20-ton axle-load, so Bulleid expanded the idea to a six-axle locomotive and offered the SR Board a more powerful and universal design. As this was developed, however, the axle-load crept up again, and the final weight was at least 130 tons.

The 'Leader' locomotive had two driving cabs, one at each end, with a separate cab amidships for the fireman. The boiler was relatively conventional, but offset from the centreline to provide a side corridor between the driver's and fireman's cabs. The firebox had no side or back water jackets and instead used four thermic siphons linking the boiler barrel with the firebox crown. The fireman's fully enclosed position was sandwiched between the firebox and the coal bunker with no opening on the non-door side, a difficult compromise that proved a problem in reality. A large live steam pipe to the rear cylinders was just one of the heat sources that added to the ambience in the fireman's cab.

The two bogies each had three axles, with 5ft 1in B-F-B wheels (as on the 'Q1') and three small cylinders inside the frames that were fed and exhausted through reciprocating and rotating sleeve valves. These had been tried out on a Brighton Atlantic before fitting to the 'Leaders'. Valve gear was another version of the compact Bulleid gear, chain driven from a lay shaft that itself was driven by a chain from the middle crank axle. Lubrication used the principle of a deep oil sump feeding virtually all moving parts from the crossheads to the cranks and valve gear. The axleboxes had plain roller bearings, which in hindsight would have been better had they been of a self-aligning type; early fatigue damage to axles was said to have been a risk with the chosen arrangement. Drive from the crank axle to the other axles was by wide chains, which proved to be a practical concept.

Class	Leader C-C
Engineer	O. V. S. Bulleid
Designed for	SR
Built by	SR and BR Brighton
BR power rating	- (unclassified)
Number in class	5*
Introduced	1949
Cylinders (6 inside)	12¼in x 15in
Coupled wheels	5ft 1in
Boiler pressure	280lb/sq in
Grate area	25.5sq ft
Tractive effort	26,350lb
Weight	130 tons 10cwt
BR number series	36001-36005

* Only one locomotive, No 36001, was completed

Construction of the five locomotives was stopped when the trials of No 36001 began to threaten expensive modifications, though No 36002 was nearly finished when placed in store, and No 36003 was well advanced. Bulleid was given plenty of support by the BRB mechanical engineer, R. A. Riddles, but the advent of a programme for building BR Standard steam classes, coupled with the realisation that only a complete redesign could save the 'Leader', resulted in the decision to stop the trials. Senior technical opinion was that the locomotive could be made operational but that its weight was so excessive for its originally intended duties that the cost of redesigning the locomotive and building new prototypes could not be supported. The project was cancelled early in 1951, and the locomotives' proposed duties were ultimately covered by new Brighton-built 2-6-4Ts of LMS and BR designs.

O. V. S. Bulleid later carried out a similar, more advanced experiment in Ireland, which is covered in the companion volume *Locomotive Compendium: Ireland*.

Left: *The experimental 'Leader' 0-6-6-0T, No 36001, photographed running light through Lewes on 31 August 1949. This view shows clearly the positions of the two driving cabs and the fireman's cab, which is on this side of the locomotive. The general heaviness of its construction is evident. In November 1950 No 36001 hauled a 480-ton test train from London to Basingstoke, holding a steady 50mph — its official speed limit — in a satisfactory manner, but by then all official interest in pursuing the project had evaporated.* C. C. B. Herbert

Being a railway that had electrified a greater portion of its route miles than any other in the UK, the Southern was interested in developing electric locomotives for heavy mixed-traffic duties. In SR management at that time, mechanical and electrical engineering was split between O. V. S. Bulleid for mechanical work and A. Raworth covering electrical engineering. Nonetheless, these two together directed an interesting and up-to-date design of Co-Co electric locomotive specifically suited to the SR type of 660V DC third-rail electrification.

Electrically the class broke new ground for locomotives in that traction current was initially passed through a pair of motor-generator sets before being fed through the six traction motors. Each motor-generator set consisted of a large DC motor fed at 660V on a common shaft with a flywheel and a DC generator. As the speed of the motor was varied, the output voltage of the generator windings was variable, almost infinitely since the controller had 26 positions. The six 245bhp traction motors were designed to receive current at a maximum of 400V. The resulting 1,470bhp locomotive output as fed to the six wheelsets was matched by a useful 75mph top speed, with a starting tractive effort of 40,000lb. Whenever a locomotive's pick-up shoes met conductor-rail gaps, the flywheels enabled the generators to continue rotating and providing some power to the traction motors. Each locomotive also had a central roof pantograph to enable it to operate under overhead wires in yards in which a side conductor rail would be unsafe for working personnel.

Mechanically the design was also original in that the bogies, which had 3ft 7in wheels, had neither bolsters nor centre pivots. Bulleid developed a bogie with four bearing segments on which the body rested, the body being held in place by centring springs.

No CC1 was outshopped in 1941 and was followed by a second, almost identical locomotive, No CC2. A third, of improved design, completed the trio in 1948: No 20003 came out after nationalisation and was slightly longer and heavier than the first two.

These useful and reliable machines were allocated to the Central Section of the SR and made their name hauling the heavy boat trains

Class	CC Co-Co electric
Engineer	O. V. S. Bulleid / A. Raworth
Designed for	SR
Built by	SR and BR Ashford
BR power rating	7P5F
Number in class	3
Introduced	1941, 1948*
Wheels	3ft 7in
Electric supply	660V direct current
Current collection	Conductor rail/overhead wire
Control	Motor-generator sets and flywheel
Tractive effort	40,000lb, 45,000lb*
Maximum speed	75mph
Train heat	Electrically heated steam boiler
Weight	99 tons 15cwt, 104 tons 14cwt*
SR number series	CC1, CC2
BR number series	20001-20003

* These figures refer to No 20003

between Victoria and Newhaven Harbour. They also headed freight trains around the central part of the region. They were equipped with electrode-heated steam boilers for train heat supply. This came in useful from 1967 when BR's Southern Region had eliminated steam heating from all its internal trains but needed something to haul the steam-heated Royal Train whenever it ventured on the region. No 20001 was the last of the three to receive a general overhaul (Eastleigh 1966) and, resplendent in BR Rail blue, undertook the occasional Royal Train duty until its final withdrawal in 1969.

Above: *Bulleid/Raworth Co-Co electric locomotive No 20002 in BR Southern Region green after general overhaul at Eastleigh Locomotive Works on 10 May 1959. Note the roof-mounted pantograph for current collection in yards. Owing to loading-gauge restrictions in the non-electrified area the third-rail collector shoes have been removed for the locomotive's transfer back to its home depot.* Author

Above right: *No 20003 was built without the domed front to the roof line, giving it a starker profile. When delivered it was painted SR malachite green, but in 1950 it emerged from overhaul in BR's simple but attractive gloss black with aluminium lining band and silver/grey paint on roof and bogies, in which condition it posed for an official photograph at Waterloo.* BR Southern Region

Right: *After its final overhaul No 20001 undergoes electrical test at Eastleigh Locomotive Works in late 1966. This was the only ex-SR Co-Co to receive BR Rail blue.* Author

0-6-0 DIESEL-ELECTRIC

Above: *Originally No 2, SR 0-6-0 350hp diesel shunting locomotive No 15202 rests at Hither Green depot on 31 May 1958. These prewar locomotives are visually distinctive by virtue of the joggled shape of the back of the cab and the small canopy over the front of the radiator.* Author

In the 1930s all the 'Big Four' railways tried out diesel shunting locomotives, the English Electric 350bhp 0-6-0 diesel-electrics becoming the firm favourite. On the SR three such locomotives were built by the Southern Railway at Ashford, to a basically similar design to those on other railways. They emerged soon after Bulleid arrived on the SR as its Chief Mechanical Engineer; but it is doubtful whether he had any significant influence on the design. The locomotives had two traction motors between the frames, each driving an outer axle through a single reduction gear. The single reduction gear was intended to enable the locomotive to be driven at speeds up to 40mph. The frames were set wider apart than on most steam locomotives in order to accommodate the traction motors. With the frames actually outside the wheels, the axles were extended so that the axleboxes also were outside the wheels and working within horn guides in the frames. Beyond the axleboxes and pressed on the ends of the axles were fly cranks which drove the coupling rods that spread the drive between all three wheelsets.

The locomotives had a commodious cab at one end. Immediately in front of the cab was a compartment for such equipment as a compressor and an electrical control system. In front of that was the power unit, an English Electric 6KT six-cylinder in-line diesel engine coupled to a DC generator. This could be accessed for maintenance by removing and storing lightweight bodyside panels which were designed for quick release. A large cooling radiator and fan at the front of the locomotive cooled the treated water that kept the engine temperature within design limits. A battery for starting and for powering auxiliaries was in a cupboard on one side running plate, and the fuel tanks on this design were in front of the cab on both side running plates. Deep steps on each side and at both ends of the locomotive enabled a shunter or other operator to stand inside the loading-gauge as the locomotive progressed around a yard.

One of the key advantages of this type of locomotive was its ability to be driven safely by one man with no driver's assistant. To this economy could be added the availability of the locomotive over almost 24 hours a day, except for the time needed to take on fuel at a servicing depot. The Southern Railway numbered these diesel locomotives 1, 2 and 3 in their own series, actually duplicating three Class T1 0-4-4T steam locomotives with the same numbers on the main SR system,

as well as three 'E1' 0-6-0Ts on the Isle of Wight (though the latter had a 'W' prefix)! The locomotives were used in freight yards such as those at Norwood and Hither Green, until their withdrawal as non-standard in 1964.

Type	0-6-0 diesel-electric
Engineer	O. V. S. Bulleid
Designed for	SR
Builder	SR Ashford
Number in class	3
Introduced	1937
Diesel engine	English Electric 6-cylinder 6KT
Diesel-engine rating	350bhp
Traction generator (DC)	EE 801/7D
Traction motors (DC)	DK129-2D (2) with single-reduction gears
Wheels	4ft 6in
Tractive effort	30,000lb*
Maximum speed	30mph*
Train heat	None
Weight	55 tons 5cwt
SR number series	1-3
BR number series	15201-15203

* These are the universally published figures, but the author believes that the tractive effort quoted is too high for the maximum speed given and for the use of single-reduction gears

Type	0-6-0 diesel-electric*
Engineer	O. V. S. Bulleid
Designed for	SR
Builder	BR Ashford
Number in class	26
Introduced	1949
Diesel engine	English Electric 6-cylinder 6KT
Diesel-engine rating	350bhp
Traction generator (DC)	EE 801/7D
Traction motors (DC)	EE506A (2) with double-reduction gears
Wheels	4ft 6in
Tractive effort	24,000lb
Maximum speed	27½mph
Train heat	None
Weight	49 tons
Number series	15211-15236

* BR designated this type Class 12, but none survived long enough to carry a number in the 12 xxx series

Below: *Shunting at Eastleigh East Yard on 2 May 1955 is Bulleid/ English Electric 350hp diesel shunter No 15235. The B-F-B wheels are very clear in this view, as is the overall similarity with the LMS and BR 350hp classes.* Author

After World War 2 had ended the SR placed orders with Ashford Works for 26 new diesel shunters. These were almost identical to the LMS and WD types that already existed in significant numbers and which had proved their effectiveness in goods-yard shunting. The most noticeable difference in the SR locomotives was the use of B-F-B wheels instead of the standard spoked variety. The SR locomotives also had a higher top speed than the LMS type, being geared to a run at a maximum of 27½mph instead of 20mph.

While the locomotives were certainly rugged and possibly over-engineered, their reliability became legendary, provided the maintainers and operators were able to keep battery and cooling equipment condition up to scratch. There were in fact few significant developments of the LMS/SR/GWR/LNER postwar 350bhp shunter designs as the type consolidated into the British Railways '13xxx'-series locomotive (later 'D3xxx' and later still known variously as Class 08 and Class 09), of which more than 1,000 were built.

The 26 locomotives of this class were scattered throughout the Southern Region of BR to places that had significant freight yards. They replaced steam locomotives on hump shunts including Classes G16 and Z and older tank engines at other locations. However, being non-standard in certain components, the SR-built diesel shunters were superseded in the 1970s by more recently built Class 08s. Only one survives in preservation, No 15224, which at the time of writing (2009) is in service on the Spa Valley Railway. This locomotive had seen industrial service after withdrawal by BR, between 1970 and 1983 working at Snowdown Colliery, in Kent.

0-6-0 DIESEL-MECHANICAL

To meet a demand for using diesel traction flexibly between shunting and general train duties O. V. S. Bulleid managed the design and building of one prototype 0-6-0 diesel-mechanical locomotive of 500bhp. No 11001 emerged from Ashford Works late in 1949. It had a Paxman 12-cylinder diesel engine driving through a fluid flywheel (otherwise called an hydraulic coupling) to a mechanical gearbox. The gearbox provided three forward and three equal reverse gears. Drive from the gearbox was fed to a jackshaft at the rear of the locomotive's plate frames. From the end of the jackshaft, connecting rods drove the centre pair of coupled wheels, the drive being transmitted to the other coupled wheels by coupling rods as in normal steam locomotive practice.

No 11001 had a long, low bonnet over the engine and transmission. The radiators were in front of the engine, and forward of them was a fuel tank.

No 11001's top speed was 36mph, just adequate for freight transfer work. The locomotive had only its own air brake, however, and so could work only unbraked trains, although in 1949 very few freight trains were through-braked, so this was only a minor disadvantage. However, in common with all other Bulleid locomotives No 11001 had clasp brakes, a type in which each wheel has two brake blocks applied in opposite positions on either side. This arrangement removes the pressure on axleboxes that less sophisticated braking arrangements cause; most locomotive designs, including the BR Standard steam locomotives, perpetuated single-block braking on coupled wheels. The locomotive had standard B-F-B-type wheels, of 4ft 6in diameter.

No 11001 worked for most of its 10-year life at Norwood yard in south London. Stories of its unreliability abound, and its end came when it was finally cut up at Ashford in December 1959.

Type	0-6-0 diesel-mechanical
Engineer	O. V. S. Bulleid
Designed for	SR
Builder	BR Ashford
Number in class	1
Introduced	1949
Diesel engine	Davey Paxman 12-cylinder RPH Series 1
Diesel-engine rating	500bhp
Fluid coupling	Vulcan Sinclair
Gearbox	SSS Powerflow three-speed
Wheels	4ft 6in
Tractive effort	33,500lb
Maximum speed	36mph
Train heat	None
Weight	49 tons 9cwt
Number	11001

Below: *No 11001 demonstrated its Bulleid pedigree by virtue of its B-F-B wheels. This prototype was built for shunting and local-train use, though its top speed of 36mph was scarcely adequate for the latter. This picture illustrates well the clasp brakes that Bulleid specified on all his locomotive designs for the SR. Note also the high cab roof and the jackshaft, with its prominent balance weight at the rear of the frame.* Ian Allan Library

Even though the Southern Railway preferred electrification of its main lines, those to the West Country and beyond were but a distant dream. The cost of electrification was high in infrastructure, and diesel locomotives were still at least four or five times the cost of an equivalent steam locomotive to build. Nevertheless, the SR wanted to test the advantages that dieselisation might offer in terms of better availability and utilisation, as well as performance on the line. O. V. S. Bulleid, together with the new electrical engineer, C. S. Cocks, was tasked with designing and building at Ashford two prototypes, later extended to three, to work express passenger trains up to 90mph and to handle heavy freight trains too.

The heart of the new locomotive was the English Electric 16SVT diesel engine that was rated at 1,750bhp, slightly uprated from that fitted to the LMS prototypes, Nos 10000 and 10001. The DC traction generator and six traction motors were also by the EE Co. The mechanical parts were pure Bulleid, the bogies each having four axles, three of them motored, the leading axle to spread the weight and keep the maximum axle load within reasonable bounds. As with the 'CC' electrics, the bodies of No 10201 and its siblings rested on lubricated segment plates held in place by centring springs. They rode very well. No 10203, built at Brighton Works, was rated at 2,000bhp, and formed the prototype for the subsequent builds of English Electric Type 4, of which 200 were constructed for BR in the period 1958-62.

The SR diesels' bodies had curved sides to match the curves of Bulleid-designed carriages. Each cab had an end door that was flush with the cab front. The door permitted crew access between locomotives in the event of multiple working. In practice this was not needed on the SR.

In Southern Region service the locomotives worked trains from Waterloo to Bournemouth and Weymouth and to Exeter. One was sometimes scheduled to haul the 'Golden Arrow' boat train from Victoria to Dover Marine. In 1953 they were joined by the LMS twins, Nos 10000 and 10001, all based at Nine Elms depot in London. No 10203 was outshopped in 1954. Late in 1954 all five big diesel-electrics were transferred to the London Midland Region and

Type	1Co-Co1 diesel-electric
Engineer	O. V. S. Bulleid / C. S. Cocks
Designed for	SR
Builder	BR Ashford / BR Brighton*
BR power rating	5P5F, 6P6F*
Number in class	3
Introduced	1951, 1954*
Diesel engine	English Electric 16SVT
Diesel-engine rating	1,750bhp, 2,000bhp*
Electric traction equipment	English Electric Co
Traction motors (six DC)	EE 526A
Driving wheels	3ft 7in
Tractive effort	48,000lb, 50,000lb*
Maximum speed	90mph
Train heat	Oil-fired steam generator
Weight	135 tons, 132 tons*
Number series	10201-10203

* These details refer to No 10203

worked out of Camden depot on the West Coast main line. While Nos 10000 with 10001 and 10201 with 10202 worked in multiple pairs on heavy trains such as the 'Royal Scot', No 10203 was able to handle such a load unaided. The locomotives were taken out of traffic in 1963. Most regrettably, none was preserved, all being scrapped by 1968. However, the SR design legacy endures in the 21st century, several Class 40, 44, 45 and 46 1Co-Co1 diesels surviving in preservation, all riding on examples of the Bulleid eight-wheeled bogie.

Right: *On 17 May 1953 1Co-Co1 diesel-electric locomotive No 10201 enters Bournemouth Central with the 2.30pm Bournemouth West–Waterloo, the load of about 12 coaches being well within the capabilities of this 1,750bhp locomotive. The carriages are Bulleid stock in carmine-and-cream livery, their bodyside curves being matched by the shape of the locomotive.* Author

Right: *Still in as-new condition, No 10203 is pictured during a visit to Eastleigh Works in 1954. Rated at 2,000bhp, this locomotive can be regarded as the prototype for all BR's subsequent builds of 1Co-Co1 diesel-electrics, particularly those from the English Electric Co, which employed the same power unit.* B. J. Swain / Colour-Rail DE1512

MISCELLANEOUS

Although the vast majority of its stock was inherited from the three main railway companies from which it was formed in 1923, the Southern Railway also inherited diverse locomotives from various 'outside' sources. Some had already been acquired by the pre-Grouping companies, notably the 0-4-0Ts that joined the LSWR when it purchased the Southampton Dock Company and the three tank engines — two 0-6-2Ts and an 0-6-0T — built for the Plymouth, Devonport & South Western Junction Railway. Others were absorbed by the SR after the Grouping, and several of these had interesting histories.

In 1932 the SR purchased a solitary 0-8-0T from the Kent & East Sussex Railway. This became SR No 949 and carried the name *Hecate*. The KESR was one of the many light railways laid under the inspiration of one Colonel Stephens, who showed that it was possible (just) to serve rural communities with railways that were both lightly laid and economically run. In 1946, besides acquiring an additional Adams radial tank from the East Kent Railway (page 9 refers), the SR seized the opportunity of purchasing 15 0-6-0Ts which, following the end of World War 2, had become surplus to the requirements of the US Army Transportation Corps and were considered ideal for shunting heavy loads on the curved tracks of Southampton's Eastern Docks.

A few odd locomotives were acquired by BR at nationalisation, although only a few of these appear to have been taken into Southern Region locomotive stock. They included East Kent Railway 0-6-0T No 4, basically an industrial locomotive, which was scrapped in 1949 before it could receive its new identity (30948). The EKR had been another of Colonel Stephens' light railways.

All the locomotives listed above are described more fully in the following pages.

Below: *With an ocean liner in the background, Class USA 0-6-0 tanks Nos 30065 and 30068 are seen at work in the Eastern Docks at Southampton on 14 May 1955. Fifteen of these locomotives were purchased by the SR after the war, having previously been part of the US Army Transportation Corps' stock.* Author

Above: *The last survivor from the Southampton Docks Co fleet was Hawthorn Leslie 0-4-0ST No 30458* Ironside, *seen at an open day at Eastleigh Works in August 1954, shortly before being broken up. Note the cutaways on the cab front and rear, an aid to visibility applied also to 'B4' 0-4-0Ts when used at Southampton Docks.* Colour-Rail BRS14

Class	0458 0-4-0ST
Engineer	W. Adams*
Designed for	Southampton Dock Co
Built by	Hawthorn Leslie
Number in class	1 (plus 1 withdrawn before 1948)
Introduced	1890
BR power rating	0F
Cylinders (2 outside)	12in x 20in
Coupled wheels	3ft 2in
Boiler pressure	120lb/sq in
Tractive effort	7,730lb
Weight	21 tons 2cwt
SR numbers	E734, 0458 / 734**, 3458
BR number	30458

* In office at time of locomotive's acquisition but not responsible for design
** Withdrawn 1945

When the LSWR took over Southampton Docks it inherited a fleet of small tank engines used for shunting. Two of these lasted much longer than the rest, the pair of Hawthorn Leslie 0-4-0STs proving most useful. Nos 457 *Clausentum* and 458 *Ironside* had been built in 1890 as the builder's Nos 2174 and 2175. When their stint at the docks came to an end they were put to use shunting the sharply curved Town Quay lines that were sited west of the docks. Later the SR built the long, straight Western Docks that stretched about three miles almost as far as Redbridge. Street working of trains was common between the two sets of docks, and the docks shunters crossed and shared tracks with the Town Quay locomotives.

The Hawthorn Leslie locomotives were displaced from their Southampton work by Class C14 0-4-0Ts (see page 25). No 457 had been renumbered 0457 in 1901, then 734 in 1920; it was withdrawn in 1945. However, No 458 (renumbered 0458 by the LSWR and 3458 by the SR) survived to become BR No 30458 and spent its last years acting as depot shunting locomotive at Guildford, where its short length was useful in moving locomotives on and off the roundhouse turntable. It was finally replaced in June 1954 by a Class B4 0-4-0T and was scrapped later that year.

CLASS 757

In 1890 the Plymouth, Devonport & South Western Junction Railway opened its double-track main line between Plymouth and Lydford, where there was an end-on junction with the LSWR main line from Exeter via Okehampton. From the outset the PD&SWJR main line was leased to the LSWR, which worked it as a through route between Exeter and Plymouth. In 1891 the PD&SWJR purchased the East Cornwall Mineral Railway, a 3ft 6in-gauge line that ran from Callington to Calstock, and in 1908 it built a standard-gauge line from Bere Alston, on the main line up to Calstock, at the same time contracting Col Stephens to convert the ECMR to standard gauge, the latter being additionally re-routed east of Gunnislake to meet the new branch at a different level in Calstock. The Bere Alston–Callington line was opened in 1908, the former ECMR being worked under light-railway regulations.

Three tank engines carried out the work on the Callington line, two of them being 0-6-2Ts supplied for the opening of the railway. These were built by Hawthorn Leslie in 1907 and were named *Lord St. Levan* and *Earl of Mount Edgcumbe*, after directors of the PD&SWJR company. (Curiously both names are mis-spelled by various sources; this book quotes the names actually carried on the nameplates on the tank sides in SR and BR days.)

Absorbed by the SR at the Grouping, the two 0-6-2Ts, which had been numbered 757 and 758 upon acquisition by the LSWR in 1922, continued to work on their 'home' railway until after nationalisation, finally being replaced in 1952 by new Ivatt Class 2 2-6-2Ts. Thereafter they found employment in the Plymouth area until 1956, when they moved to Eastleigh, where both took up shunting duties at the locomotive works, No 30757 being the more regularly used. No 30758 was withdrawn in 1956, No 30757 following in 1957, both being scrapped by the end of that year.

Class	757 0-6-2T
Purchasing agent	Col H. Stephens
Designed for	PD&SWJR
Built by	Hawthorn Leslie
Number in class	2
Introduced	1907
BR power rating	1P2F
Cylinders (2 outside)	16in x 24in
Coupled wheels	4ft 0in
Boiler pressure	170lb/sq in
Tractive effort	18,495lb
Weight	49 tons 19cwt
SR numbers	E757, E758 / 757, 758
BR numbers	30757, 30758

Below: Chunky and useful, Plymouth, Devonport & South Western Junction Railway 0-6-2T No 30758 Lord St. Levan *was photographed stabled at Eastleigh depot on 13 June 1956. Note that BR deemed these mixed-traffic locomotives and painted them lined black.* Author

When placing his order for locomotives for the Plymouth, Devonport & South Western Junction Railway Col Stephens, who had been contracted to convert the East Cornwall Mineral Railway from 3ft 6in gauge to 4ft 8½in, requested alongside the two 0-6-2Ts a smaller locomotive in the form of an outside-cylinder 0-6-0T. Named *A. S. Harris* after one of the PD&SWJR's directors, this was a straightforward, simple locomotive and was intended to work goods traffic. However, being of light weight and having a lower tractive effort, it was a bit short on power compared with the 0-6-2Ts, so the latter did most of the line work between Calstock and Callington, and *A. S. Harris* spent most of its time shunting at Callington.

Acquired by the LSWR in 1922 as No 756, the 0-6-0T remained in use at Callington until displaced in 1929 by a Class O2 0-4-4T, after which it put in a stint on the Wadebridge–Wenford Bridge line. Its subsequent allocations read like a listing of key Southern Railway locations, for in the years that followed it worked at Winchester, Eastleigh, Stewarts Lane, Fratton, Bournemouth, Brighton, Tonbridge, Folkestone and Dover before spending a lengthy period (from 1931 to at least 1939) as shed shunter at Nine Elms, eventually withdrawn from Stewarts Lane depot in November 1951 and scrapped that same month. Like the 0-6-2Ts it retained its nameplates throughout its career, neither the SR nor BR taking any steps to remove them.

Class	756 0-6-0T
Purchasing agent	Col H. Stephens
Designed for	PD&SWJR
Built by	Hawthorn Leslie
Number in class	1
Introduced	1907
BR power rating	1F
Cylinders (2 outside)	14in x 22in
Coupled wheels	3ft 10in
Boiler pressure	170lb/sq in
Tractive effort	13,545lb
Weight	35 tons 15cwt
SR number	E756 / 756
BR number	30756

Below: *Seen between shunting duties in early SR days, ex-PD&SWJR Hawthorn Leslie 0-6-0T No 756* A. S. Harris *is in Maunsell lined green livery and looks well cared for.* Ian Allan Library

CLASS KES

The Kent & East Sussex Railway was one of the light railways promoted by Col Stephens. In 1904 a heavy goods tank engine was delivered by Hawthorn Leslie as that railway's No 4. It had an 0-8-0T wheel arrangement (unusual for a light railway) and, as delivered, was an apparently chunky beast, weighing 47 tons — not excessively heavy for its size, though a locomotive with a shorter wheelbase would surely have been preferred by the line's track-maintenance team. No 4 did its work successfully, although it was indeed reported to be heavy for the track of the KESR.

For inexplicable reasons the locomotive was named *Hecate* after the Greek goddess of magic, witchcraft, necromancy (spiritual communication with the dead) and also protector of the newly born. Despite carrying this occult burden No 4 served the KESR until the company went into administration in 1932, at which time the locomotive was sold to the SR, exchanged for an ex-LSWR 0-6-0ST (No 0330) that would be easier on the KESR's track and which took over the number 4.

Numbered by the SR as 949, the 0-8-0T retained its name (mispronounced 'hee-kate' by most SR crews; it should be 'he-kat-ee'), doing plenty of work in the London area around Nine Elms yard and depot, and entered BR service only to be withdrawn in 1950.

Class	KES 0-8-0T
Purchasing agent	Col H. Stephens
Designed for	KESR
Built by	Hawthorn Leslie
Number in class	1
Introduced	1904
BR power rating	unclassified
Cylinders (2 outside)	16in x 24in
Coupled wheels	4ft 3in
Boiler pressure	160lb/sq in
Tractive effort	16,385lb
Weight	47 tons 10cwt
SR number	949
BR number*	30949

*   Never carried

Below: Built in 1905 for the ex-Kent & East Sussex Railway but probably too rigid for the track of a Col Stephens light railway, 0-8-0T Hecate *was acquired by the Southern Railway as No 949 in 1932 and for most of its life worked in the London area, being seen here at Nine Elms. It would be withdrawn in 1950 without receiving its allocated BR number.*
P. Ransome-Wallis

At nationalisation the East Kent Railway became part of British Railways, which thus inherited an 0-6-0T with an interesting history. Built by Kerr Stuart in 1917 as one of a batch of 10 'Victory'-class locomotives, EKR No 4 had first been owned by the Inland Waterways & Docks Department as that organisation's No 11 and was used for shunting at Richborough in Kent. In 1919, after the war had ended, it was transferred to the East Kent Railway, which used it for transferring coal wagons to and from the collieries it served.

Being impecunious, the EKR did not buy the locomotive, and it was paid for jointly by the East Kent and Golford & Waldershare collieries, which affixed a plate on the locomotive affirming their ownership. A rental agreement was signed in 1920, but the EKR stopped paying rent during 1921. Then came the General Strike, followed by the two collieries' going into receivership, and it was not until 1929 that the

locomotive finally became the EKR's property, for a nominal payment of one shilling! No 4 was normally employed on coal runs between Shepherdswell and Tilmanstone Colliery. On nationalisation it was allotted the BR number 30948, although this was never physically applied, the locomotive being withdrawn and scrapped in 1949.

For completeness it should be recorded that the other nine 'Victory' 0-6-0Ts were also disposed of by the Railway Operating Division (ROD), mainly into industrial use, for which they were well suited, and their subsequent careers are summarised in the second table below.

Note: The class name 'Victory' was that applied by Kerr Stuart to this design of 0-6-0T; as far as the author is aware the example inherited by the Southern Region was never given a formal BR classification.

Class	Victory 0-6-0T
Purchasing agent	Col H. Stephens
Designed for	industrial/military use
Built by	Kerr Stuart
Number in class	1*
Introduced	1917
BR power rating	unclassified
Cylinders (2 outside)	17in x 24in
Coupled wheels	4ft 0in
Boiler pressure	160lb/sq in
Grate area	20.5sq ft
Tractive effort	19,650lb
Weight	49 tons 0cwt
EKR number	4
BR number**	30948**

* Of an overall total of 10 locomotives built to this design a further two entered BR service on the Western Region *(see separate table)*

** Never carried

'Victory' 0-6-0T: Historical notes

IW&D No	History
10	Duffryn Aberaman Colliery No 18, scrapped 1969
11	EKR No 4, BR 30948, scrapped 1949
12	Manchester Collieries *Francis*
13	Alexandra Docks Railway No 34, then GWR/BR No 666, withdrawn 1955
14	Brecon & Merthyr Railway No 35, GWR No 2161, sold to Ashington Colliery in 1929
15	Duffryn Aberaman Colliery No 19, scrapped by NCB in 1969
16	Tirpentwys Coal & Coke Co, scrapped by NCB *c*1964
17	Alexandra Docks Railway No 35, then GWR/BR No 667, withdrawn 1954
18	Lambton, Hetton & Joicey Railway No 41, scrapped 1964
19	Rothervale No 8 at United Steel Co, then to NCB Orgreave Colliery

Right: *Kerr Stuart 'Victory' 0-6-0T No 4 of the East Kent Railway was used for coal traffic from local collieries. It is pictured here having received an SECR chimney and smokebox door during an overhaul at Ashford Works. In 1948 — when, along with the 'Big Four' railways and a few other small lines, the EKR was nationalised — No 4 entered BR stock as No 30948, but it was destined to be withdrawn in 1949 without physically receiving its new number.* Don Townsley collection

CLASS USA

As World War 2 progressed, the US Army Transportation Corps needed additional locomotives to serve in Europe during the build-up to D-Day and subsequently. From 1942 two classes were built that fitted within the British loading-gauge — about 800 of the 2-8-0 tender engines that are nowadays known universally as the 'S160s' and a class of 382 0-6-0Ts for shunting. The 2-8-0s did a great deal of work around Britain during the war, but after D-Day the USATC had them all shipped to the Continent, where railways were in need of locomotives to help with postwar reconstruction. However, some of the 0-6-0Ts were retained by Britain's War Department for shunting work, and Bulleid saw them as an opportunity to replacing the Adams 'B4' 0-4-0Ts that were still needed at Southampton Docks.

The US-built tanks (or 'Yankee tanks', as they became colloquially known) were considered preferable to the British WD 0-6-0STs by virtue of their shorter wheelbase, better condition (few had seen much use) and their basic design simplicity, together with their outside cylinders and full accessibility of moving parts. From the summer of 1946 No WD4326 was tried out at Southampton Docks and proved ideal for the curved tracks and heavy loads being shifted. The SR therefore purchased this locomotive along with a further 14 and proceeded to send them through Eastleigh Works for modification to suit British requirements. There they received enlarged bunkers, cabs with sliding side windows, lamp irons, vacuum-brake controls, steam-heating equipment and changes to regulators and cylinder drain cocks. (Later they were also modified with hinged plates at the front for shed staff to stand on when cleaning out the smokeboxes.) The first 13 to be modified were given SR numbers 61-73; the trial locomotive,

the aforementioned WD4326, was the last to be modified and did not return to traffic until after nationalisation, finally entering service as BR No 30074. The 15th locomotive purchased was never taken into stock: No WD1261 was used as a source of spare parts, and after a few years very little of it remained except the frame, which for many years languished behind Eastleigh Works.

Carrying radio aerials for operational control of their crews, the 'USA' tanks became a common sight in and around the Eastern and Western Docks at Southampton and on the connecting lines that ran through the streets between them. They performed their tasks well, enabling the 'B4' dock tanks to be withdrawn or redeployed (see page 12).

Class	USA 0-6-0T
Engineer	O. V. S. Bulleid*
Designed for	US Army Transportation Corps
Built by	H. K. Porter (61 and WD1261) / Vulcan Ironworks (62-74)
BR power rating	3F
Number in class	14**
Introduced	1946**
Cylinders (2 outside)	16½in x 24in
Coupled wheels	4ft 6in
Boiler pressure	210lb/sq in
Grate area	20sq ft
Tractive effort	21,600lb
Weight	46 tons 10cwt
SR number series***	61-73, WD4326
BR number series***	30061-30074

*   In office at time of locomotives' acquisition but not responsible for original design
**   382 built 1942/3, of which 15 purchased by the SR in 1946/7 (No WD1261 used only for spares)
***   See separate table for locomotive renumbering

Below: *Pausing during shunting at Southampton Eastern Docks on 14 May 1955, 'USA' 0-6-0T No 30063 is in the early BR livery with 'cycling lion' logo on the tank sides. Note that, contrasting with normal British practice, the connecting rods drive the rear coupled wheels. The light construction enabled a low weight of 46½tons to be achieved, sometimes causing the locomotives to slip on starting or to skid when trying to check heavy unbraked trains! The wide plate beneath the smokebox door was hinged at the bottom and could be let down to bridge the gap between the buffers and thus provide a platform for cleaning out the smokebox.* Author

In 1962 BR began to take delivery of 14 Ruston & Hornsby 0-6-0 diesel-electric shunting locomotives to replace the 'USA' tanks at Southampton. No 30063 was withdrawn that year but was not quickly followed by others. So useful were these locomotives that other duties were foreseen for the surplus examples, notably as works shunters at Eastleigh, Ashford and Lancing. No 30072 went to be Guildford shed shunter, thus releasing another Class B4 0-4-0T.

The 'USA' locomotive that was proposed for Lancing Carriage Works to replace the last BR 'A1' 0-6-0T No DS680 (page 55) presented a problem because the curves around which carriages had to be shunted were left-hand curves, and the 'USA' design was right-hand-drive. When No 30073 was tested there early in 1963 it faced away from the shops so that the driver could look back along the curve, but that was not ideal. The author, as a junior engineer then based at Brighton, discovered on inspecting the locomotive that it would be a simple matter to relocate the reversing gear and driver's controls to the left-hand side. Eastleigh Works quickly took No 30074 into the erecting shop and effected the conversion, at the same time, under the instruction of the acting Assistant Works Manager, John Click, repainting the locomotive in carriage-stock green lined out in the postwar style associated with SR malachite green. As the locomotive was always single-manned at Lancing it was most convenient that the injector controls were now grouped neatly under the new position of the driver's seat. Once it eventually reached Lancing Works (having suffered a hot axlebox on the way) No DS236 performed well and was joined there by No DS235 (formerly 30066). Both were finally withdrawn in 1965. Two others, Nos 30065 and 30070, which became respectively Nos DS237 *Maunsell* and DS238 *Wainwright*, were repainted green for shunting at Ashford Works (more hot axleboxes on the way), and yet two more, Nos 30064 and 30073, for Eastleigh Works, though these latter remained in capital stock. No DS233 (formerly No 30061) was the replacement at Redbridge depot, releasing Class C14 No 77S for a spell at Southampton Town Quay, while No DS234 (30062) went to Meldon Quarry (after running hot twice!).

Nine of the 'USA's lasted until the end of steam on the Southern Region, not being withdrawn until 1967. Four are preserved — No 30072 on the Keighley & Worth Valley Railway, No 30064 on the Bluebell Railway and Nos DS237 and DS238 on the Kent & East Sussex Railway. The K&WVR replaced No 30072's gravity lubricator with a mechanically driven one and thereby finally solved the problem of these locomotives' running hot when travelling long distances.

Class USA 0-6-0T: numbers and names

WD number	SR number	BR number	Departmental number and name
1264	61	30061	DS233
1277	62	30062	DS234
1284	63	30063	
1959	64	30064	
1968	65	30065	DS237 *Maunsell*
1279	66	30066	DS235
1282	67	30067	
1971	68	30068	
1952	69	30069	
1960	70	30070	DS238 *Wainwright*
1966	71	30071	
1973	72	30072	
1974	73	30073	
4326	-	30074	DS236
1261*	-	-	

*   Not formally taken into SR or BR stock, being used only for spares

Below: *Resplendent in Southern Region carriage-stock green, the former No 30074 shunts carriages at Lancing Works on 15 May 1963 after its transfer to departmental stock as No DS236. By now converted to left-hand drive, this locomotive was once No WD4326, the successful trial of which at Southampton Docks in 1946 prompted the SR to purchase 14 examples specifically for such work. Author*

DEPARTMENTAL

This section describes individual locomotives that were either inherited by British Railways from the Southern Railway's service stock or which were acquired subsequently by the Southern Region; it does not include traffic locomotives that were allocated subsequently to service or departmental stock, which are described elsewhere in this volume. As none of these individual types had official class designations they are identified here by the locomotive running numbers. They are grouped according to their traction system and described and illustrated therein in numerical order with or without prefixes and suffixes. Where technical details have been discovered these are tabulated, but this had not proved possible with most departmental locomotives, and, where this is the case, such information as has been found is included in the text. Three of the vehicles in this section were actually not departmental locomotives (two being items of plant, and one listed as a road vehicle) but are included for completeness.

DS74   ELECTRIC LOCOMOTIVES

Built in 1899, probably locally, this Bo-Bo electric locomotive spent its long career working in the environs of Durnsford Road power station at Wimbledon. The power station was built to supply direct current for the LSWR's electrification system, which fed trains with a 660V DC supply through side conductor rails. It was coal-fired, and No 74S was provided to handle the inevitable shunting of coal wagons, loaded and empty. If their appearance is a guide, the low-slung bogies may have been intended for (or come from) underground railway motor coaches. The central cab had an access door on one side only, the other side carrying two long air reservoirs to support the locomotive's braking system. Outside the end of each cab was a ventilated structure that looked rather like a toolbox but in fact housed equipment, probably starting resistances.

When No 74S was taken into BR Southern Region departmental stock it was officially renumbered DS74, but there is no evidence that this was ever carried. Durnsford Road power station closed at around the time the Southern Region upgraded its main lines to 750V DC and began to take the supply from the National Grid, and the locomotive was withdrawn for scrap in 1965 after a life of 66 years.

Right: *Built in 1899, Bo-Bo electric No 74S spent most of its life shunting coal wagons at Durnsford Road power station. This view shows the side with no cab door, the space being blocked by two long air reservoirs.*
Ian Allan Library

Left: *Photographed on 9 February 1957, No 74S shows its cab-door side and step. The locomotive was particularly low-slung.*
R. C. Riley

No 75S, as it was numbered when in Southern Railway service stock, was built by Siemens Bros, London, in 1898 for shunting movements around the Waterloo & City Railway. The W&CR was unique among London's underground railways in having only two stations, at Waterloo and Bank, both of them being termini. At the Waterloo end, after arrival from Bank trains were run empty beyond the station to the underground depot sidings immediately beyond the platform ends.

No 75S was a Bo electric shunting locomotive, small enough to prevent siding capacity from being compromised by its presence. It weighed 35 tons, and its four wheels measured 3ft 9in in diameter. Its main duty performed in its earlier years was to haul coal wagons from the wagon lift alongside Waterloo main-line station to and from the railway's own power station, believed by the author to have been on the south bank of the Thames: a contemporary map shows a stub siding off the W&C line just south of the river before the line crosses under it.

In 1940, coinciding with the introduction of new Bulleid-designed rolling stock, the W&C's electric supply was changed from the old centre third rail to the Southern Railway's standard side conductor rail.

Above: Underneath Waterloo station is the depot that used to be host to four-wheeled electric locomotive No 75S, pictured in January 1964 wearing clean malachite green livery and displaying the old BR lion-over-wheel emblem. Bruce Chapman collection / Colour-Rail DE1330

Locomotive No 75S was sent to Peckham Rye to be fitted with side collection shoes, but the war intervened, and it did not resume its duties on the W&C line until 1943.

Renumbered DS75 by BR, the locomotive was withdrawn in 1968 after a fire and stored at Brighton until moved in 1977 to be restored as part of the National Collection. It was exhibited for some years in the National Railway Museum at York but is currently looked after by the Middleton Railway at Leeds. The Waterloo & City line nowadays forms part of the London Underground network.

DS400 AND DS600 DIESEL LOCOMOTIVES

Postwar the Southern Railway purchased two Fowler 0-4-0 diesel shunting locomotives — No 400S in 1946 and No 600S in 1947. The former was for use by the Docks Engineer's Department at Southampton, the latter in the sawmill area at Eastleigh Carriage Works. Built to a manufacturer's standard model for industrial use, the pair exhibited detail differences, notably the exhaust scrubber that was prominent on the leading left side of No 600S to remove the risk of exhaust sparks' causing a timber fire. No 400S was withdrawn in 1957 as BR No DS400. No 600S kept its SR number into the 1960s even when repainted locally in BR days; it was officially withdrawn as No DS600 in 1963 — four years before the transfer of the carriage works to the site of the adjacent locomotive works — but was not scrapped until 1969.

Type	Fowler 0-4-0DM
Designed for	industrial use
Built by	John Fowler & Co
Number in class	2
Introduced	1946
Diesel engine	Fowler 4C, 150bhp
Coupled wheels	3ft 3in
Transmission	mechanical four-speed gearbox
Tractive effort	15,000lb
Weight	29 tons 0cwt
SR numbers	400S, 600S
BR numbers	DS400, DS600

Right: *Fowler 0-4-0 diesel-mechanical shunter No 400S worked for the Docks Engineer at Southampton, being seen at the Western Docks on 17 May 1947.* A. F. Cook

Below: *Resplendent in a coat of fresh green paint, Fowler 0-4-0DM No 600S stands outside Eastleigh Carriage Works on 1 February 1960. Only later would it gain its official BR number (DS600).* Author

Purchased in 1948 from Ruston & Hornsby Ltd, 0-4-0 No DS1169 was an example of the Type 48DS, the smallest standard-gauge locomotive design produced by that manufacturer. Powered by a 48bhp diesel engine driving the wheels through a gearbox and chain drive, it was intended for work at Broad Clyst civil-engineering depot, located on the West of England main line between Pinhoe and Whimple, replacing petrol 0-4-0 No 49 (see page 122). BR decided in 1965 to close Broad Clyst station, depot and yard, concentrating the work at Exeter, and after a period at Folkestone No DS1169 was eventually withdrawn in 1972, being scrapped the following year.

For completeness it should be noted that from 1958 another locomotive of this type, numbered ED10, worked in departmental service at Beeston creosote works, on the London Midland Region.

Type	Ruston 0-4-0DM
Designed for	industrial use
Built by	Ruston & Hornsby
Maker's type	48DS
Number in class	1 *
Introduced	1948
Diesel engine	Ruston 4YC, 48bhp
Coupled wheels	2ft 6in
Transmission	mechanical four-speed gearbox and chain drive
Tractive effort	4,200lb
Weight	8 tons 4cwt
BR number	DS1169

*   A similar locomotive worked in departmental service on the LMR as No ED10

Below: *An example of the smallest type of Ruston & Hornsby standard industrial diesel shunter, No DS1169 spent many years shunting at Broad Clyst before ending up at Folkestone.* Martyn Thresh

DS1173

Above: *Pre-dating by five years BR's purchase of Drewry diesel shunting locomotives, No DS1173 was bought to shunt at Hither Green, where it is seen in October 1962. In 1967 this locomotive would be taken into capital stock as No D2341.* C. R. Gordon Stuart / Colour-Rail DE2333

Type	Drewry 0-6-0DM*
Designed for	industrial use
Built by	Drewry Car Co, Vulcan Foundry
Number in class	1*
Introduced	1948
Diesel locomotive	Gardner 8L3, 204bhp
Coupled wheels	3ft 3in
Transmission	mechanical five-speed gearbox
Tractive effort	16,850lb
Weight	24 tons 15cwt
BR number	DS1173 / D2341

*   From 1952 BR received a further 141 similar locomotives, later designating them Class 04, to which DS1173 was transferred in 1967

Built in 1947, this Drewry standard 204bhp 0-6-0 diesel-mechanical shunting locomotive appears to have been acquired around 1948 and spent most of its life working from Hither Green depot in south-east London. Numbered DS1173 in BR's departmental series, it had a Gardner 8L3 eight-cylinder diesel engine driving through a driver-operated five-speed epicyclic gearbox with hydraulic coupling and cardan shaft to a bevel gearbox on the jackshaft, which drove the coupled wheels by means of side coupling rods. Maximum speed was 26mph. The need to throttle back to change gear was a problem for this type in some locations, particularly when shunting more delicate vehicles such as partially repaired carriages, but for light goods duties the inconvenience appears to have been generally bearable.

In 1952 BR began to purchase locomotives of the same type from Drewry for capital stock as its standard smaller 0-6-0 shunting locomotives. In 1967 No DS1173 was taken into capital stock as Class 04 No D2341, but was withdrawn a year later. BR's last '04' was withdrawn in 1971.

Introduced on trial in 1967, a four-wheeled modern diesel shunting locomotive from Secmafer in France spent just over a year on the Southern Region. Numbered DS209, it had two unusual features, employing a high-pressure hydrostatic transmission (probably a first for BR) and being intended for unmanned use under radio control, though whether this was put into practice is uncertain. The locomotive had a maximum speed of 50mph and so might have been useful in moving civil-engineering works trains around the network, although during its stay it was reported shunting in a yard at East Shalford, near Guildford.

Hydrostatic transmission may have been a little early in development at the time of these trials. It relies on very high-pressure fluid with small-bore piping to supply a theoretically simple and compact form of transmission; the diesel engine drives a high-pressure pump (3,000lb/sq in or higher) which feeds high-pressure oil through piping to an oil motor (or motors) that drive the locomotive axles. The transmission is able to change constant-speed engine output into variable output to the wheels. It replaces a conventional mechanical or hydraulic transmission or electric generator and motors. Hydrostatic drive has seldom been used successfully for locomotive traction and has more commonly been applied to driving auxiliary equipment such as cooling fans.

No DS209's BR career was a short one, the locomotive returning to France in 1968.

Below: *This Secmafer four-wheeled diesel demonstrator spent nearly two years on loan to the Southern Region Civil Engineer's Department. It had hydrostatic transmission and was intended to be radio-controlled when unmanned. Photographed at Eastleigh Works shortly after delivery in February 1967, it would later be numbered DS209.* Author

In 1930 a small four-wheeled diesel-mechanical shunting locomotive was built at Southall by Hardy Rail Motors Ltd (works number 943) to shunt the sawmill area at Eastleigh Carriage Works. Numbered 343S, it was powered by a 45bhp Karrier petrol engine driving through a mechanical gearbox and had solid disc wheels. Each end of the locomotive had a bonnet; beneath one was the petrol engine, and at one end was a cooling water radiator. The vehicle was built around rolled-steel-joist frames with end buffer-beams, but the frame's low height above rail level meant that the buffers, which were conventional, were set higher than the frame, rather like those on the Stroudley 'A1' and 'A1X' classes (pages 55 and 56). No 343S was withdrawn for scrap in 1952, having become redundant following the successful introduction in 1947 of Fowler 0-4-0 No 600S.

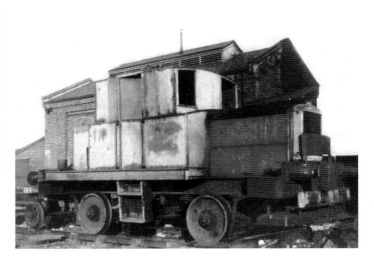

Right: *Small locomotive tractor No 343 was a four-wheeled petrol vehicle used for shunting behind the sawmill at Eastleigh Carriage Works. It lasted from 1930 to 1952.* John Harvey collection / Southern Railways Group

S112

Left: *Not really a locomotive, No S112 was a Fordson petrol tractor converted for railway operation. It worked at Ashford but was scrapped three years after conversion.* W. M. J. Jackson / Barry Fletcher collection / Southern Railways Group

Nine Elms goods depot once employed a Fordson petrol-engined road tractor, numbered S112 in the SR road fleet. Around the year 1946 someone changed its wheels for flanged ones so that it could be used as a rail-mounted shunting locomotive (albeit a small one); the smaller, leading carrying wheels were cast solid but with half-relief 'spokes', whilst the rear, driven wheels were also solid but plain. A simple roof was supported over the driver's seat by lengths of angle iron, and behind the cab was a drawhook, but there were no buffers at either end, nor was there a drawhook at the front. Its wheel arrangement can be described as 2-2-0 (or 1A).

After conversion No S112 went to Ashford Works, retaining its road fleet number, but its duties there are unclear. It was withdrawn from use in 1948 and scrapped the following year.

In 1935 Lancing Carriage Works, needing a small locomotive to move carriages between tracks at the rear of the complex, built a four-wheeled rail tractor based on what appears to have been the underframe of a 15-ton short-wheelbase goods brake van; it had LBSCR axlebox covers. Given the Plant & Machinery stock number 499, it was powered by a 25bhp Karrier petrol engine that was protected by a bonnet from a Thornycroft vehicle, misleading many observers over what power unit lurked beneath! At the rear was a similar bonnet, which may have covered equipment but was essentially a dummy. Both bonnets had attractive cast plates at the top of the front, with the word 'SOUTHERN' on a curve that fitted the bonnet top and 'RLY' beneath. At each end of the vehicle was a riveted buffer-beam with a full set of buffers and three-link couplings. The cab had three glass windows front and rear and a steam-locomotive-style opening on each side for access and egress.

The locomotive was used mainly to shunt carriages in varying states of overhaul from the end of one 'progressive' line to the beginning of the next, this being at the back end of the works buildings. In its 1962 Workshops Plan BR outlined its intention to transfer new construction and overhauls from Lancing to Eastleigh; this was duly done, enabling Lancing Works to close in 1965, and No 499, no longer required, was withdrawn that same year.

Below: Four-wheeled diesel shunter No 499 was quite a pretty little thing for a home-grown locomotive. Built in 1935 by the staff at Lancing Carriage Works, it lasted until closure of the works in 1965. This photograph was taken in 1964. D. A. Hope / Colour-Rail DE1670

No 49 was a 'home-made' four-wheeled petrol shunting locomotive built in 1940 at Exmouth Junction wagon-repair shops. It was assembled on a former SECR carriage bogie, itself originally built by Pressed Steel, and had an eight-cylinder 40bhp Dorman petrol locomotive driving through a mechanical gearbox. The buffer-beams (or 'headstocks' to carriage engineers) looked like carriage types riveted onto the side frames via trunnion brackets, but the drawgear and buffers were entirely conventional. The locomotive did not have continuous brakes, but a study of photographs shows that the wheels, which appear to be 3ft 7in standard carriage wheels, did have clasp brake blocks, presumably operated by a handbrake. The body was designed and built in the wagon shops and was functional yet æsthetically pleasing, as long as one did not look too closely at the roof, which was corrugated iron. The whole ensemble weighed about 8 or 10 tons, according to different sources. In later years the body was painted malachite green and lettered 'ENGINEERS DEPT' in full capitals (with no apostrophe).

Above: Spells at Yeovil and Meldon aside, petrol-engined four-wheeled shunter No 49 served at Broad Clyst from 1940 to 1959. It was painted in malachite green, and its cab was well lit by windows all round.
John Harvey collection / Southern Railways Group

While many publications have recorded this locomotive as No 49S, or even DS49 under British Railways, it appears always to have carried just the number 49, because it was numbered in the Plant & Machinery list and not as a service or departmental locomotive. Its duties were centred mainly on Broad Clyst civil-engineering depot, but it served also for a shorter time at Meldon Quarry (where it proved capable of hauling nine wagons in bottom gear) and at the permanent-way yard at Yeovil Junction. It was withdrawn for scrap in 1959, rendered surplus because No DS1169 (page 117) was well able to handle the reducing workload at Broad Clyst.

SR Number	BR Number	Name
Class B4 0-4-0T		
E81 / 81	30081	*Jersey*
E85 / 85	30085	*Alderney*
E86 / 86	30086	*Havre*
E89 / 89	30089	*Trouville*
E90 / 90	30090	*Caen*
E93 / 93	30093	*St Malo*
E95 / 95	30095	*Honfleur*
E96 / 96	30096	*Normandy* *
E97 / 97	30097	*Brittany*
E98 / 98	30098	*Cherbourg*
E101 / 101	30101	*Dinan*
E102 / 102	30102	*Granville*
E147 / 147	30147	*Dinard*
E176 / 176	30176	*Guernsey*

* Named *Corrall Queen* after sale to Corrall Ltd at Northam

Note: Names not carried after repainting in BR livery

No 92 was sold in 1949 to the Ministry of Fuel & Power and worked near Wakefield until 1961, with name *Pepper* painted on tank sides

SR Number	BR Number	Name
Class N15 4-6-0 'King Arthur'		
E448 / 448	30448	*Sir Tristram*
E449 / 449	30449	*Sir Torre*
E450 / 450	30450	*Sir Kay*
E451 / 451	30451	*Sir Lamorak*
E452 / 452	30452	*Sir Meliagrance*
E453 / 453	30453	*King Arthur*
E454 / 454	30454	*Queen Guinevere*
E455 / 455	30455	*Sir Launcelot*
E456 / 456	30456	*Sir Galahad*
E457 / 457	30457	*Sir Bedivere*
Class 0458 0-4-0ST		
0458 / 3458	30458	*Ironside*
Class N15 4-6-0 'Urie Arthur'		
E736 / 736	30736	*Excalibur*
E737 / 737	30737	*King Uther*
E738 / 738	30738	*King Pellinore*
E739 / 739	30739	*King Leodegrance*
E740 / 740	30740	*Merlin*
E741 / 741	30741	*Joyous Gard*
E742 / 742	30742	*Camelot*
E743 / 743	30743	*Lyonnesse*
E744 / 744	30744	*Maid of Astolat*
E745 / 745	30745	*Tintagel*
E746 / 746	30746	*Pendragon*
E747 / 747	30747	*Elaine*
E748 / 748	30748	*Vivien*
E749 / 749	30749	*Iseult*
E750 / 750	30750	*Morgan le Fay*
E751 / 751	30751	*Etarre*
E752 / 752	30752	*Linette*
E753 / 753	30753	*Melisande*
E754 / 754	30754	*The Green Knight*
E755 / 755	30755	*The Red Knight*

SR Number	BR Number	Name
Class 756 0-6-0T		
E756 / 756	30756	*A. S. Harris*
Class 757 0-6-2T		
E757 / 757	30757	*Earl of Mount Edgcumbe*
E758 / 758	30758	*Lord St. Levan*
Class N15 4-6-0 'Scotch Arthur'		
E763 / 763	30763	*Sir Bors de Ganis*
E764 / 764	30764	*Sir Gawain*
E765 / 765	30765	*Sir Gareth*
E766 / 766	30766	*Sir Geraint*
E767 / 767	30767	*Sir Valence*
E768 / 768	30768	*Sir Balin*
E769 / 769	30769	*Sir Balan*
E770 / 770	30770	*Sir Prianius*
E771 / 771	30771	*Sir Sagramore*
E772 / 772	30772	*Sir Percivale*
E773 / 773	30773	*Sir Lavaine*
E774 / 774	30774	*Sir Gaheris*
E775 / 775	30775	*Sir Agravaine*
E776 / 776	30776	*Sir Galagars*
E777 / 777	30777	*Sir Lamiel*
E778 / 778	30778	*Sir Pelleas*
E779 / 779	30779	*Sir Colgrevance*
E780 / 780	30780	*Sir Persant*
E781 / 781	30781	*Sir Aglovale*
E782 / 782	30782	*Sir Brian*
E783 / 783	30783	*Sir Gillemere*
E784 / 784	30784	*Sir Nerovens*
E785 / 785	30785	*Sir Mador de la Porte*
E786 / 786	30786	*Sir Lionel*
E787 / 787	30787	*Sir Menadeuke*
E788 / 788	30788	*Sir Urre of the Mount*
E789 / 789	30789	*Sir Guy*
E790 / 790	30790	*Sir Villiars*
E791 / 791	30791	*Sir Uwaine*
E792 / 792	30792	*Sir Hervis de Revel*
E793 / 793	30793	*Sir Ontzlake*
E794 / 794	30794	*Sir Ector de Maris*
E795 / 795	30795	*Sir Dinadan*
E796 / 796	30796	*Sir Dodinas le Savage*
E797 / 797	30797	*Sir Blamor de Ganis*
E798 / 798	30798	*Sir Hectimere*
E799 / 799	30799	*Sir Ironside*
E800 / 800	30800	*Sir Meleaus de Lile*
E801 / 801	30801	*Sir Meliot de Logres*
E802 / 802	30802	*Sir Durnore*
E803 / 803	30803	*Sir Harry le Fise Lake*
E804 / 804	30804	*Sir Cador of Cornwall*
E805 / 805	30805	*Sir Constantine*
E806 / 806	30806	*Sir Galleron*
Class LN 4-6-0		
E850 / 850	30850	*Lord Nelson*
E851 / 851	30851	*Sir Francis Drake*
E852 / 852	30852	*Sir Walter Raleigh*
E853 / 853	30853	*Sir Richard Grenville*
E854 / 854	30854	*Howard of Effingham*
E855 / 855	30855	*Robert Blake*

SR Number	BR Number	Name
E856 / 856	30856	*Lord St Vincent*
E857 / 857	30857	*Lord Howe*
E858 / 858	30858	*Lord Duncan*
E859 / 859	30859	*Lord Hood*
E860 / 860	30860	*Lord Hawke*
E861 / 861	30861	*Lord Anson*
E862 / 862	30862	*Lord Collingwood*
E863 / 863	30863	*Lord Rodney*
E864 / 864	30864	*Sir Martin Frobisher*
E865 / 865	30865	*Sir John Hawkins*

Class V 4-4-0 'Schools'

SR Number	BR Number	Name
E900 / 900	30900	*Eton*
E901 / 901	30901	*Winchester*
E902 / 902	30902	*Wellington*
E903 / 903	30903	*Charterhouse*
E904 / 904	30904	*Lancing*
E905 / 905	30905	*Tonbridge*
E906 / 906	30906	*Sherborne*
E907 / 907	30907	*Dulwich*
E908 / 908	30908	*Westminster*
E909 / 909	30909	*St. Paul's*
910	30910	*Merchant Taylors*
911	30911	*Dover*
912	30912	*Downside*
913	30913	*Christ's Hospital*
914	30914	*Eastbourne*
915	30915	*Brighton*
916	30916	*Whitgift*
917	30917	*Ardingly*
918	30918	*Hurstpierpoint*
919	30919	*Harrow*
920	30920	*Rugby*
921	30921	*Shrewsbury*
922	30922	*Marlborough*
923	30923	*Bradfield* *
924	30924	*Haileybury*
925	30925	*Cheltenham*
926	30926	*Repton*
927	30927	*Clifton*
928	30928	*Stowe*
929	30929	*Malvern*
930	30930	*Radley*
931	30931	*King's-Wimbledon*
932	30932	*Blundell's*
933	30933	*King's-Canterbury*
934	30934	*St. Lawrence*
935	30935	*Sevenoaks*
936	30936	*Cranleigh*
937	30937	*Epsom*
938	30938	*St Olave's*
939	30939	*Leatherhead*

* Originally *Uppingham*; renamed August 1934 following protest from Uppingham School

Class KES

	949	30949 *	*Hecate*

* BR number never carried

Class K / K1* 2-6-4T

SR Number	BR Number	Name
A790		*River Avon*
A791		*River Adur*
A792		*River Arun*
A793		*River Ouse*
A794		*River Rother*
A795		*River Medway*
A796		*River Stour*
A797		*River Mole*
A798		*River Wey*
A799		*River Test*
A800		*River Cray*
A801		*River Darenth*
A802		*River Cuckmere*
A803		*River Itchen*
A804		*River Tamar*
A805		*River Camel*
A806		*River Torridge*
A807		*River Axe*
A808		*River Char*
A809		*River Dart*
A890*		*River Frome*

Note: Names included for completeness; all removed when locomotives rebuilt as Class U / U1* 2-6-0s

Class H1 4-4-2

SR Number	BR Number	Name
B37 / 2037	32037	*Selsey Bill*
B38 / 2038	32038	*Portland Bill*
B39 / 2039	32039	*Hartland Point* *
B40 / 2040		*St. Catherine's Point*
B41 / 2041		*Peveril Point*

* Named *La France* by the LBSCR in 1913 for hauling the French president's special train; name retained until 1923

Class H2 4-4-2

SR Number	BR Number	Name
B421 / 2421	32421	*South Foreland*
B422 / 2422	32422	*North Foreland*
B423 / 2423	32423*	*The Needles*
B424 / 2424	32424	*Beachy Head*
B425 / 2425	32425	*Trevose Head*
B426 / 2426	32426	*St. Alban's Head*

* BR number never carried

Class N15X 4-6-0

SR Number	BR Number	Name
B327 / 2327	32327	*Trevithick* *
B328 / 2328	32328	*Hackworth*
B329 / 2329	32329	*Stephenson* **
B330 / 2330	32330	*Cudworth*
B331 / 2331	32331	*Beattie*
B332 / 2332	32332	*Stroudley*
B333 / 2333	32333	*Remembrance* **

* Originally *Charles C. Macrae*; renamed on rebuilding
** Names carried both before and after rebuilding; others applied on rebuilding as 4-6-0s

SR Number	BR Number	Name
Class WC and BB 4-6-2		
21C101	34001	*Exeter*
21C102	34002	*Salisbury*
21C103	34003	*Plymouth*
21C104	34004	*Yeovil*
21C105	34005	*Barnstaple*
21C106	34006	*Bude*
21C107	34007	*Wadebridge*
21C108	34008	*Padstow*
21C109	34009	*Lyme Regis*
21C110	34010	*Sidmouth*
21C111	34011	*Tavistock*
21C112	34012	*Launceston*
21C113	34013	*Okehampton*
21C114	34014	*Budleigh Salterton*
21C115	34015	*Exmouth*
21C116	34016	*Bodmin*
21C117	34017	*Ilfracombe*
21C118	34018	*Axminster*
21C119	34019	*Bideford*
21C120	34020	*Seaton*
21C121	34021	*Dartmoor*
21C122	34022	*Exmoor*
21C123	34023	*Blackmoor Vale / Blackmore Vale**
21C124	34024	*Tamar Valley*
21C125	34025	*Rough Tor / Whimple ***
21C126	34026	*Yes Tor*
21C127	34027	*Taw Valley*
21C128	34028	*Eddystone*
21C129	34029	*Lundy*
21C130	34030	*Watersmeet*
21C131	34031	*Torrington*
21C132	34032	*Camelford*
21C133	34033	*Chard*
21C134	34034	*Honiton*
21C135	34035	*Shaftesbury*
21C136	34036	*Westward Ho*
21C137	34037	*Clovelly*
21C138	34038	*Lynton*
21C139	34039	*Boscastle*
21C140	34040	*Crewkerne*
21C141	34041	*Wilton*
21C142	34042	*Dorchester*
21C143	34043	*Combe Martin*
21C144	34044	*Woolacombe*
21C145	34045	*Ottery St. Mary*
21C146	34046	*Braunton*
21C147	34047	*Callington*
21C148	34048	*Crediton*
21C149	34049	*Anti-Aircraft Command*
21C150	34050	*Royal Observer Corps*
21C151	34051	*Winston Churchill*
21C152	34052	*Lord Dowding*
21C153	34053	*Sir Keith Park*
21C154	34054	*Lord Beaverbrook*
21C155	34055	*Fighter Pilot*
21C156	34056	*Croydon*
21C157	34057	*Biggin Hill*
21C158	34058	*Sir Frederick Pile*
21C159	34059	*Sir Archibald Sinclair*
21C160	34060	*25 Squadron*
21C161	34061	*73 Squadron*
21C162	34062	*17 Squadron*
21C163	34063	*229 Squadron*
21C164	34064	*Fighter Command*
21C165	34065	*Hurricane*
21C166	34066	*Spitfire*
21C167	34067	*Tangmere*
21C168	34068	*Kenley*
21C169	34069	*Hawkinge*
21C170	34070	*Manston*
	34071	*615 Squadron / 601 Squadron* ***
	34072	*257 Squadron*
	34073	*249 Squadron*
	34074	*46 Squadron*
	34075	*264 Squadron*
	34076	*41 Squadron*
	34077	*603 Squadron*
	34078	*222 Squadron*
	34079	*141 Squadron*
	34080	*74 Squadron*
	34081	*92 Squadron*
	34082	*615 Squadron*
	34083	*605 Squadron*
	34084	*253 Squadron*
	34085	*501 Squadron*
	34086	*219 Squadron*
	34087	*145 Squadron*
	34088	*213 Squadron*
	34089	*602 Squadron*
	34090	*Sir Eustace Missenden* Southern Railway
	34091	*Weymouth*
	34092	*Wells / City of Wells #*
	34093	*Saunton*
	34094	*Mortehoe*
	34095	*Brentor*
	34096	*Trevone*
	34097	*Holsworthy*
	34098	*Templecombe*
	34099	*Lynmouth*
	34100	*Appledore*
	34101	*Hartland*
	34102	*Lapford*
	34103	*Calstock*
	34104	*Bere Alston*
	34105	*Swanage*
	34106	*Lydford*
	34107	*Blandford / Blandford Forum ##*
	34108	*Wincanton*
	34109	*Sir Trafford Leigh Mallory*
	34110	*66 Squadron*

*	Spelling amended in 1948 at request of local council
**	Original name carried for only a few days in 1948
***	Original name transferred in 1948 to No 34082
#	Altered in 1950 to recognise Wells' city status
##	Altered in 1952 at request of town council

SR Number	BR Number	Name
Class MN 4-6-2		
21C1	35001	*Channel Packet*
21C2	35002	*Union Castle*
21C3	35003	*Royal Mail*
21C4	35004	*Cunard White Star*
21C5	35005	*Canadian Pacific*
21C6	35006	*Peninsular & Oriental S.N. Co.*
21C7	35007	*Aberdeen Commonwealth*
21C8	35008	*Orient Line*
21C9	35009	*Shaw Savill*
21C10	35010	*Blue Star*
21C11	35011	*General Steam Navigation*
21C12	35012	*United States Line*
21C13	35013	*Blue Funnel Certum Pete Finem* *
21C14	35014	*Nederland Line*
21C15	35015	*Rotterdam Lloyd*
21C16	35016	*Elders Fyffes*
21C17	35017	*Belgian Marine*
21C18	35018	*British India Line*
21C19	35019	*French Line C.G.T.* **
21C20	35020	*Bibby Line*
	35021	*New Zealand Line*
	35022	*Holland America Line*
	35023	*Holland-Afrika Line*
	35024	*East Asiatic Company*
	35025	*Brocklebank Line*
	35026	*Lamport & Holt Line*
	35027	*Port Line*
	35028	*Clan Line*
	35029	*Ellerman Lines*
	35030	*Elder-Dempster Lines*

* Originally *Blue Funnel Line*: amended within three months of naming in 1945
** Name in cursive script (rest of class in sans-serif capitals)

Above: *Each 'Merchant Navy' had a striking nameplate cast in solid gunmetal (brass) with an enamelled plaque showing the flag of the relevant shipping line. This was the plate on No 35005* Canadian Pacific, *photographed on 3 June 1959 as the locomotive was outshopped from rebuilding at Eastleigh Works. Nameplates would later gain a red backing.* Author

SR Number	BR Number	Name
Isle of Wight locomotives		
Class E1 0-6-0T		
(B136) / W1	W1	*Medina*
(B152) / W2	W2	*Yarmouth*
(B154) / W3	W3	*Ryde*
(B131) / W4	W4	*Wroxall*
Class A1X 0-6-0T		
2 * / W2	W8	*Freshwater*
(B677) / W3 / W13	W13	*Carisbrooke*

* FY&NR number
** IWCR number

SR Number	BR Number	Name
Class O2 0-4-4T		
(178) / W14	W14	*Fishbourne*
(195) / W15	W15	*Cowes*
(217) / W16	W16	*Ventnor*
(208) / W17	W17	*Seaview*
(220) / W18	W18	*Ningwood*
(206) / W19	W19	*Osborne*
(211) / W20	W20	*Shanklin*
(205) / W21	W21	*Sandown*
(215) / W22	W22	*Brading*
(188) / W23	W23	*Totland*
(209) / W24	W24	*Calbourne*
(190) / W25	W25	*Godshill*
(210) / W26	W26	*Whitwell*
(184) / W27	W27	*Merstone*
(186) / W28	W28	*Ashey*
(202) / W29	W29	*Alverstone*
(219) / W30	W30	*Shorwell*
(180) / W31	W31	*Chale*
(226) / W32	W32	*Bonchurch*
(218) / W33	W33	*Bembridge*
(201) / W34	W34	*Newport*
	(30181) / W35	*Freshwater*
	(30198) / W36	*Carisbrooke*

Note: Names carried only when locomotives numbered in Isle of Wight 'W' series (bracketed numbers are those carried immediately before transfer to Isle of Wight)

Departmental locomotives

Class A1X 0-6-0T

B635 / 2635 / 377S DS377		*Brighton Works*

Not named thus until in service stock (in Stroudley yellow livery)

BIBLIOGRAPHY

During his research for this compendium the author consulted many sources of information on Southern locomotives. The following are particularly recommended for further reading.

The ABC of Southern Locomotives (Ian Allan, 1942),
ABC British Railways Locomotives (Ian Allan, 1951)

ABC British Locomotives 1957 (Ian Allan, 1957, reprinted 1993 [ISBN 0 7110 2203 8]). These booklets are accurate sources of details of SR locomotives, developed when Ian Allan worked for the Southern Railway and had access to official data.

Nameplates of the Big Four by Frank Burridge (Oxford Publishing Co, 1975 [ISBN 0 902888 43 9]). This lists all names and gives details of the design and dimensions of nameplates of locomotives of the 'Big Four' railways and early British Railways. It is the definitive publication on this subject.

Bulleid of the Southern by H. A. V. Bulleid (Ian Allan, 1977 [ISBN 0 7110 0689 X]). This is a mine of information and includes some succinct reports on the evolution of the 'Leader' class.

A Pictorial Record of the Diesel Shunter by Colin Marsden (Oxford Publishing Co, 1981 [ISBN 0 86093 108 0]). This gives useful background, technical details and pictures of the wide variety of diesel and petrol shunting locomotives operated by the 'Big Four' and BR.

Maunsell Locomotives — A Pictorial History by Brian Haresnape (Ian Allan, 1977 [ISBN 0 7110 0743 8]). Lots of background research went into this very useful book, which contains diagrams, data and many photographs. It is more definitive than its title suggests.

Drummond Locomotives — A Pictorial History by Brian Haresnape and Peter Rowledge (Ian Allan, 1982 [ISBN 0 7110 1206 7]). Covers the LSWR and the Scottish railways which operated Drummond locomotives.

Built at Eastleigh by Eric Forge, Colin Asprey and Gavin Bowle (Kingfisher Railway Publications, 1985 [ISBN 0 946184 17 8], updated in 1992 by Waterfront Publications [ISBN unchanged]). Lists all Eastleigh-built steam locomotives giving dates new, rebuilt and withdrawn. Many pictures.

LB&SCR Locomotives by F. Burtt (Ian Allan, 1946). Detailed account of all LBSCR locomotives from 1870. Highly recommended.

SE&CR Locomotives by F. Burtt (Ian Allan, 1947). Detailed account of all locomotives built or inherited by the SECR, the earliest dating from 1874. Highly recommended.

L&SWR Locomotives by F. Burtt (Ian Allan, 1949). Detailed account of all LSWR locomotives from 1872. Highly recommended.

The LSWR at Nine Elms — The Works and its Products 1830 to 1909 by Barry Curl (KRB Publications, 2004 [ISBN 0954203577]). Highly detailed description of Nine Elms Locomotive Works and the locomotives it built and overhauled. Superbly illustrated with rare period photographs, drawings and sketches. Lists every LSWR locomotive built at Nine Elms.

The Leader Project — Fiasco or Triumph? by Kevin Robertson (Oxford Publishing Co, 2007 [ISBN 978 0 86093 628 2]). Detailed and profusely illustrated discussion on the merits and demerits of O. V. S. Bulleid's 'Leader' project, with figures from dynamometer-car tests. Recommended.

The Southern Railways Group magazine *Southern Notebook* (ISSN 0308 9991) contains regular updates of all things Southern Railway and Region. Visit www.srg.org.uk.

The Southern E-Group website www.semgonline.com contains painstakingly researched details of most Southern Railway and BR Southern Region locomotives and multiple-units, illustrated with apposite photographs and supported by brief technical and historical notes and number lists.

Below: *Three Maunsell 4-6-0s stand impressively outside the shed at Eastleigh depot in April 1957. From left to right are Nos 30787* Sir Menaduke, *30784* Sir Nerovens *and 30859* Lord Hood.
Colour-Rail BRS1455

INDEX

Adams, W.	6-14, 16, 19, 58, 106
Armstrong Whitworth	86
Ashford	5, 33, 36-51, 69, 76, 77, 79, 82, 83, 85-87, 90-92, 101-105, 113, 118
Balancing	21, 88, 94
Beattie, J.	6
Beattie, W. G.	6, 7, 11
Beyer Peacock	7, 10, 47, 52, 53, 57
Borsig	47
Billinton, L. B.	54, 71-73, 79
Billinton, R. J.	54, 59-65, 68, 69
Brighton	4, 5, 47, 54, 55, 59-61, 63, 64, 66-70, 73, 77, 79, 84, 96, 100, 105, 109, 113, 115
Broad Clyst	117, 122
Bulleid, O. V. S.	4, 29, 30, 50, 66, 74, 75, 77, 80, 82, 89, 92-106, 115
Chain-driven	94, 100, 117
Click, J. G.	113
Comparative trials	70
Departmental stock	10, 14, 25, 35, 36, 39, 58, 113-122
Diesel locomotives	4, 73, 75, 102-105, 113, 116-119
Drewry Car Co	118
Drummond, D.	6-8, 12, 14-26, 28-31, 53, 76
Dübs & Co	15, 16, 40
Durnsford Road	114
East Kent Railway	5, 9, 106, 111
Eastleigh	5, 6, 8, 10, 16, 17, 23, 24, 26-32, 62, 67, 76-79, 81, 83, 87, 88, 90-92, 94-99, 101, 108, 109, 112, 113, 116, 119, 121
Electric locomotives	4, 75, 101, 116, 119
Exmouth Junction	9, 14, 85, 90, 122
Experiments	26, 41, 50, 62, 66, 70, 75, 77, 80, 92, 95, 98, 100, 112, 119
Giesl exhaust	98
Hastings-line gauge	50, 74, 88, 97
Hawthorn Leslie	107-110
Industrial service	12, 25, 57, 67, 103, 106, 111, 116
Isle of Wight	5, 11, 13, 54, 55, 57, 62, 102
Jarvis, R. G.	96
John Fowler & Co	116
KESR	5, 110, 112
Kerr Stuart	111
Kirtley, W.	33-35
Kitson & Co	66
Kylchap exhaust	80
LSWR	4-33, 47, 54, 55, 74-76, 83, 106, 107, 109, 110, 114
LBSCR	5, 10, 16, 44, 54-74, 79, 84, 85, 90, 112, 121
LCDR	14, 33-35
Lancing Works	36, 55, 94, 113, 121
'Leader' class	4, 66, 75, 100

Lemaître exhaust	29, 66, 74, 77, 80, 89, 92-94, 100
Longhedge Works	35, 38, 61
Lyme Regis branch	9, 56, 58
Marsh, D. E.	54, 55, 57-60, 62, 64-71
Maunsell, R. E. L.	6, 15, 18, 22-24, 26, 28-30, 33, 37, 40-44, 47-53, 67, 71, 74, 76-93, 113
Neilson/Neilson Reid	8, 10, 36-38, 51, 58
Nine Elms	6, 8-22, 25, 26, 30, 39, 79, 83, 105, 109, 110, 120
North British Locomotive Co	77, 78, 82
PD&SWJR	5, 8, 108, 109
Petrol locomotives	120-122
Porter, H. K.	112
Preserved locomotives	7, 9, 11, 12, 15, 16, 30, 33, 39, 40, 42-44, 49, 55, 57, 62, 80, 89, 77, 83, 86, 92, 93, 99, 103, 122, 115
Radial truck	7, 9, 61, 64, 65, 85, 106
Rebuilding	4, 6, 16, 18, 21, 23, 28, 33, 34, 37, 38, 40-42, 45, 51-53, 55, 57, 58, 60, 64, 65, 69, 76, 79, 80, 84-87, 95-97, 99
Replica 'Atlantic'	67
Robert Stephenson	40
Ruston & Hornsby	117
SER	33, 34, 36, 46, 52, 54, 86
SECR	4, 5, 33-35, 37-53, 55, 74, 75, 82, 86, 91, 122
Self-trimming coal bunker	80
Self-weighing tender	96, 98
Service stock	10, 14, 25, 35, 36, 39, 58, 113, 116-122
Sevenoaks derailment	74, 86
Sharp Stewart	34, 38, 40, 42, 63
Sleeve valves	66, 100
Southampton Docks	14, 25, 27, 30, 57, 73, 75, 83, 106, 107, 112, 113, 117
Southampton Town Quay	25, 107, 113
Stirling, J.	33, 37, 42, 45
Stroudley, W.	44, 54-59, 61, 85, 106
Urie, R. W.	6, 15-19, 21-32, 74, 94, 76, 79, 86, 90
Vulcan Foundry	40, 60
Vulcan Ironworks	112
Wainwright, H. S.	33-35, 37-47, 51
War: 1914-18	8, 9, 25, 31, 35, 36, 44, 47, 48, 51, 62, 72, 79, 111
War: 1939-45	4, 10, 19, 28, 40, 60, 63, 75, 79, 94, 97, 100, 104, 106, 112, 115
'Watercart' tenders	15, 19-24, 28, 76
WC&PR	55
Woolwich Arsenal	48, 49